"Gender Diversity and Sport is an essential addition to the field around non-conforming people in sport at all levels. Its interdisciplinary research, and acknowledgement of more work needed across disciplines is clear, and should be seen as a calling to those working in social sciences."

– **Rachael Bullingham,** *Senior Lecturer of Sport and Exercise, University of Gloucestershire, UK*

"This is a well constructed and timely book on a very important, and widely discussed, topic. Rather than focus on exclusionary practices, this book draws on a range of interdisciplinary perspectives that address inclusivity to explain the diverse relationship between gender and sport in the 21st century. The quality of it is in its accessibility to students, researchers, and all who seek to develop their knowledge in this research area."

– **Jamie Cleland,** *Senior Lecturer in Sport and Management, University of South Australia*

"This book provides the reader with a critical insight into the realm of gender diversity in sport; offering new perspectives beyond the polarised view and established 'norm' challenging what we thought we already knew. The chapters provide a well-considered introduction into the field for those how may be starting out in this area of interest as well as contributing to our understanding of the sector and the challenges sport faces to provide opportunities for everyone to be active. Congratulations to Witcomb and Peel in producing such a comprehensive consideration of environments; from educational experiences to the nuances of the legal system and the impact of the media. *Gender Diversity and Sport* is a must read for those not only interested in gender diversity but for everyone working within sport."

– **Helen Ives,** *Senior Lecturer in Sport, Exercise and Health Sciences, Brunel University London*

"Witcomb and Peel have delivered a provocative and contemporary book that will be a prized asset for anyone interested in gender and sport. It is an invaluable interdisciplinary contribution that enriches our understanding and practice of gender, diversity and inclusivity."

– **Brett Smith,** *Professor of Disability and Physical Activity and co-author of the Routledge International Handbook of Sport Psychology, Durham University, UK*

"Gender Diversity and Sport really gets to the heart of why inclusion and gender diversity in sport matters for trans and non-binary people. It's accessible and relatable, and covers a rainbow of perspectives from social justice, human rights, university and school sport, to the ways gendered sports clothing can make gender diverse people feel excluded. Most importantly, the themes in this book are addressed sympathetically and draw on trans and non-binary people's lived experiences in sport. Gender Diversity and Sport shows a genuine commitment to move the discussion away from historical hostilities, and reflects a passion for improving inclusion and celebrating diversity in sport for all."

– **Verity Smith**, *Rugby Player/Trans Inclusion in Sports Youth Worker, Mermaids*

"At a time when gender diverse people are being targeting politically, Gemma Witcomb and Elizabeth Peel provide an insightful and compassionate view into the grand diversity of gender within sport. The ground-breaking essays highlight the experiences of a broad range of gender diverse people in sport; identify challenges and barriers facing trans, non-binary, and intersex people in sport; and point to strategies for inclusion. This engaging collection is a call to action that will challenge and inspire readers to envision a gender diverse and inclusive sport."

– **Vikki Krane,** *Professor of Teaching Excellence and author of Sex, Gender and Sexuality in Sport: Queer Inquiries, Bowling Green State University, USA*

Gender Diversity and Sport

This timely and urgent text presents cutting-edge research exploring the complexities of barriers to inclusive access to sport and physical activity, and discusses how sport, and society, can move forward beyond the gender binary, in both theory and practice.

Sport is one of the most influential, powerful, and visible institutions upholding the gender binary, even as the number of people identifying as transgender and non-binary increases rapidly worldwide. With this rising visibility, societal pressure has been increasing for the equal acceptance of gender diverse people, but while gains have been made in many areas, the participation of intersex, trans and non-binary people in sport remains harshly contested. Bringing together a world-leading team of established and emerging scholars from the UK, USA, and Australia, this collection presents an interdisciplinary analysis of current issues related to the participation of gender diverse individuals in sport and physical activity. Engaging with psychological ideas around identity, prejudice and discrimination, and sports psychology and performance, authors examine evidence that the rules, regulations, and practices that surround physical activity participation – from elite sport to sport in schools, universities, and society at large – are grounded in heteronormative, cisgendered, and sexist practices which unfairly discriminate against gender diverse people.

Also including analysis of personal accounts from non-binary and transgender athletes from a range of sports, this is fascinating and essential reading for education, health, and sports professionals who work with and support gender diverse children and adults, as well as academics and students in the fields of psychology, sport psychology, sociology, law, and sports science, and those participating in, and navigating, sport and physical activity spaces.

Gemma L. Witcomb is a Senior Lecturer in Psychology at Loughborough University, UK. Her research interests are broadly centred around gender and mental health across a broad spectrum of populations, including trans and non-binary individuals. She has a particular interest in the interplay between physical activity and wellbeing, and thus inclusion. She is the founder of the Gender and Sport mini-Centre for Doctoral Training at Loughborough University, with six PhD students all researching the critical issue of trans and non-binary inclusion in sport.

Elizabeth Peel is Professor of Communication and Social Interaction and Associate Pro Vice Chancellor (Doctoral College), Loughborough University, UK. Her research areas are within critical health and social psychology and focus on LGBTIQ psychology and chronic illness. Her latest books are *Lesbian, Gay, Bisexual, Trans, Queer & Intersex Psychology* (with Sonja Ellis and Damien Riggs, 2020), *Psychologies of Ageing* (2018) and *Critical Kinship Studies* (2016).

Gender and Sexualities in Psychology
Series Editors: Elizabeth Peel and Elizabeth Stokoe

Gender and Sexualities in Psychology is a book series showcasing scholarly work over a wide range of areas within gender and sexualities in psychology, and the intersection of gender, feminism, sexualities and LGBTQI psychology with other areas of the discipline.

The series includes theoretically and empirically informed scholarship including critical, feminist, queer, trans, social, and intersectional perspectives, and encourages creative and innovative methodological approaches. The series adopts an inclusive approach to the discipline of psychology, as well as its cross-cutting relationship to related disciplines, and recognizes diversity in research on genders and sexualities.

Titles in the series:

Gender Diversity and Sport
Interdisciplinary Perspectives
Gemma Witcomb & Elizabeth Peel

Bisexual and Pansexual Identities
Exploring and Challenging Invisibility and Invalidation, 1st Edition
Nikki Hayfield

Queer Ink
A Blotted History Towards Liberation
Katherine Hubbard

Reproductive Losses
Challenges to LGBTQ Family-Making
Christa Craven

Emergent Identities
New Sexualities, Genders and Relationships in a Digital Era
Rob Cover

For further information about this series please visit: https://www.routledge.com/Gender-and-Sexualities-in-Psychology/book-series/GSP

Gender Diversity and Sport

Interdisciplinary Perspectives on Increasing Inclusivity

Edited by
Gemma L. Witcomb and Elizabeth Peel

Routledge
Taylor & Francis Group
LONDON AND NEW YORK

Cover image: TBC

First published 2022
by Routledge
4 Park Square, Milton Park, Abingdon, Oxon OX14 4RN

and by Routledge
605 Third Avenue, New York, NY 10158

Routledge is an imprint of the Taylor & Francis Group, an informa business

British Library Cataloguing-in-Publication Data
A catalogue record for this book is available from the British Library

Library of Congress Cataloging-in-Publication Data
A catalog record has been requested for this book

ISBN: 978-0-367-50629-2 (hbk)
ISBN: 978-0-367-50628-5 (pbk)
ISBN: 978-1-003-05056-8 (ebk)

DOI: 10.4324/9781003050568

Typeset in Sabon
by Taylor & Francis Books

Dedication: For our children Ellie, Alex and Martha – the future is yours

Contents

Tables

Contributors

Catherine Armstrong is Reader in Modern History at Loughborough University (UK) and an oral historian working on Trans Lives: East Mids, a project to create an archive of trans experience in the English East Midlands. She is also an historian of colonial North America and the United States especially around the history of slavery in a transnational context. In 2020 her third monograph was published by Cambridge University Press, entitled *American Slavery, American Imperialism*. In the field of book history, she is editor of the journal *Publishing History*, and part of the organising committee of the Print Networks conference series.

Janine Coates is a Senior Lecturer in Qualitative Research Methods at Loughborough University UK. Her research focuses on issues relating to the inclusion of marginalised young people in Physical Education, sport and physical activity. She has a particular interest in the visibility of marginalised youth in research and the use of participatory research methods, with much of her work focusing on young people with special educational needs and disabilities.

Jennifer Cooke is Senior Lecturer in English at Loughborough University UK. She is author of *Contemporary Feminist Life-Writing: The New Audacity* (CUP, 2020) and editor of *The New Feminist Literary Studies* (CUP, 2020), *Scenes of Intimacy: Reading, Writing and Theorizing Contemporary Literature* (Bloomsbury Academic, 2013), and a special issue of *Textual Practice* on challenging intimacies and psychoanalysis (September 2013). Her first monograph was *Legacies of Plague in Literature, Theory and Film* (Palgrave, 2009). Her research interests lie in theories of intimacy; the affective turn and theories of the emotions; queer, trans, and feminist theories; and contemporary literature. She chaired the Gendered Lives Research Group from 2015–2020.

Hannah Kettley-Linsell is a PhD candidate at Loughborough University (UK) currently researching the experiences of transgender and non-binary people in Physical Education, the perceptions of parents towards gender diversity, and the attitudes of teachers towards transgender and non-binary students.

Gabriel Knott-Fayle is a Research Assistant at Leeds Beckett University (UK) following the completion of his doctoral research at Loughborough University's department for Communication and Media. Primarily drawing on theories of discourse and rhetoric, his research focuses on media representations of trans, intersex and gender diverse sportspeople in sports media and communication as well as on masculinities and homophobia in sport.

Hannah J.H. Newman is a Research Associate in the School of Sport, Exercise, and Health Sciences at Loughborough University, UK. Their research focuses on inclusivity in sport and exercise, and the promotion of sport, exercise, and physical activity in marginalised populations. In particular, Hannah's research to date has focused on gender diversity in sport and exercise, as well as sporting activities, athletes and bodies that transgress gender norms and societal ideals (i.e., muscularity for men and thinness for women).

Paul O'Halloran is discipline lead of Rehabilitation Counselling in the School of Psychology and Public Health at La Trobe University Australia. Paul is also a practising Psychologist, specialising in Sport and Exercise Psychology and Health Psychology. Paul has published extensively in the sport participation research and has a particular interest in promoting wellbeing through participation in sport and physical activity.

Jennifer Oates is Emeritus Professor of Speech Pathology in the Department of Speech Pathology, Orthoptics and Audiology at La Trobe University Australia. She is a Certified Practicing Speech Pathologist and a Life Member of Speech Pathology Australia. Jenni practices clinically at the Melbourne Voice Analysis Centre and Voice Medicine Australia. Her research focuses on perception, physiology and acoustics of typical and impaired voice, epidemiology of voice disorders, and prevention and management of voice and middle airway disorders. She also has clinical and research interests in counselling training for speech pathologists and in voice, communication and social participation support for people who identify as trans, gender diverse and non-binary. Jenni is a member of the Voice and Communication Standards of Care Committee of the World Professional Association of Transgender Health. She has published 78 journal papers and book chapters and presented 140 conference papers.

Seema Patel is a Senior Lecturer in Law at Nottingham Law School, Nottingham Trent University, UK. Her research field is sports law, with specific focus on discrimination and the regulatory balance between inclusion and exclusion in competitive sport. Seema is an international expert on gender discrimination in sport, where she has offered extensive media commentary on the legal implications of gender eligibility rules. Her recent academic publications examine the regulatory gaps in the protection of athletes' human rights in sport. Seema has been involved in sport policy in this field and she has also contributed to government consultation on inclusion and participation in sport.

Elizabeth Peel is Professor of Communication and Social Interaction and Associate Pro Vice Chancellor (Doctoral College), Loughborough University, UK. Her research areas are within critical health and social psychology and focus on LGBTIQ psychology and chronic illness. Her latest books are *Lesbian, Gay, Bisexual, Trans, Queer & Intersex Psychology* (with Sonja Ellis and Damien Riggs, 2020), *Psychologies of Ageing* (2018) and *Critical Kinship Studies* (2016).

Catherine Phipps is a Senior Lecturer in Sport and Physical Education at Solent University, UK. Her research centres around women, gender relations and LGBT+ issues in sport, physical activity and physical education. She has published a number of book chapters and journal articles, and is currently focussed on research around social media abuse directed towards elite athletes.

Rachel Sandford is a Senior Lecturer in Young People and Sport at Loughborough University, UK. Her research centres on issues related to young people's experiences of and development in/through sport, physical activity, and Physical Education. She has a particular interest in issues around popular culture, embodied identity, and positive youth development, with recent work focused on the experiences of marginalised youth.

Jaime Schultz is a professor of Kinesiology at Pennsylvania State University, USA, with an affiliate faculty appointment in Women's, Gender, and Sexuality Studies. She is the author or editor of six books, including *Qualifying Times: Points of Change in U.S. Women's Sport History* (University of Illinois Press, 2014), *Women's Sports: What Everyone Needs to Know* (Oxford University Press, 2018), and *Women and Sports in the United States: A Documentary Reader* (Lebanon, NH: University Press of New England, 2019), co-edited with Jean O'Reilly and Susan K. Cahn. In addition, she has published more than fifty article and chapters, the majority of which focus on the history and politics of women's sports. An award-winning teacher and a recipient of the Fulbright Senior Scholar Award, Schultz serves as the academic editor of the *International Journal of the History of Sport* and as co-editor for the University of Illinois Sport and Society book series.

Lauryn Stewart is an experienced university teacher in the School of Psychology and Public Health at La Trobe University, Australia, she is also a clinical supervisor at the Australian Catholic University in the department of Allied Health. Lauryn is a practising speech pathologist and a member of Speech Pathology Australia. Lauryn has a clinical and research interest in communication and promoting health and wellbeing in individuals as well as in voice and voice disorders.

Lauren Whitehouse is a PhD candidate in the School of Social Sciences and Humanities at Loughborough University, UK. Lauren researches non-binary experiences in sport, exercise and physical activity and has a keen interest in LGBTQI+ people's experiences of sport, exercise, and physical activity participation.

Gemma L. Witcomb is a Senior Lecturer in Psychology at Loughborough University, UK. Her research interests are broadly centred around gender and mental health across a broad spectrum of populations, including trans and non-binary individuals. She has a particular interest in the interplay between physical activity and wellbeing, and thus inclusion. She is the founder of the Gender and Sport mini-Centre for Doctoral Training at Loughborough University, with six PhD students all researching the critical issue of trans and non-binary inclusion in sport.

Acknowledgements

It is rather stating the obvious but producing a book during a pandemic is not something any of us have experienced before. Gemma and Elizabeth are very grateful to all the contributors to this volume for their work under these circumstances and for their patience and good will in engaging with our feedback. Timelines have invariably slipped, and there have been losses and chapter substitutions, so a warm thanks also to the team at Routledge – Eleanor Taylor and Alex Howard, and series co-editor Elizabeth Stokoe. It may not be exactly the book you contracted, though it is a finished book nonetheless. A number of the contributors wrote their chapter while engaging in doctoral programmes funded by Loughborough University via the *Gender and Sport* mini-Centre for Doctoral Training; thanks go to Loughborough Doctoral College for funding the CDT. Finally, we wish to express gratitude to all of the individuals who have given their time so generously to take part in the research studies that are reported within some of these chapters.

Chapter 1

Introduction

Situating Gender Diversity and Sport

G.L. Witcomb and E. Peel

If you enter a sporting event, what are you asked to disclose about yourself? Which categories are salient and influential? 'Gender' is an undisputed category participants engaging in sports are typically mandated to disclose. This is a real example of how gender is approached by a sport events listing service in 2021:

Gender

- Male
- Female
- Other/Prefer not to say (Selecting this may affect prize eligibility)

This UK company lists various types of running races, walking, cycling, athletics track and field, aquathon, duathlon and triathlon events. We can see in the way that disclosing gender as part of the registration process is constructed that, on the one hand, gender beyond the two binary options of 'female' and 'male' is recognised by the presence of a third category. On the other hand, however, if a competitor lists their gender as 'other' or does not wish to identify as either 'male' or 'female' the implication is that they forfeit their opportunity to win any prize associated with the race or event. Ultimately, then, though there is acknowledgement that gender is more complex than dimorphic sex, the only legitimate forms of sporting engagement are in the women's or men's categories. This example illustrates the liminality that gender diversity inhabits in sports spaces and raises important questions about how recognition *per se* does not necessarily translate into inclusion.

Interdisciplinarity and psychological spheres

Gender Diversity and Sport aims to showcase interdisciplinary perspectives in order to further the inclusivity of trans, non-binary and diverse genders in discussion of sport and physical activity. Indeed, cultural studies (Shultz, Chapter 2), law (Patel, Chapter 3), sociology (Phipps, Chapter 4; Newman & Witcomb, Chapter 9), and speech pathology (Stewart et al., Chapter 7) are all represented. Nevertheless, a number of contributors, and ourselves, orient the discussion of

DOI: 10.4324/9781003050568-1

gender diversity and sport with reference to psychology – especially concerns germane to the psychology of women and equalities, and the psychology of sexualities.[1] The discipline of psychology in the UK, and elsewhere, has had a chequered history regarding representation and inclusions of trans and gender diverse people and concerns (e.g., Tosh, 2016). Rather than offer an extensive critique of mainstream psychology and the 'psy' discipline's failings, omissions and harms regarding those minoritised on the basis of gender, a brief genealogy of the development of the key (and affirmative) sub-field of psychology of sexualities is illuminating.[2]

When the field of lesbian and gay psychology – as it was known then – was established in 1998 there was limited consideration of trans and gender non-conforming topics and concerns (e.g., Coyle & Kitzinger, 2002; Clarke & Peel, 2007a). By 2007 there was explicit inclusion of 'trans' and 'queer' in the field (Clarke & Peel, 2007b), and, as a key collection at that time stressed, the time had come to be "outing" psychology as already, if sometimes ambivalently or unwillingly, incorporate[ing] LGBTQ perspectives' (Clarke & Peel, 2007c, p. 1). Nevertheless, if we take this substantial four-part 21 chapter volume (Clarke & Peel, 2007b) as a litmus test of the state of the field at that time, there were only three chapters devoted to trans people and a single chapter that focused on sport, centering on the experiences of lesbian sportswomen (Krane & Kauer, 2007). When the first textbook in the psychology of sexualities field was published in 2010 there was acknowledgement that the existing research focused on sport and exercise highlighted 'the challenges faced by non-heterosexual sportswomen and men in a world infused with ideals of hegemonic masculinity and heterosexuality; and in which sportswomen who display qualities associated with masculinity (such as aggression, strength and confidence) are (negatively) assumed to be lesbian' (Clarke et al., 2010, p. 253). Notable, then, by its absence was research focused on trans and gender-nonconforming experiences with and in sports contexts, beyond their intersection with gendered stereotypes impacting lesbians. And whilst discussion of gender diversity is thoroughly integrated into the second edition of the *Lesbian, Gay, Bisexual, Trans, Intersex, and Queer Psychology* (Ellis et al., 2020) textbook, sport only gets mentioned tangentially in the context of discussion of gender inequality in sports being a site for the discursive production of prejudice.

In terms of sport psychology, while there have been recent efforts to offer intersectional feminist perspectives (e.g., Carter, 2019), there are also renewed calls to frame the sub-field away from its positivist, androcentric routes toward being a field which actively foregrounds 'compassionate inclusion' (Krane & Waldron, 2021, p. 469). In their throughgoing critique of the current state of the field of sport psychology Krane and Waldron (2021, p. 470) flag the 'glaring lack of attention to inclusion and diversity' and emphasise the 'largely non-existent' nature of LGBTQ psychological research within sport psychology. By contrast, their call to action stresses that the:

> field should be on the cutting edge of advancing inclusive sport environments. [...] given the widespread scrutiny surrounding transgender people in sport and the common narrative of their unfair advantages or locker room politics, there is a deafening silence from sport psychology professionals. [...] We should be at the forefront of supporting trans athletes.
>
> (Krane & Waldron, 2021, pp. 470 and 485)

Although we position ourselves as feminist psychologists and not sport psychologists, there is much to be said for heeding the clarion call of Vikki Krane and Jennifer Waldron. Given this book's focus on sport we encourage sport psychologists – broadly conceived – to consider how centring perspectives that emphasise inclusion in sports for trans and non-binary people and concerns might de-centre taken-for-granted assumptions in sport, sports psychology, and also in wider society.

Though we have situated the interdisciplinary research contained in *Gender Diversity and Sport* in psychological spheres this should not be read as exclusive. The boundaries of social science disciplines should be porous ones; and similar debates about inclusion and exclusion and the relationship between the marginalised and the mainstream occur in numerous disciplinary contexts.

Axes of Exclusion and Inclusion

Gender has been leveraged throughout history to explain and justify inequality. Most notably, early psychology and neuroscience provided 'evidence' of inherent differences between the sexes, with women having marked deficiencies compared to men (cf. Rippon, 2019). While it is now acknowledged that sex-correlated biological processes do play a role in behaviour, it is largely recognised that they do so flexibly, bi-directionally, and in ways that fluctuate across the life course, rather than having a fixed and enduring polarising effect (Rogers, 1999). That said, societal beliefs regarding traditional gender roles still pervade modern society and are evident in opinions about the participation of gender diverse individuals within sport, with those holding more traditional gender role beliefs espousing less support (Flores et al., 2020).

Understandings of gender and sex have shifted largely due to feminist thought from the 1960s onwards. In the contemporary West, often sex is viewed as foundational, dimorphic and wholly linked to biology whereas gender is seen as culturally and socially produced. At times sex/gender are used interchangeably, at other times gender is used as the sole signifier acknowledging that 'sex' is subject to the same regulatory norms and discursive practices which produce the material as well as the social (Butler, 1993). Gender, and sexism and cisgenderism, are produced in and through various contexts (e.g., Speer & Stokoe, 2011); fluid, contestable and contingent on the one hand, and structurally embedded and resistant to change on the other. While debate continues about what is included and excluded within the edifice of Gender[3] – at all levels of normative practice – the progressive view is that there is no inevitable mapping of biological sex onto a singular gendered identity. The disaggregation of biological sex and gender identity has shaped social practices in many spheres, such as the instantiation of gender-neutral toilets in many organisational spaces and legislative frameworks to support binary trans peoples' sense of self. Though the widening and troubling of sex and gender is a welcome move forward in understanding gender as influenced by, and 'performed' (Butler, 1988; 1990) within our cultural boundaries, and thus also constrained by them, it has presented problems in areas that are firmly rooted to sex difference politics, such as sport.

Sporting contexts are often characterised by exclusivity rather than inclusivity and can 'completely negate the possibility of inclusion for people with non-binary or intersex identities' (Krane & Waldron, 2021, pp. 472–473). Although latterly there has been 'some progress toward greater inclusivity for transgender people in relation to Sport' (Hargie et al., 2017; p. 224) genuine inclusion of diverse genders in sports settings and, especially, competitive contexts requires transformative thinking and practice. Given the prestige and power of sport we might question whether there is the ideological and political will to affect change in support of minoritised groups and individuals. For many nations around the world, sport is a central part of their national identity. Success in sport is not only a source of national pride for fans, but is seen as a visible, tangible illustration of international ranking and status to the wider world. The international media coverage of the (postponed) 2020 Olympic and Paralympic Games in Tokyo (July–September 2021) is testament to the importance bestowed upon sport as part of a nation's identity.

At an individual level, sport is also central to identity for many people – whether through personal identity as a participant (e.g., identifying as a sports person) or social identity of being a fan (e.g., identifying with a particular team or sport). Both are significant identities that are enacted through sport, and which have many benefits for mental wellbeing and quality of life. Self-esteem (Jetten et al., 2015), social support (Häusser et al., 2020), meaning and purpose (Steffens et al., 2017) and personal growth (Greenaway et al., 2015) are all associated with connection to sport. Thus, a shared sporting identity can act as vehicle through which people connect with one another. Connectedness is a fundamental human need and desire of all (Baumeister & Leary, 1995) and exclusion in sport may render this more difficult for gender diverse people to achieve; arguably those who have perhaps the greatest need, due to their marginalised status, to connect with both the LGBTQ+ and non-LGBTQ+ communities. Unfortunately, these sporting identities remain harder for gender diverse people to connect with others through, which is concerning since research has shown that trans people's wellbeing suffers from lack of connectedness with communities and peers (Pflum et al., 2015; Witcomb et al., 2019).

The physiological benefits of sport and physical activity are also central to the achievement of optimal physical and mental health. Decades of research have highlighted the link between physical activity and the release of endorphins which serve to boost mood (Schuch et al., 2016), something that can be of particular benefit for trans people who experience higher levels of depression (Witcomb et al., 2018), anxiety (Thorne et al., 2019; Bouman et al., 2017) and non-suicidal self-injury (Marshall et al., 2016) than cis people. Furthermore, there are obvious long-term benefits to morbidity and mortality as a result of having a strong, healthy body (Kujala, 2018) and maintaining functional capacity into older age (Merchant et al., 2021). Indeed, the immunological benefits of being physically active have never been as salient as they are now during the COVID-19 pandemic (Nieman, 2021). Thus, the exclusion of gender diverse people from sporting spheres is a direct infringement on their physical and mental health. Additionally, changes to the physical body – through exercise-induced weight loss or increased lean body mass – can bring the body more in line with the physicality that is desired. Such congruence can provide additional mental health benefits related to the alleviation of dysphoric and incongruent body image (Teti et al., 2020), leaving gender diverse people less reliant on maladaptive eating behaviours to manage their bodies (Witcomb et al., 2015).

The Olympic Charter (IOC, 2020) states that 'the practice of sport is a human right. Every individual must have the possibility of practising sport, without discrimination of any kind and in the Olympic spirit, which requires mutual understanding with a spirit of friendship, solidarity and fair play'. Similarly, Article 1 of UNESCO's 1978 International Charter of Physical Education and Sport (mostly recently updated in 2015; International Charter of Physical Education, Physical Activity and Sport) deems that 'the practice of physical education, physical activity and sport is a fundamental right for all' (UNESCO, 2015; 1978). However, at present, policies are largely exclusionary and facilities are not inclusive (e.g., Jones et al., 2017) and trans people overall engage in less physical activity than their cis counterparts (Jones et al., 2018). In *Gender Diversity and Sport*, the extent to which gender diverse individuals' human rights are being undermined is presented in a multitude of ways, and all chapters address the issue of barriers to inclusion – be that directly (e.g., sports kit, Chapter 5; voice, Chapter 7) or in a more nuanced way (e.g., media representation, Chapter 8; progressive sporting events, Chapter 9).

Of course, sex and gender play a critical role in the extent to which personal and social identity can be built around sport for trans and cis people alike. For example, biological sex, and the socially constructed gender roles that have been imposed upon this, have long been a barrier – for both women and men – to the watching of, commentating on, working in, or indeed engaging in sports that are deemed for 'the opposite sex'. For example, female commentators often face abuse and harassment online when giving their professional opinion on the male game, as though their sex renders their expertise worthless (Antunovic, 2019; Chen et al., 2020). Similarly, analysis of Twitter threads from four Spanish media accounts regarding women in the 2016 Olympic Games in Rio found that a third promulgated negative content around women athlete's 'failures' and nine per cent included images of highly sexualised content (Adá-Lameiras & Rodríguez-Castro, 2021). Furthermore, in the absence of any live sport during the COVID-19 pandemic, the skewed coverage of male sport content versus female sport content highlighted how male sport is centered as the dominant consumer/ viewer interest and female sport positioned as secondary (Symons et al., 2021).

Such examples are recent and thus illustrate how these fundamental sexist attitudes still continue to colour how sport is experienced in the 2020s. If this were not enough, another threat to the freedom to participate in, and consume and enjoy, sport relates to gender identity. Sport is predominantly organised around a cisgender framework. In other words, most sports are sex segregated based on two beliefs; that first there are only two binary genders, namely male and female; and second males are always physically superior to females and therefore mixed competition would be unfair. This leads to a situation where, despite increasing numbers of people identifying outside of the gender binary, sport is struggling to accommodate individuals with diverse genders within this framework. Therefore a cisgenderist, binary conceptualisation of gender does not lend itself well to inclusive sports. The reasons for this, and the barriers to be overcome, are numerous and complex and this book brings together scholars to explore these issues in depth.

While notions of two binary genders and the dominance of male physicality conceptualise the problem as related to only two issues which foreground fairness and physical injury risk, there are significant wider factors at play. To this end, this book is not concerned with unpacking arguments for and against inclusion that centre on physiology (for example the effects of testosterone or gender-affirming hormone therapy[4]), despite this being the predicating factor in policies that govern elite level sports (see Chapters 2 and 3). Rather, *Gender Diversity and Sport* seeks to centre the additional factors that are significant in discussions around gender inclusivity in sport, from grassroots to the elite level. That is, those issues that are concerned with how gender diversity in sport is, and is not, mandated, organised, experienced, and documented, with the aim of considering how gender inclusivity can be promoted. You will find, then, that this book speaks to the current concerns around the challenges of gender diversity in all sporting contexts.

The Contents

This book has brought together scholars from the UK, the USA, and Australia. It therefore offers a partial perspective from the West, rather than a global perspective. The absence of non-Western and intersectional perspectives is apologetically acknowledged, and certainly there is space for considerations of gender diversity and sport which focus on the global South and use an intersectional lens (e.g., Tice-Brown, 2019). Nevertheless, *Gender Diversity and Sport* does offer a broad brush of issues affecting the participation of trans, non-binary, and intersex individuals across the lifespan; from history, the law, and the media, sport in educational settings, the influence of voice, to analysis of real-life experiences. These distinct contributions sit together within this contemporary debate[5] and highlight the plethora of ways in which exclusion and inclusion can be enacted; the former through a narrow focus on reductive biological-informed debates to drive policy, and the latter via overdue challenges to societal norms. They speak to the concerns around whether trans, non-binary and gender diverse people can be incorporated into existing frameworks governing sports, or if radical transformation is needed. And where do the boundaries of inclusion and exclusion in sport lie.

In Chapter 2, Jaime Schultz from the USA explores the history of sex segregation in sport, focused on the Northern America context and international sports stage, particularly the International Olympic Committee (IOC) and World Athletics (WA). Focusing on interrogating the representation of intersex and trans athletes in women's sports, Shultz highlights the systemic rigidity in elite sports policy. The implications of international sports regulations are explored with regard to the ongoing subordination of female athletes, and the problematic erasure of non-binary sport participation.

In Chapter 3, UK scholar Seema Patel develops the theme of exclusion in their discussion of the law pertaining to human rights, inclusion and sports participation. Patel focuses particularly on regulatory barriers to trans athletes' inclusion in sport applying international human rights frameworks. They suggest that in the sport context human rights and legal obligations are especially difficult to enforce, to the detriment of gender diverse sports people.

Regulatory frameworks, their implementation, and effects are explored in a national context of University sport by Catherine Phipps in Chapter 4. They examine the exclusionary nature of the British Universities and Colleges Sport (BUCS) policies and the experiences of those implementing and/or affected by them. Drawing on focus group and questionnaire data with trans and non-binary students and student union officers Phipps highlights how binary gender in national and international sports policy constrains University sport and stifles desire to innovate to increase inclusion.

As Chapter 4 considers lived experience of exclusion so too does Chapter 5. In Chapter 5 Lauren Whitehouse, Catherine Armstrong and Jennifer Cooke explore non-binary individuals' experiences of sport in the UK, focused particularly on the embodied practices associated with navigating sports kit. Whitehouse et al.'s interviewees articulated the dysphoria inducing nature of gendered sportswear as young people, but through experimentation and adaptation of kit and equipment had moved subsequently from gender dysphoria to euphoria. Challenging gendered sports clothing stipulations, Whitehouse et al. argue, would be beneficial for all not just non-binary people.

Hannah Kettley-Linsell, Janine Coates and Rachel Sandford explore the barriers and facilitators to gender diverse pupil inclusion in secondary schools in the UK in Chapter 6. Drawing on data from trans and non-binary people's experiences of PE and school sport (PESS) they focus on the physical education curriculum and class as a troubling environment to negotiate and navigate gender performances. They advocate for a gender inclusive approach to PESS, suggesting practical strategies for change.

Moving briefly to Australia in Chapter 7, Lauryn Stewart, Jennifer Oates and Paul O'Halloran articulate the importance of voice as a significant (dis) enabler for participation. After making the case for the importance of, and challenges to, voice in sports contexts – particularly team sports – they draw our attention to the voice associated challenges for trans women in enacting belonging in the team. They conclude their chapter on a practical note suggesting voice feminisation training might be beneficial for these sports women.

While Stewart et al. focus on a strategy trans women could themselves adopt to promote inclusion in Chapter 8 Gabriel Knott-Fayle, Elizabeth Peel and Gemma Witcomb interrogate the production of cisgenderism. In focusing on the discursive production of cisgenderism they offer an analysis of the UK media's coverage of trans, non-binary, and intersex athletes. They explore the themes of un/natural athletic bodies, contested rights, and deviation from gender norms signalling deviancy and in so doing demonstrate how media representation invisibilises non-binary athletes and perpetuates cisgender men and women as uncontestable.

In the final chapter, Chapter 9, Hannah Newman and Gemma Witcomb scrutinise a context where normative gender practices in sporting contexts are configured differently. Rather than an incremental approach to inclusion of gender diverse people Newman and Witcomb's examination of a gender-free sporting event that took place in the UK invites us to consider how sport, especially competitive sport, could be enacted differently. Through interviews with participants and spectators they illuminate the advantages and disadvantages associated with operationalising a strength athletics event without sex segregation. This case study of a sports competition beyond binary gender serves not only as a model of how to do things differently, but importantly as a challenge to move beyond inclusion to the transformation of normative sporting practices.

Taken together, then, this edited collection showcases interdisciplinary fields of thought at the level of policy and governance (Shultz; Patel; Phipps), media representation (Knott-Fayle et al.), in significant – and potentially transformative – settings (Kettley-Linsell et al.; Newman & Witcomb) and through lived experience (Whitehouse et al.; Stewart et al.). This is critical to understanding the complexity of the challenge faced by gender diverse people in their pursuit of inclusive participation, and those that are responsible for pushing forward the change needed to facilitate this. As well as offering new research extending the germinal literature on the perspectives of gender diverse people with respect to sport, in what follows there are many practical suggestions and recommendations to genuinely increase inclusivity for trans, non-binary, and intersex sportspeople.

We share in the frustration about how sport and physical activity is still organised in 2021. Gemma, a heterosexual cisgender woman (she/her), found her early experiences of physical education stiflingly gendered. In more recent years Gemma has witnessed heteronormative and objectifying attitudes in the traditionally 'masculine' sports that she has engaged in, leading to withdrawal in protest. Elizabeth, a queer woman (she/they) who took up sport later in life, finds the persistence of the 'Ladies' category in running clubs and teams frustratingly pejorative. And a 'non-binary' option alongside 'female' or 'male' at running event registration remains incredibly rare. These two personal accounts underscore how far a distance there is to travel before there is a degree of gender equity in sports that is appropriately and fully inclusive of all genders.

Ultimately, as you will see, many of the issues discussed in *Gender Diversity and Sport* transcend the gender diversity sphere and are firmly rooted within a long-standing and problematic history of gender discrimination. It is our hope that this book will be received not only as an educational text around the issues affecting gender diverse people in sport, but as a call to action to facilitate a transformative and equality-driven approach to how we organise, participate in, and consume sport.

Notes

1 We use the phrases 'psychology of women and equalities' and 'psychology of sexualities' as these are the labels used at time of writing for the two Sections of the British Psychological Society (BPS) especially concerned with diverse genders (although a membership consultation is under way regarding changing the name of psychology of sexualities).

2 This genealogy of the development of the inclusion of transgender, intersex and diverse genders in psychology is limited to the UK context but a broadly similar trajectory has occurred in other Western contexts, such as Australia and the USA.

3 Judith Butler (2004, p. 42) has suggested, for instance, that 'those permutations of gender which do not fit the binary are as much a part of gender as its most normative instance'.

4 To date, there is a paucity of data on the effects of gender-affirming cross-sex hormone therapy on the athletic performance of gender-diverse athletes. This is for a number of reasons, including the logistical difficulties in executing a rigorous study that requires sufficient numbers of gender-diverse *athletes* to be recruited internationally and before any hormonal intervention has taken place in order to track physiological and performance changes. Even with non-athlete samples, the relatively recent call for evidence precludes, as yet, longitudinal data. While some studies do exist, these are lacking rigour (e.g., Harper, 2015) or are based on non-athletic samples (e.g., Harper et al., 2021; Hilton & Lundberg, 2021; Roberts et al., 2020, Wiik et al., 2020).

5 While we label this a 'contemporary debate' we recognise that there is a longer history of trans people's participation in sport since the mid-1970s (e.g., Riseman, 2021).

References

Adá-Lameiras, A., & Rodríguez-Castro, Y. (2021). Analysis from a gender perspective of the Olympic Games on Twitter. *European Sport Management Quarterly*, 1–17.

Antunovic, D. (2019). 'We wouldn't say it to their faces': Online harassment, women sports journalists, and feminism. *Feminist Media Studies*, 19(3), 428–442.

Baumeister, R.F., & Leary, M.R. (1995). The need to belong: Desire for interpersonal attachments as a fundamental human motivation. *Psychological Bulletin*, 117(3), 497.

Bouman, W.P., Claes, L., Brewin, N., Crawford, J.R., Millet, N., Fernandez-Aranda, F., & Arcelus, J. (2017). Transgender and anxiety: A comparative study between transgender people and the general population. *International Journal of Transgenderism*, 18(1), 16–26.

Butler, J. (1988). Performative acts and gender constitution: An essay in phenomenology and feminist theory. *Theatre Journal*, 40(4), 519–531.

Butler, J. (1990). *Gender Trouble: Feminism and the Subversion of Identity*. London and New York: Routledge.

Butler, J. (1993). *Bodies that Matter: On the Discursive Limits of 'Sex'*. London and New York: Routledge.

Carter, L. (Ed.) (2019). *Feminist Applied Sports Psychology: From Theory to Practice*. London and New York: Routledge.

Chen, G.M., Pain, P., Chen, V.Y., Mekelburg, M., Springer, N., & Troger, F. (2020). 'You really have to have a thick skin': A cross-cultural perspective on how online harassment influences female journalists. *Journalism*, 21(7), 877–895.

Clarke, V. & Peel, E. (2007a). From lesbian and gay psychology to LGBTQ psychologies: A journey into the unknown (or unknowable)? In V. Clarke & E. Peel (Eds.) *Out in Psychology* (pp. 11–35). Chichester: Wiley.

Clarke, V. & Peel, E. (Eds.) (2007b). *Out in Psychology: Lesbian, Gay, Bisexual, Trans and Queer Perspectives*. Chichester: Wiley.

Clarke, V. & Peel, E. (2007c). Introducing Out in Psychology. In V. Clarke & E. Peel (Eds.) *Out in Psychology* (pp. 1–9). Chichester: Wiley.

Clarke, V., Ellis, S.J., Peel, E. & Riggs, D.W. (2010). *Lesbian, Gay, Bisexual, Trans and Queer Psychology: An Introduction*. Cambridge: Cambridge University Press.

Coyle, A. & Kitzinger, C. (2002). *Lesbian and Gay Psychology: New Perspectives*. Blackwell.

Ellis, S.J., Riggs, D.W. & Peel, E. (2020). *Lesbian, Gay, Bisexual, Trans, Intersex and Queer Psychology: An Introduction*. Cambridge: Cambridge University Press. Second Edition.

Flores, A.R., Haider-Markel, D.P., Lewis, D.C., Miller, P.R., Tadlock, B.L., & Taylor, J.K. (2020). Public attitudes about transgender participation in sports: The roles of gender, gender identity conformity, and sports fandom. *Sex Roles*, 83, 382–398.

Greenaway, K.H., Haslam, S.A., Cruwys, T., Branscombe, N.R., Ysseldyk, R., & Heldreth, C. (2015). From "we" to "me": Group identification enhances perceived personal control with consequences for health and well-being. *Journal of Personality and Social Psychology*, 109(1), 53–74.

Hargie, O.D.W., Mitchell, D.H., & Somerville, I.J.A. (2017). 'People have a knack of making you feel excluded if they catch on to your difference': Transgender experiences of exclusion in sport. *International Review for the Sociology of Sport*, 52(2), 223–239.

Harper, J. (2015). Race times for transgender athletes. *Journal of Sport, Culture & Identities*, 6(1), 1–9.

Harper, J., O'Donnell, E., Khorashad, B.S., McDermott, H., & Witcomb, G.L. (2021). How does hormone transition in transgender women change body composition, muscle strength and haemoglobin? Systematic review with a focus on the implications for sport participation. *British Journal of Sports Medicine*, 55, 865–872.

Häusser, J. A., Junker, N. M., & van Dick, R. (2020). The how and the when of the social cure: A conceptual model of group- and individual- level mechanisms linking social identity to health and well-being. *European Journal of Social Psychology*, 50(4), 721–732.

Hilton, E. N., & Lundberg, T. R. (2021). Transgender women in the female category of sport: perspectives on testosterone suppression and performance advantage. *Sports Medicine*, 51(2), 199–214.

IOC. (2020). *Olympic Charter*. Retrieved on 9 September 2021 from https://stillmed.olympic.org/media/Document%20Library/OlympicOrg/General/EN-Olympic-Charter.pdf.

Jetten, J., Branscombe, N.R., Haslam, S.A., Haslam, C., Cruwys, T., Jones, J.M., ... & Zhang, A. (2015). Having a lot of a good thing: Multiple important group memberships as a source of self-esteem. *PloS one*, 10(5), e0124609.

Jones, B.A., Arcelus, J., Bouman, W.P., & Haycraft, E. (2017). Barriers and facilitators of physical activity and sport participation among young transgender adults who are medically transitioning. *International Journal of Transgenderism*, 18(2), 227–238.

Jones, B.A., Haycraft, E., Bouman, W.P., & Arcelus, J. (2018). The levels and predictors of physical activity engagement within the treatment-seeking transgender population: A matched control study. *Journal of Physical Activity and Health*, 15(2), 99–107.

Krane, V. & Kauer, K.J. (2007). Out on the ball fields: lesbians in sport. In V. Clarke & E. Peel (Eds.) *Out in Psychology* (pp. 273–290). Chichester: Wiley.

Krane, V. & Waldron, J.J. (2021). A renewed call to queer sport psychology. *Journal of Applied Sport Psychology*, 33(5), 469–490.

Kujala, U.M. (2018). Is physical activity a cause of longevity? It is not as straightforward as some would believe. A critical analysis. *British Journal of Sports Medicine*, 52(14), 914–918.

Marshall, E., Claes, L., Bouman, W.P., Witcomb, G.L., & Arcelus, J. (2016). Non-suicidal self-injury and suicidality in trans people: A systematic review of the literature. *International Review of Psychiatry*, 28(1), 58–69.

Merchant, R.A., Morley, J.E., & Izquierdo, M. (2021). Exercise, aging and frailty: Guidelines for increasing function. *The Journal of Nutrition, Health & Aging*, 25, 405–409.

Nieman, D.C. (2021). Exercise is medicine for immune function: Implication for COVID-19. *Current Sports Medicine Reports*, 20(8), 395–401.

Pflum, S.R., Testa, R.J., Balsam, K.F., Goldblum, P.B., & Bongar, B. (2015). Social support, trans community connectedness, and mental health symptoms among transgender and gender nonconforming adults. *Psychology of Sexual Orientation and Gender Diversity*, 2(3), 281.

Rippon, G. (2019). *The Gendered Brain: The New Neuroscience that Shatters the Myth of the Female Brain*. London: Vantage.

Riseman, N. (2021). A history of transgender women in Australian Sports, 1976–2017. *Sport in History*. doi:10.1080/17460263.2021.1938194.

Rogers, L. (1999). *Sexing the Brain.* London: Weidenfeld & Nicolson.

Roberts, T.A., Smalley, J., & Ahrendt, D. (2020). Effect of gender affirming hormones on athletic performance in transwomen and transmen: Implications for sporting organisations and legislators. *British Journal of Sports Medicine*, 55, 577–583.

Schuch, F.B., Vancampfort, D., Richards, J., Rosenbaum, S., Ward, P.B., & Stubbs, B. (2016). Exercise as a treatment for depression: A meta-analysis adjusting for publication bias. *Journal of Psychiatric Research*, 77, 42–51.

Speer, S.A. & Stokoe, E. (Eds.) (2011). *Conversation and Gender.* Cambridge University Press.

Symons, K., Breitbarth, T., Zubcevic-Basic, N., Wilson, K., Sherry, E., & Karg, A. (2021). The (un)level playing field: Sport media during COVID-19. *European Sport Management Quarterly*, 1–17.

Steffens, N.K., Haslam, S.A., Schuh, S.C., Jetten, J., & van Dick, R. (2017). A meta-analytic review of social identification and health in organizational contexts. *Personality and Social Psychology Review*, 21(4), 303–335.

Teti, M., Bauerband, L.A., Rolbiecki, A., & Young, C. (2020). Physical activity and body image: Intertwined health priorities identified by transmasculine young people in a non-metropolitan area. *International Journal of Transgender Health*, 21(2), 209–219.

Thorne, N., Witcomb, G.L., Nieder, T., Nixon, E., Yip, A., & Arcelus, J. (2019). A comparison of mental health symptomatology and levels of social support in young treatment seeking transgender individuals who identify as binary and non-binary. *International Journal of Transgenderism*, 20(2–3),241–250.

Tice-Brown, D. (2019). A life of paradoxes: Transwomen of color in sport. In L. Carter (Ed.) *Feminist Applied Sports Psychology: From Theory to Practice.* London and New York: Routledge.

Tosh, G. (2016). *Psychology and Gender Dysporia: Feminist and Transgender Perspectives.* London: Routledge.

UNESCO (1978). International Charter of Physical Education and Sport. Retrieved 9 September 2021 from http://www.icsspe.org/sites/default/files/International%20Charter%20of%20Physical%20Education%20and%20Sport.pdf.

UNESCO (2015). International Charter of Physical Education, Physical Activity and Sport. Retrieved 9 September 2021 from https://unesdoc.unesco.org/ark:/48223/pf0000235409_eng.

Wiik, A., Lundberg, T.R., Rullman, E., Andersson, D.P., Holmberg, M., Mandić, M., … & Gustafsson, T. (2020). Muscle strength, size, and composition following 12 months of gender-affirming treatment in transgender individuals. *The Journal of Clinical Endocrinology & Metabolism*, 105(3), e805–e813.

Witcomb, G.L., Bouman, W.P., Brewin, N., Richards, C., Fernandez-Aranda, F., & Arcelus, J. (2015). Body image dissatisfaction and eating-related psychopathology in trans individuals: A matched control study. *European Eating Disorders Review*, 23(4), 287–293.

Witcomb, G.L., Bouman, W.P., Claes, L., Brewin, N., Crawford, J.R., & Arcelus, J. (2018). Levels of depression in transgender people and its predictors: Results of a large matched control study with transgender people accessing clinical services. *Journal of Affective Disorders*, 235, 308–315.

Witcomb, G.L., Claes, L., Bouman, W.P., Nixon, E., Motmans, J., & Arcelus, J. (2019). Experiences and psychological wellbeing outcomes associated with bullying in treatment-seeking transgender and gender-diverse youth. *LGBT Health*, 6(5), 216–226.

Chapter 2

Sex Segregation in Elite Sport

What's the Problem?

Jaime Schultz

Introduction

Elite sport is one of the few global institutions still guided by policies that mandate sex segregation. It has always been that way, but is that the way it will always be? In recent history, activists have challenged segregationist policies, calling for their modification and even obliteration to better include gender diverse athletes.[1] Sporting authorities have responded to these challenges in various ways, but have consistently left intact a two-sex model of sport and insisted sporting bodies conform to that binary.

Political scientist Carol Lee Bacchi's (2009) 'What's the problem represented to be?' (WPR) methodology offers valuable insight into elite sport's policies on gender diversity. As Bacchi argues, policymakers do not react to fixed, external, or independent problems, but rather 'constitute (or give shape to) "problems"' through policy discourse (p. 1). Additionally, Bacchi continues, 'the way in which the "problem" is represented carries all sorts of implications for how the issue is thought about and for how the people involved are treated, and are evoked to think about themselves' (p. 1). A WPR analysis of the policies, regulations, expert commentary, and consensus statements concerning gender diversity illuminates how sport's governing bodies—specifically the International Olympic Committee (IOC) and the International Association of Athletics Federations (IAAF, now World Athletics) – *problematize* intersex and trans athletes in women's sport.[2]

This chapter begins with the recognition that the genealogy of the 'problem' does not begin with the first policy regarding gender diversity. Instead, it begins with the organization of elite sport by and for men to the exclusion of women. After establishing some of the early rationales against women's involvement, I address women's push for greater access to sport throughout the twentieth century. With new opportunities, however, came questions about competitors' sex. Consequently, organizers developed a number of strategies to maintain sex segregation and, simultaneously, to define essentialized notions of femininity and 'femaleness'.

A WPR approach to policies regarding intersex and transgender athletes yields that the discourse of 'fairness' and maintaining an 'even playing field', the

DOI: 10.4324/9781003050568-2

policies in question presuppose male biological athletic superiority. According to this logic, any indicator of 'maleness' in women's sport grants a competitor an unfair advantage. Ultimately, I argue that representing the 'problem' of gender diversity in women's sport elicits two significant effects. First, it suggests the physical inferiority of female athletes, which justifies and sustains their subordinate status in sport. Second, it stigmatizes and ultimately erases non-binary sport participation, which can have devastating consequences for athletes and non-athletes alike.

Historical Rationales against Women in Sport

From the beginning, sport has been organized for men in ways that privilege culturally sanctioned versions of masculinity. The ancient Olympic Games (776 BCE to 393 CE), for instance, barred women not just as athletes, but also as spectators. Girls and young women might have competed in the Heraean Games and similar festivals, but these were not only separate from what men did, but also perceived to be inferior and insignificant (Spears, 1984).

When Baron Pierre de Coubertin and his aristocratic compatriots sought to revive the Games in the 1890s, they adopted the Greeks' position on distaff competitors. As de Coubertin remarked in 1912:

> [T]he Olympic Games must be reserved for men ... we have tried and must continue to try to achieve the following definition: the solemn and periodic exaltation of male athleticism with internationalism as a base, loyalty as a means, art for its setting, and female applause as reward.
>
> (in Chatziefstathiou, 2008, pp. 101–2)

Women could watch and cheer, but competition was unequivocally for male athletes only. Like de Coubertin, other nineteenth-century organizers of modern sport took their cues from classical antiquity and denounced women's participation. In the throes of industrialization, sport became a masculine refuge from social tumult, a practice to build up one's body in the absence of manual labour, and an inoculation against society's 'feminizing' influences (Messner, 1988).

Not everyone subscribed to the influential Baron's point of view. He had no authority to keep women from carving out their own athletic spaces and opportunities, although he consistently expressed dismay, if not outright disgust over their efforts. The 'indecency, ugliness and impropriety' of women in the Games, he believed, would only result in 'destroying their feminine charm and leading to the downfall and degradation of sport' (in Loy, et al., 2009, p. 12). Sport ruins women; women ruin sport.

Sport officials drew on a pernicious mix of medical, social, and aesthetic rationales to maintain women's exclusion (Kay & Jeanes, 2008). The primary medical concern, although not one backed by any actual medical study, was that sport would damage women's reproductive capabilities. Strenuous activity, according to an 1898 article in the German *Journal of Physical Education*, 'can cause a shift in the position and a loosening of the uterus as well as prolapse and bleeding, with resulting sterility, thus defeating a woman's true purpose in life, i.e. the bringing forth of strong children' (quoted in Pfister, 1990, p. 191). To engage in sport was to sacrifice one's maternal mission.

Pseudo-medical myths about women's delicate 'nature' further prevented women from vigorous physical activity—as well as from education, politics, certain jobs, and other aspects of the public sphere (Theberge, 1989; Dowling, 2000). In 1921, English Football Association leaders argued that the game was 'quite unsuitable for females' and banned women's teams from club grounds for the next fifty years (in Hargreaves, 1989, p. 142). A decade later, the same 'unsuitability' argument was used against Australian women in rugby (Downes et al., 2015, p. 2153). Members of Brazil's National Sports Council similarly decreed in 1941 that women would 'not be allowed to practice sports incompatible with the conditions of their nature' and barred women from organized football until 1979 (Rial, 2012).

These justifications dovetailed with aesthetic rationales against women's sport participation, most of which followed along three lines. First, as American sportswriter Paul Gallico argued in 1938, only 'unattractive girls' were any good at sport. 'Pretty girls are not. The ugly ducklings, have taken to sport as an escape and to compensate for whatever it is they lack, sex appeal, charm, ready-made beauty' (p. 233). Second, detractors worried that sport *made* girls and women unattractive. In 'masculine' sports such as track and field, women's 'charms shrink to something less than zero', assessed one journalist ('Things seen', 1936, p. 18). Third, women's sport performance was an unsightly spectacle. On women's participation in bobsleigh, de Coubertin decried, 'that sight represents a true offense to the eyes. Nothing uglier could be imagined' (in Leigh, 1974, p. 61).

Finally, social rationales against female athletes had to do with the gendered expectations about what was appropriate for men and women. If athletic prowess signified hegemonic masculinity, how could one reconcile that trait in girls and women? And if girls and women could become skilled and accomplished athletes, what would that mean for sport's status as a 'man maker', as sporting goods magnate A.G. Spalding (1911, p. 533) characterized baseball.

Early Questions of Gender Diversity in Women's Sport

Of course, women have always found ways to participate in sport—including baseball. At American women's colleges, safely sheltered from public scrutiny, women took to the diamond with great enthusiasm. Basketball, too, was an early favourite. Shortly after James Naismith invented the game in 1891, women physical educators adapted it to suit their students' 'feminine' constitutions—devising less strenuous nine- and six-player versions in the US or, as in the UK, creating netball (Taylor, 2001; Grundy & Shackelford, 2017). Both physical education and sport developed differently for men and women in ways that naturalized the perceived social and biological differences between the sexes.

Rebuffed by the rationales that constrained their athletic potential, women had 'no solution other than to create their own societies and own sports federations', as the French athlete and organizer Alice Milliat warned the establishment (in Ferez, 2012, p. 274). True to her word, Milliat established the *Fédération Sportive Féminine Internationale* in 1921 and hosted the First Women's World Olympic Games the following year (the event became the Women's World Games after the IOC objected to the use of the word *Olympic*). The games proved successful in terms of participation, member nations, and spectatorship (Leigh & Bonin, 1977). Moreover, they spurred the IOC to action. The committee, no longer willing to rest on the ideals of de Coubertin, moved to create new opportunities for women. Yet, as soon as these opportunities materialized, so too did questions about competitors' sex.

These questions were especially pronounced with the addition of women's athletics to the 1928 Olympic programme. Commenting on the inaugural women's 800-metre race, for example, journalists speculated that Japan's silver medallist, Hitomi Kinue, was '40 or 50 percent male' (in Pieper, 2016, p. 19). American Olympic Committee president Avery Brundage likewise assumed that sportswomen's sex could be gauged by degrees. In 1936, he 'roundly recommended that all women athletes entered in the Olympics be subjected to a thorough physical examination to make sure they were really 100% female' ('Olympic Games', 1936, p. 28).

At the same time, a number of sensationalized events amplified gender anxieties, including reports in *Time* that 'two athletes who recently competed in European track events as women were later transformed into men by sex operations'. According to the article, the athletes, who both retired before undergoing gender affirming surgeries, were 'hermaphrodites' or 'pseudo-hermaphrodites' who had been raised as females ('Change of Sex', 1936; Tebbutt, 2015). Based on these and other media accounts, early concerns about gender diversity evidently fixated on athletes with differences of sex development and their eligibility to compete in women's sport.

Observers expressed related concerns over American sprinter Helen Stephens, who beat Polish rival, Stella Walsh (Stanisława Walasiewicz) in the 1936 Olympic 100-metre race. Polish journalists alternatively reported that Stephens was either a man, or so masculine in appearance that Frederick the Great would have drafted her 'into the grenadier's regiment' (in Anderson, 2017, p. 107). The American press defended their champion, asserting that 'German Olympic officials had ascertained her true sex before admitting her participation in the 1936 Games' ('Helen Stephens a Man', 1936, p. 20; see also Kinney-Hanson, 2004, p. 96; Gallico, 1938, pp. 233–4). Although unconfirmed, the statement alludes to an early iteration of sex testing.

If Stephens did undergo some type of examination, it was neither official IOC policy nor comprehensively applied to all competitors, for it might have disqualified Walsh. In 1980, after a long, decorated athletic career that included five gold and four silver Olympic medals, assailants shot and killed Walsh during a robbery. Although both her birth and death certificates identify her as female, upon autopsy, a coroner determined that Walsh possessed 'tiny', 'incomplete', non-functioning male sex organs, as well genetic mosaicism: 'The majority of her cells examined had a normal X and Y chromosome, and a minority of her cells contained a single X chromosome and no Y chromosome' ('Tests Show' 1981, sec. A, p. 2). Despite her difference of sex development, observers generally interpreted the coroner's report in one way: 'that Stella Walsh was a man' (Guttmann, 1991, p. 169; Cohn, 1981, sec. A, p. 1).

Based on that misinterpretation, critics lobbied to posthumously revoke Walsh's Olympic medals. 'Fair is fair', reasoned Roxanne Atkins Andersen, a hurdling champion of the 1930s turned athletics administrator. 'If Stella was a man, she had an unfair advantage' (in Diadiun, 1991). Track and field officials ultimately let Walsh's medals stand, primarily because there were no sex-based regulations in place during the peak of her career. Just the same, comments like Andersen's show the rigidity of the sex binary—that any difference of sex development made Walsh un-female and therefore male—and the presumption that any element of 'maleness' confers 'unfair' advantage in women's sport.

As with Walsh, an exam used to 'ascertain' the sex of Helen Stephens might have also disqualified Heinrich Ratjen, who took fourth in the 1936 Olympic women's high jump and, two years later, set a world record in the event. Shortly thereafter, police arrested the athlete for impersonating a woman, judging his feminine clothing incongruent with his masculine features. Although a midwife had declared Ratjen female at birth and his official documents identified him as a woman, a post-arrest medical examination re-classified Ratjen as male, and he lived the remainder of his life as a man (Berg, 2009).

'Of course', asserts historian Vanessa Heggie (2010), 'neither Walsh nor Ratjen had anything whatsoever to do with the introduction of sex testing'. As Heggie explains, the 'stories were revealed years, in one case nearly thirty years, after they had stopped competing, and neither were made broadly public until after systematic sex testing had already been introduced into international sports' (p. 158). Furthermore, neither athlete was a 'gender fraud', as many accounts have unjustly characterized them (e.g., Cameron, 1996, p. 8; Jönsson, 2007; Schultz, 2014). Rather, they did not fit neatly into the sex/gender binary.

For a system predicated on the maintenance and segregation of two sexes, gender diversity posed a problem, or, more accurately, the organizers of elite women's sport *represented* gender diversity as a problem. So did women's sport advocates, who worried that female athletes who seemed 'masculine' in appearance or performance might set back any progress they made. Consequently, athletic administrators began to devise policies to assure competitors and the public that women athletes were, in fact, women.

Importantly, these policies have had almost no effect on men's sport. A successful performance against other men is the only 'sex test' needed. Thus, any regulations designed to keep women out of men's sport take on a decidedly different cast. They are not about ensuring a 'level playing field', but about protecting sanctity of a male preserve and, simultaneously, protecting the 'weaker sex' from the injuries they would invariably sustain when competing with men—a slight variation on the historical refrain: women ruin men's sport; men's sport ruins women.

Determining Femaleness

Initially, there was no official policy for determining sex in elite sport. That began to change as international sport took on additional significance in the Cold War era. In 1946, the IAAF required all athletes competing in women-only events to present medical certificates confirming that they were women. The IOC followed suit for the 1948 Summer Games, though neither organization detailed what criteria physicians should endorse (Heggie, 2010).

In 1966, the IAAF initiated its first standardized, pre-competition sex test, 'because', *Life* reported in an article titled 'Are girl athletes really girls?' (1966), 'there had been persistent speculation through the years about women who turn in manly performances' (pp. 64–65). Put differently, successful women athletes were too fast, too strong, too good to be 'real' women. For the same reason, officials insisted that female athletes undergo gynaecological examinations at the British Empire and Commonwealth Games in Kingston, Jamaica. The exam, as one competitor characterized it, was the 'most crude and degrading experience I have even known in my life' (Peters, 1974, pp. 55–6; see also Stratford, 1988, p. 199).

Later that year, at the 1966 European Athletics Championships in Budapest, Hungary, authorities compelled female athletes to present themselves in a 'nude parade' before a panel of physicians. The inspection, *Time* reported, 'was perfunctory. Lined up in single file, the 234 female athletes paraded past three female gynaecologists. "They let you walk by," said one competitor afterward. "Then they asked you to turn and face them, and that was it'" ('Preserving', 1966, p. 74). That several Eastern Bloc women refused to comply and dropped out of elite sport only fuelled suspicions about their sex. The test, crowed IAAF president David Burghley, 'has been successful in frightening the doubtful ones away' (in Pieper, 2016, p. 54).

The discovery of the Barr body—the second X chromosome in the sex chromosome pair—presented IAAF authorities with what they regarded as a 'simpler, objective and more dignified' way to determine sex (Hay, 1972, p. 998). Inaugurated at the 1967 European Cup in Kiev, testers swabbed female competitors' cheeks to analyse for the presence of the Barr body. Anything other than XX spelled disqualification.

Such was the case for Polish sprinter Ewa Kłobukowska, who became the test's first athletic casualty. Although she passed the visual inspection the previous year, testers in Kiev, Soviet Union, determined that Kłobukowska had 'one chromosome too many' (presumed to be 46,XY/47,XXY mosaicism), disqualified her from sport, rescinded her medals, and wiped her name from the record books ('Sex Test', 1967, p. 28; see also Simpson et al., 1993). 'It's a dirty and stupid thing to do to me', the twenty-one-year-old athlete said at the time. 'I know what I am and how I feel' (in 'Records', 1968, p. 40). Yet, throughout the history of sex determination, what an athlete knows and how she feels has been largely irrelevant to where she can compete in sport.

Despite objections from scientists and physicians, including Murray Barr of the eponymous Barr body, the sex chromatin test remained in place for the next three decades (Moore, 1968; De la Chapelle, 1987; Ferris, 1992). As Eduardo Hay (1972), chief of testing for the IOC's Medical Commission explained, the exam 'verifies that the athletes are competing on an equal basis considering their physical status. In the cases of intersexuality or hermaphroditism, the athlete must be barred from competition in order to insure [*sic*] *fair* play' (p. 999).

The discourse of 'fair play', equality, and 'physical status' appears throughout the policies designed to determine femaleness. In effect, the regulations brand gender diverse athletes as 'cheats', 'freaks', or both—representing individual athletes as the 'problem' that must be addressed, rather than problematizing a sport system that will not accommodate them (Bacchi, 2009). After the 'Kłobukowska affair', for example, IOC executive Monique Berlioux urged the continuation of sex testing to identify any 'sexual mutation'. This would 'put an end to the cheating, which takes place, whether intentionally or not' and was also necessary to keep women's athletics on 'the road to progress' in the face of speculation about 'virile' women athletes. 'Nothing is more prejudicial to female sport [than] this charlatanry; nothing can kill it more surely' (Berlioux, 1967, p. 1). Women with differences of sex development were not only female imposters, Berlioux suggested, but also saboteurs of women's sport.

Following Kłobukowska's humiliating and undoubtedly devastating disqualification, sports officials pledged confidentiality. As a result, sex testing (and its looming threat) excluded an untold number of women. Athletes who produced 'abnormal' test results at local, regional, or national levels were often counselled to quietly retire from sport. It was only when someone openly challenged her results, as hurdler María José Martínez-Patiño did, that the public learned about adverse results. After undergoing assessment at the 1985 World University Games in Kobe, Japan, officials advised Martínez-Patiño to drop out of the competition and await their decision. She complied and later received word: 'Karyotype is decided 46, XY' (Martínez-Patiño, 2005, p. S38). Male sex chromosomes branded her a man and made her ineligible for women's sport.

The news came as a shock to the Spanish athlete. 'I could hardly pretend to be a man', Martínez-Patiño (2005) later wrote. 'I have breasts and a vagina. I never cheated. I fought my disqualification' (p. S38). During the course of that fight, she learned that she has complete androgen insensitivity syndrome, a condition in which cells do not form typical androgen receptors and, consequently, cannot respond to testosterone. She was, as one expert put it, 'disqualified for having an advantage that she didn't have' (in Carlson, 1988, p. 29). Martínez-Patiño successfully fought to be reinstated to women's sport and the IAAF subsequently dropped the sex chromatin test, conceding that two Xs were not enough to determine femaleness. The IOC followed suit in 1999.[3]

Testosterone and Other 'Suspicious' Problems

In the early 1990s, the IAAF recognized that 'women athletes have been excluded unfairly from competition because of erroneous sex chromatin testing and medical ignorance' and announced, 'We have no femininity list—the file is closed' (Ljungqvist & Simpson, 1992, p. 852; Vines, 1992, p. 39). However, officials maintained a sex-testing 'reserve clause' in order to pacify lingering concerns 'about men masquerading as women' (Elsas, et al., 2000; Ljungqvist & Simpson, 1992, p. 850). Yet, as Dickinson et al. (2002, p. 1542) point out, '[g]enuine sex-impostors have not been uncovered by laboratory-based genetic testing'. Quite frankly, 'men masquerading as women' was never really the issue, despite persistent rumours to the contrary. Nevertheless, as Dickinson and colleagues continue, 'gender verification procedures have resulted in substantial harm to a number of women athletes' with various differences of sex development (Ibid.).

Since the turn of the twenty-first century, sex testing has persisted in a less comprehensive but perhaps more 'wicked' manifestation (Schultz, 2021). According to the IAAF's 2006 *IAAF Policy on Gender Verification*, although there was 'no compulsory, standard or regular gender verification', officials reserved the right to test female athletes in order 'to be able to address the occasional anomalies that do surface'. Specifically, 'if there is any "suspicion" or if there is a "challenge" by a competitor', the athlete in question must submit to a medical evaluation before a panel comprised of a gynecologist, endocrinologist, psychologist, internal medicine specialist, expert on gender/transgender issues'. If the athlete refused the evaluation, she forfeited her right to compete as a woman. The policy, its authors explained, was designed to offer 'proper guidelines to organizers, national associations, athletes and officials' for 'how to approach this *problem*' (IAAF, 2006, emphasis added). 'Suspicious' (read: 'masculine') women, by dint of performance or appearance, were the problem.

Middle-distance runner Santhi Soundarajan found herself in the crosshairs of suspicion-based testing after the 2006 Asian Games, when the Indian Olympic Association disclosed that she 'did not possess the sexual characteristics of a woman' ('Indian Runner', 2006). Without explaining what those characteristics were, officials stripped Soundarajan of the silver medal and banned her from future competitions. The athlete attempted suicide not long after that, telling reporters that she was 'physically and mentally totally broken' (in Bhowmick & Thottam, 2009; see Mitra, 2014). As Bacchi (2009) stresses, 'How "problems" are represented directly affects people's lives' (p. 17).

Representation also affected the life of South Africa's Caster Semenya, who similarly struck observers as 'suspicious' at the 2009 World Championships. Shortly before the finals of the 800-meter race, IAAF officials broke confidentiality to confirm rumours that Semenya did 'not meet the requirements to compete as a woman' ('Semenya', 2009; see also Schultz, 2011; Schultz, 2012a). Semenya went on to win the race, after which administrators requested she abstain from further competition while 'a group of medical experts' reviewed her 'gender verification test results'. In language eerily like that of the 1920s and 1930s, IAAF secretary Pierre Wiess commented, 'It is clear that she is a woman but maybe not 100 per cent' (in 'Semenya', 2009).

As with Soundarajan, officials did not explain what 'requirements' they deemed necessary 'to compete as a woman'. This did not stop muckraking journalists and social media commentators from speculating that it had something to do with Semenya's testosterone (Harrell, 2009; Schultz, 2012b). The IAAF's 2011 *Regulations Governing Eligibility of Females with Hyperandrogenism to Compete in Women's Competition* all but confirmed those rumours. Specifically, the regulations reframed the 'problem' as women with *hyperandrogenism*, a condition the federation defined as female athletes whose blood tests measured 10 or more nanomoles of testosterone per litre of serum (10nmol/L)—a measure that exceeded the 'normal' female range and registered at the low end of 'normal' male range (p. 12). The regulations stipulated that women diagnosed with hyperandrogenism must comply with a 'prescribed medical treatment' to lower their testosterone below 10nmol/L in order to compete in women's events (p. 13; for critiques see Karkazis et al., 2012; Sudai, 2017; Karkazis & Carpenter, 2018; Sönksen et al., 2018). Refusal of treatment was a disqualifying offence.

Although the IAAF attempted to represent the 'problem' as testosterone, not sex, it nevertheless justified its policy by upholding the tradition and importance of sex segregation in sport:

> Since 1928, competition in Athletics has been strictly divided into male and female classifications and females have competed in Athletics in a separate category designed to recognize their specific physical aptitude and performance.
>
> The difference in athletic performance between males and females is known to be predominantly due to higher levels of androgenic hormones in males resulting in increased strength and muscle development.
>
> (IAAF, 2011)

Whereas the IAAF announced it had 'abandoned all reference to the terminology "gender verification" and "gender policy" in its Rules', the test for hyperandrogenism produced the same effect: to detect and exclude gender diversity in order to 'respect ... the very essence if male and female classifications in Athletics' as the 'fundamental notion of fairness of competition in female Athletics' (Ibid.).

The hyperandrogenism rule remained in place, for both the IAAF and the IOC, until nineteen-year-old sprinter Dutee Chand challenged it in the Court of Arbitration for Sport (CAS). In 2014, the Athletics Federation of India ruled Chand ineligible to compete as a woman due to hyperandrogenism. Chand refused to submit to treatment, maintaining that the 'high androgen level produced by my body is natural. I have not doped or cheated'. She went on to explain that experts advised that any medical intervention to lower her androgen levels was 'unscientific', 'invasive', 'often irreversible and will harm my health now and into the future' (*Dutee Chand v. Athletics Federation of India*, 2015). The IAAF's insistence that she bring her biology into compliance with the latest definition of femaleness could have significant adverse effects.

At the CAS hearing, the IAAF's legal team defended the hyperandrogenism policy on the grounds that women with 'male levels' of testosterone would turn in 'male levels' of performance and undermine the principles of sex segregation. They pointed to research that found the average performance gap between elite male and female athletes in comparable events is 12.64 per cent, and concluded that '[d]ifferences in testosterone are the most significant factor in explaining the performance differences between male and female athletes' (p. 59; 36). Based on the testimony of bioethicist Thomas Murray, the IAAF maintained that 'women are to be treated as a "*protected class*" in athletics competition'. Hence, the federation has '*an ethical obligation to assure that women athletes … do not have to compete against athletes with hormone-related performance advantages commonly associated with men*"' (p. 70, emphasis in original).

The CAS arbiters agreed with the IAAF's reasoning, but ruled in Chand's favour because the IAAF had 'insufficient evidence about the *degree* of the advantage that androgen-sensitive hyperandrogenic females enjoy over non-hyperandrogenic females' (*Dutee Chand v. Athletics Federation of India*, 2015, emphasis in original). Specifically, the IAAF lacked the scientific backing to argue that hyperandrogenic women enjoyed 'commensurate significance to the competitive advantage that male athletes enjoy over female athletes' – that women with 'high' testosterone were not out-performing women with 'normal' testosterone by anything approximating a 12.64 per cent margin (p. 154). The court gave the IAAF two years to find research to support its policy.

Just as the IAAF's grace period was about to expire, it replaced the hyperandrogenism policy with the 2018 *Eligibility Regulations for the Female Classification (Athletes with Differences of Sex Development)*, which effectively dismissed Chand's case. In brief, the new regulations specifically and, perhaps, suspiciously concern athletes who: 1) show serum testosterone equal to or greater than 5nmol/L (half that of the previous regulations); 2) are sensitive to testosterone; 3) compete in international competitions in the 400m, 400m hurdles, 800m, 1500-meter, and mile races. In any other events, the regulations do not apply, leading some analysts to denounce the regulations as 'Semenya targeting'. Even more, critics argue, the regulations seem to disproportionately affect women of colour from the Global South (Hoad, 2010; Magubane, 2014;

Munro, 2010; Nyong'o, 2010; Henne & Pape, 2018; Karkazis & Jordan-Young, 2018).

Semenya fought back against the new regulations in CAS, arguing that forcing women to suppress their natural testosterone is discriminatory, unnecessary, lacks scientific grounding, and does 'irreparable harm to affected female athletes' (*Mokgadi Caster Semenya v. International Association of Athletics Federations*, 2019). As before, the IAAF countered because of 'the significant advantages in size, strength and power enjoyed (on average) by men over women', it must 'place conditions' on the female category in order 'to ensure fair and meaningful competition' (Ibid.). CAS's three-person panel voted 2–1 in favour of the IAAF. The regulations stand. As of the writing of this chapter, several organizations, including the Union Cycliste Internationale and the International Tennis Federation, have adopted comparable standards and it seems likely that others will follow suit.

Since at least 2011, then, the measure of testosterone has become, in effect, the measure of femaleness. Indeed, the hormone has become the defining characteristic for both intersex and trans athletes, despite their significant differences. And although policies, regulations, and consensus statements about the eligibility of trans athletes are relatively new developments, trans athletes have always been implicitly implicated in sex testing policies.

Eligibility Policies for Trans Athletes

The United States Tennis Association (USTA) explicitly made the connection between athletes with differences of sex development and trans athletes upon receipt of Renée Richards's application to compete in the 1976 US Open. Although Richards provided 'gynecological affirmation that she is a woman', the USTA, the Women's Tennis Association, and the US Open Committee sought to bar the trans woman's participation by initiating the Barr Body test for all female competitors ('U.S. Open', 1976, p. 52). In an official statement, the USTA explained 'that the entry into women's events … of persons not genetically female would introduce an element of inequality and unfairness into championships' (in 'MD Tennis star's sex surgery', 1979).

The charge of inequality and unfairness centered squarely on Richards's biological advantage—those associated with her natal maleness. But, as Birrell and Cole (1990) note, absent from the discussion were Richards's advantages associated with 'white male privilege, including attendance at a boys' prep school, graduation from Yale … and access to highly competitive tennis' (p. 12). For all the concern of 'fairness' in policies about gender diversity in sport, there is very little concern for the social and cultural advantages many elite athletes enjoy over others—regardless of sex.

Richards refused the test and sued the USTA for gender discrimination. The New York Supreme Court ruled in her favour, finding that the Association's insistence upon the exam was 'grossly unfair, discriminatory and inequitable and violative of her rights' (*Reneé Richards v USTA* 1977). Richards subsequently played in the 1977 US Open, where she lost in the first round and temporarily quelled anxieties about any influx of 'young male players with transsexual tendencies' (Amdur, 1976, p. 17). Still, it is worth noting that although Richards challenges sporting definitions of femaleness, she does not disrupt the sporting binary. As Birrell and Cole (1990) argue, Richards instead 'unravels and rebinds our cultural notion that there are two and only two, mutually exclusive, naturally occurring, immutable, *opposite* sexes' (p. 4, emphasis in original; see also Travers, 2006).

As trans athletes continued to fight for inclusion, the IOC's 2004 *Statement of the Stockholm Consensus on Sex Reassignment in Sports* was 'important', according to Cavanagh and Sykes (2006) because, until then, 'most sport governing bodies either had no policy designed to admit transsexual or intersexed persons into competition or defaulted into a reactionary "female at birth" policy' (p. 89). Specifically, the *Stockholm Consensus* recommended that trans athletes undergo 'surgical anatomical changes', 'legal recognition of their assigned sex', and 'hormonal therapy appropriate for their assigned sex' in order to be eligible to compete as their lived gender. Seemingly progressive, the document offered a 'very narrow definition of transsexuality' that excluded many trans and gender diverse athletes (Cavanagh & Sykes, 2006, p. 78). The solution to the 'problem' of trans eligibility was neither an option for, nor necessarily desired by the spectrum of athletes to which it applied. And although the statement was not official policy, it nevertheless provided a template that multiple sports organizations soon followed (Genel, 2017; Jones et al., 2017).

Over a decade later, the IOC reversed its position on surgery and legal recognition in its 2015 *Consensus Meeting on Sex Reassignment and Hyperandrogenism*, a document that consolidated and unfortunately conflated intersex and trans considerations. The document clearly identifies trans and hyperandrogenic *women* as the 'problem' in sport. The diagnosis of hyperandrogenism does not apply to men and, according to the statement's 'Transgender Guidelines', athletes 'who transition from female to male are eligible to compete in the male category without restriction' (p. 2). Conversely, athletes 'who transition from male to female' are only eligible to compete as women if they have 'declared that [their] gender identity is female' and do not change that declaration for a minimum of four years. Trans women must also maintain their testosterone level in serum below 10 noml/L—the same stipulation as appears under the document's 'Hyperandrogenism' guidelines—all in the name of 'fairness' and 'the protection of women in sport' (IOC, 2015, pp. 2–3; see also Pitsiladis, et al., 2016).

Although some organizations have followed the IOC's 2015 recommendations, policies devoted to trans athletes are decidedly inconsistent, vary by sport, and change from one organization to another, one level and one place to the next. The Fédération Internationale de Volleyball (2014), for example, defaults to the sex designated on an athlete's birth certificate, while World Rugby (n.d.) requires gender-affirming surgery and legal recognition of assigned sex. The International Powerlifting Federation follows the IOC's 2015 *Consensus Statement*, but USA Powerlifting breaks rank to specifically exclude trans women (USA Powerlifting, n.d.). As the US organization explains on its website, 'powerlifting is a sport of strength .... While MTF [male-to-female transgender athlete] may be weaker and less muscle [*sic*] than they once were, the biological benefits given them at birth still remain over than [*sic*] of a female'. USA Powerlifting does, however, 'allow transgender men' to compete in the men's category, presumably because there are no 'biological benefits' associated with natal females in strength sports.

Although it is difficult to draw conclusions from these and other competing positions, they have at least one element in common: policies regarding gender diverse athletes—no matter how seemingly sensitive or progressive—ultimately sanction discrimination and 'othering'. Simply having a policy and naming it according to a particular 'condition' or identity renders that condition or identity problematic.

Conclusion: The Effects of Problem Representation

Integral to the WPR approach, Bacchi (2009) asks researchers to consider 'what effects are produced by the representation of the problem' (p. 2). Certainly, representing gender diverse athletes as threats to women's sport and to the spirit of fair play produces any number of effects, but two are most germane to this chapter. The first is that a system that insists upon a binary sex model unavoidably establishes hierarchy because, as evidenced in the IAAF's defence against Chand and Semenya, it is upheld by the comparison of gendered athletic performances. If women are to have a sporting chance, proponents of sex segregation argue, both segregation and a clear definition of femaleness are imperative (Coleman, 2017; Harper, 2017).

Still, history has repeatedly shown that separate is not equal (McDonagh & Pappano, 2007; Milner & Braddock, 2016). This dichotomy was particularly conspicuous in the US women's national football team's fight against 'institutionalized gender discrimination'. Just before the 2019 World Cup, team members collectively filed suit against the US Soccer Federation for paying them substantially less than the men, even though the two teams perform 'substantially equal work' (in Lardieri, 2019).

In a motion to dismiss the case, the US federation argued to the contrary. The two teams did not perform equal work because the men's game requires more 'skill, effort, and responsibility' than the women's (*Alex Morgan. et al. v. US Soccer Federation*, 2020, p. 10). As the federation's legal team asserted:

> It must ... be acknowledged that senior men's and women's international soccer require different levels of certain fundamental physical skills central

> to the game (e.g., speed and strength), which is why FIFA requires separate-sex teams in the first place, and no one is arguing that this sex-based separation, which is designed to ensure women a fair opportunity to play and compete, is unlawful (which it would be in almost any other circumstance).
>
> (*Alex Morgan. et al. v. US Soccer Federation* 2020, p. 18)

Because women cannot compete against men—because they are not as fast and strong as men, the federation argued—they are not 'engaged in equal work requiring equal skill under the law' and, for this reason, they are not entitled to equal pay (p. 19). This is just one example of the many ways that sex segregation positions female athletes and women's sport in a secondary position to justify their secondary treatment (see Pape, 2020; Sharrow, 2017).

A second effect of representing gender diverse athletes as threats to sport's spirit of fair play is that it pathologizes, stigmatizes, and erases gender diversity. Athletes must identify as either male or female for the purpose of sport and must ensure that their bodies conform to the biological parameters of those categories, as constructed by sport's governing bodies. This 'symbolically annihilates' gender diverse individuals, the effects of which reverberate well beyond the playing field (Tuchman, 1978). Sport sends a powerful message about which bodies count. Even for those individuals who have no chance or inclination to become elite athletes, the lack of their representation in elite sport matters.

According to the Human Rights Campaign Foundation (2020), transgender and gender non-conforming individuals are disproportionately affected by discrimination, social stigma, hate crimes, and violence, which 'is pervasive and often deadly in every part of the world' (p. 14). They are also 'more susceptible to elevated mental health risks including depression, anxiety and suicide' and are 'more likely to face physical health conditions' (p. 23). Sport may provide a refuge from the abuse and discrimination, yet, in order to compete, gender diverse individuals must often set aside their personal identities in order to adhere to sport's mutually exclusive sex categories. In the process, athletes may be forced 'to choose between a body that was home and a sport they loved', as one trans athlete put it (in Sosin, 2020).

Within sport and physical activity, research shows that gender diverse individuals experience physical and verbal abuse, discrimination, abjection, and exclusion (Semerjian & Cohen, 2006; Cohen & Semerjian, 2008; Lucas-Carr & Krane, 2011; Hargie et al., 2017; Jones et al., 2017; Pérez-Samaniego et al., 2019; Ingram & Thomas, 2019). These experiences can have devastating effects on individuals' health and wellbeing, not least of which is an avoidance of sport and physical activity, along with the many social, psychological, emotional and physical benefits that active pursuits can bring.

In response to these and other concerns, scholars have proposed reframing the 'problem' in terms of sport's rigidly sex-segregated model. Some recommend eliminating 'coercive' sex segregation in favour of 'voluntary' separation

(McDonagh & Pappano, 2009; Tännsjö, 2007). Others advise the equal representation of men and women on team sports (George, 2002), or that sports officials create 'third gender' categories for those who do not or will not conform to the two-sex model (Harper et al., 2018). In the end, these proposals leave intact the male and female categories, which both devalues women's athleticism and denigrates gender diversity.

Alternatively, Krane and Barber (2019) argue that a 'radical transformation of sport is necessary to become truly inclusive' (p. 231; see also Kane, 1995; Amy-Chinn, 2012; Archibald, 2019). To that end, Bianchi (2017) proposes a 'handicap system' similar to that used in golf but determined by athletes' 'levels of effective testosterone' (p. 230). In related proposals, scholars have looked to para sport and the use of 'sport classes' to re-organize sport (Kerr & Obel, 2017; ; Anderson et al., 2019).

These are interesting alternatives to sex segregation, but sport cannot be divorced from its larger context. Certainly, times are changing, yet male and female categories continue to hold sway. Without first undergoing a 'radical transformation' of society, it is difficult to imagine that sport officials will begin to problematize sex segregation. Sport, one might argue, could lead the charge. Perhaps. But, at least in the foreseeable future, policy makers will continue to represent gender diversity as a 'problem', which will, no matter the 'solution', engender significant and long-lasting effects.

Notes

1 Consistent with the editors' definition, 'gender diversity' is used here as an umbrella term that refers to individuals whose gender does not align with their birth-assigned sex and/or who may experience gender outside of a binary framework.

2 See L. Dawn Bavington's (2019) work on a WPR approach to regulations on hyperandrogenism in women's sport.

3 In 1992, the IOC's Medical Commission continued by looking for a specific gene on the Y chromosome—the *SRY* gene—associated with sex differentiation. At the 1996 Games in Atlanta, Georgia, eight female athletes out of a total 3,387 (1 in 423) exhibited the *SRY* gene. Additional examinations determined that seven of those women had androgen insensitivity syndrome (four complete, three partial), and one woman had 5α-reductase deficiency, in which testosterone cannot be converted to its active metabolite, dihydrotestosterone. Medical authorities cleared all eight women to compete as women. In light of the time, expense, disturbance, and ultimate futility of genetic sex testing, the IOC declared its cessation in 1999 (Serrat & Herreros, 1993; Elsas et al., 1997; Genel, 2000).

References

Alex Morgan, et al. v. US Soccer Federation, Inc., 2:19-cv-0717-RGK-AGR. Defendant's memorandum of points and authorities in support of its motion for summary judgement. (United States District Court, Central District of California, 2020). Retrieved 16 June, 2021, from https://static.reuters.com/resources/media/editorial/20200224/morganvussoccer–soccerSJmotion.pdf.

Amdur, N. (1976). Women's tennis. *New York Times*, 31 December, 17.

Amy-Chinn, D. (2012). The taxonomy and ontology of sexual difference: Implications for sport. *Sport in Society*, 15(9), 1291–1305.

Anderson, L., Knox, T., & Heather, A. (2019). Trans-athletes in elite sport: inclusion and fairness. *Emerging Topics in Life Sciences*, 3(6), 759–762.

Anderson, S. (2017). *The forgotten legacy of Stella Walsh: The greatest female athlete of her time*. Rowman & Littlefield.

Archibald, C.J. (2019). Transgender and intersex sports rights. *Virginia Journal of Social Policy and the Law*, 26(3), 246–276.

Are girl athletes really girls? (1966). *Life*, 7 October, 63–65.

Bacchi, C. (2009) *Analysing policy: What's the problem represented to be?*Melbourne: Pearson Education.

Bavington, L.D. (2019). Sex control in women's sport: a history of the present regulations on hyperandrogenism in female athletes. In V. Krane (Ed.), *Sex, gender, and sexuality in sport: Queer inquiries* (pp. 181–201). London: Routledge.

Berg, S. (2009). How Dora the man competed in the women's high jump. *Spiegel*, 15 September. Retrieved 16 June, 2021, from http://www.spiegel.de/international/germany/1936-berlin-olympics-how-dora-the-man-competed-in-the-woman-s-high-jump-a-649104.html.

Berlioux, M. (1967). Femininity. *IOC Newsletter*, December, 1–2.

Bhowmick, N., & Thottam, J. (2009). Gender and athletics: India's own Caster Semenya. *Time*, 1 September. Retrieved 16 June, 2021, from http://www.time.com/time/world/article/0,8599,1919562,00.html.

Bianchi, A. (2017). Transgender women in sport. *Journal of the Philosophy of Sport*, 44 (2), 229–242.

Birrell, S., & Cole, C.L. (1990). Double fault: Renee Richards and the construction and naturalization of difference. *Sociology of Sport Journal*, 7(1), 1–21.

Cameron, J. (1996). For women's own good: Gender verification of female athletes. *Women's Studies Journal*, 12(1), 7.

Carlson, A. (1988). Chromosome count. *Ms.*, October, 40–44.

Cavanagh, S.L., & Sykes, H. (2006). Transsexual bodies at the Olympics: The International Olympic Committee's policy on transsexual athletes at the 2004 Athens Summer Games. *Body & Society*, 12(3), 75–102.

Dutee Chand v. Athletics Federation of India and the International Association of Athletics Federation, CAS 2014/A/3759. (Court of Arbitration for Sport 2015). Retrieved 16 June, 2021, from https://www.doping.nl/media/kb/3317/CAS%202014_A_3759%20Dutee%20Chand%20vs.%20AFI%20%26%20IAAF%20%28S%29.pdf.

Change of sex. (1936). *Time*, 24 August, 28.

Chatziefstathiou, D. (2008). Reading Baron Pierre de Coubertin: Issues of gender and race. *Aethlon*, 25(2), 95–116.

Cohen, J.H., & Semerjian, T.Z. (2008). The collision of trans-experience and the politics of women's ice hockey. *International Journal of Transgenderism*, 10(3–4), 133–145.

Cohn, V. (1981). Famed Olympic medalist Stella Walsh wasn't a 'she', autopsy finds. *Washington Post*, 24 January, sec. A, p. 5.

Coleman, D.L. (2017). Sex in sport. *Law and Contemporary Problems*, 80(63), 63–126.

De la Chapelle, A. (1987). The use and misuse of sex chromatin screen for 'gender identification' of female athletes. *Journal of the American Medical Association*, 137 (4), 812.

Diadiun, T. (1991). Walsh's dignity assaulted. *Plain Dealer* (Cleveland, OH), 9 June. Retrieved 16 June, 2021, from ProQuest database.

Dickinson, B.D., Genel, M., Robinowitz, C.B., Turner, P.L., & Woods, G.L. (2002). Gender verification of female Olympic athletes. *Medicine & Science in Sports & Exercise*, 34(10), 1539–1542.

Dowling, C. (2000). *The frailty myth: Women approaching physical equality*. New York: Random House.

Downes, G., Syson, I., & Hay, R. (2015). 'Not merely an isolated game': Women's association football in Australia. *International Journal of the History of Sport*, 32(18), 2150–2170.

Elsas, L.J., Ljungqvist, A., Ferguson-Smit, M.A., Simpson, J.L., Genel, M., Carlson, A. S., Ferris, E., De La Chapelle, A., & Ehrhardt, A.A. (2000). Gender verification of female athletes. *Genetics in Medicine*, 2(4), 249–254.

Elsas, L.J., Hayes, R.P., & Muralidharan, K. (1997). Gender verification at the Centennial Olympic Games. *Journal of the Medical Association of Georgia*, 86(1), 50–54.

Evans, R.K., Scoville, C.R., Ito, M.A., & Mello, R.P. (2003). Upper body fatiguing exercise and shooting performance. *Military Medicine*, 168(6), 451–456.

Fédération Internationale de Volleyball. (2014). Sports regulations. Retrieved 16 June, 2021, from https://13248aea-16f8-fc0a-cf26-a9339dd2a3f0.filesusr.com/ugd/2bc3fc_d72b0af75a4840ac8e27a424e7e94691.pdf

Ferez, S. (2012). From women's exclusion to gender institution: A brief history of the sexual categorisation process within sport. *International Journal of the History of Sport*, 29(2), 272–285.

Ferris, E.A. (1992). Gender verification testing in sport. *British Medical Bulletin*, 48(3), 683–697.

Gallico, P. (1938). *A farewell to sport*. New York: Alfred A. Knopf.

Genel, M. (2017). Transgender athletes: how can they be accommodated? *Current Sports Medicine Reports*, 16(1), 12–13.

Genel, M. (2000). Gender verification no more. *Medscape Women's Health*, 5(3), E2.

George, B.G. (2002). Fifty/fifty: Ending sex segregation in school sports. *Ohio State Law Journal*, 63(4), 1107–1163.

Grundy, P., & Shackelford, S. (2017). *Shattering the glass: The remarkable history of women's basketball*. Chapel Hill: University of North Carolina Press.

Guttmann, A. (1991). *Women's sports: A history*. New York: Columbia University Press.

Hanson, S.K. (2004). *The life of Helen Stephens: The Fulton Flash*. Carbondale: Southern Illinois University Press.

Hargreaves, J. (1989). *Sporting females: Critical issues in the history and sociology of women's sports*. London: Routledge.

Hargie, O.D., Mitchell, D.H., & Somerville, I.J. (2017). 'People have a knack of making you feel excluded if they catch on to your difference': Transgender experiences of exclusion in sport. *International Review for the Sociology of Sport*, 52(2), 223–239.

Harper, J. (2017). Athletic gender. *Law and Contemporary Problems*, 80(63), 139–153.

Harper, J., Martinez-Patino, M., Pigozzi, F., & Pitsiladis, Y. (2018). Implications of a third gender for elite sports. *Current Sports Medicine Reports*, 17(2), 42–44.

Harrell, E. (2009). Is female track star a man? No simple answer. *Time*, 25 August. Retrieved 16 June, 2021, from http://content.time.com/time/health/article/0,8599,1918668,00.html

Hay, E. (1972). Sex determination in putative female athletes. *Journal of the American Medical Association*, 221(9), 998–999.

Heggie, V. (2010). Testing sex and gender in sports; reinventing reimagining and reconstructing histories. *Endeavour*, 34(4), 157–163.

Helen Stephens a man, Polish writer thinks. (1936). *Chicago Daily Tribune*, 6 August, 20.

Henne, K., & Pape, M. (2018). Dilemmas of gender and global sports governance: An invitation to Southern Theory. *Sociology of Sport Journal*, 35(3), 216–225.

Hoad, N. (2010). 'Run, Caster Semenya, run!' Nativism and the translations of gender variance. *Safundi*, 11(4), 397–405.

Human Rights Campaign Foundation. (2020). Dismantling a culture of violence: Understanding anti-transgender violence and ending the crisis. Retrieved 16 June, 2021, from https://assets2.hrc.org/files/assets/resources/2018AntiTransViolenceReportSHORTENED.pdf?_ga=2.6803889.2056750860.1585330013-1153193232.1585330013.

Indian runner fails gender test, loses medal. (2006). *ESPN*, 18 December. Retrieved 16 June, 2021, from https://www.espn.com/olympics/trackandfield/news/story?id=2701018.

Ingram, B.J., & Thomas, C.L. (2019). Transgender policy in sport, a review of current policy and commentary of the challenges of policy creation. *Current Sports Medicine Reports*, 18(6), 239–247.

International Association of Athletics Federation. (2006). IAAF policy on gender verification. Retrieved March 24, 2011 from https://ihra.org.au/wp-content/uploads/2009/01/iaaf_policy_on_gender_verification.pdf.

International Association of Athletics Federation. (2011). IAAF regulations governing eligibility of females with hyperandrogenism to compete in women's competition. Retrieved 17 December, 2014 from http://www.iaaf.org/medical/policy/.

International Olympic Committee. (2003). Statement of the Stockholm Consensus on sex reassignment in sports. Retrieved 16 June, 2021, from https://stillmed.olympic.org/Documents/Reports/EN/en_report_905.pdf.

International Olympic Committee. (2015). IOC consensus meeting on sex reassignment and hyperandrogenism. Retrieved 16 June, 2021, from https://stillmed.olympic.org/media/Document%20Library/OlympicOrg/IOC/Who-We-Are/Commissions/Medical-and-Scientific-Commission/EN-IOC-Consensus-Meeting-on-Sex-Reassignment-and-Hyperandrogenism.pdf#_ga=2.128536648.597943528.1525642719-1063924041.1525642719.

Jones, B.A., Arcelus, J., Bouman, W.P., & Haycraft, E. (2017). Sport and transgender people: A systematic review of the literature relating to sport participation and competitive sport policies. *Sports Medicine*, 47(4), 701–716.

Jönsson, K. (2007). Who's afraid of Stella Walsh? On gender, 'gene cheaters', and the promises of cyborg athletes. *Sports, Ethics and Philosophy*, 1(2), 239–262.

Kane, M.J. (1995). Resistance/transformation of the oppositional binary: Exposing sport as a continuum. *Journal of Sport and Social Issues*, 19(2), 191–218.

Karkazis, K., & Carpenter, M. (2018). Impossible 'choices': The inherent harms of regulating women's testosterone in sport. *Journal of Bioethical Inquiry*, 15(4), 579.

Karkazis, K., & Jordan-Young, R.M. (2018). The powers of testosterone: Obscuring race and regional bias in the regulation of women athletes. *Feminist Formations*, 30(2), 1–39.

Karkazis, K., Jordan-Young, R., Davis, G., & Camporesi, S. (2012). Out of bounds? A critique of the new policies on hyperandrogenism in elite female athletes. *American Journal of Bioethics*, 12(7), 3–16.

Kay, T., & Jeanes, R. (2008). Women, sport, and gender inequity. In B. Houlihan (Ed.), *Sport and Society: A Student Introduction* (pp. 130–154). Thousand Oaks, CA: Sage.

Kerr, R., & Obel, C. (2017). Reassembling sex: Reconsidering sex segregation policies in sport. *International Journal of Sport Policy and Politics*, 10(2), 305–320.

Kinney-Hanson, S.(2004). *The Life of Helen Stephens: The Fulton Flash*. Carbondale: Southern Illinois University Press.

Knox, T., Anderson, L.C., & Heather, A. (2019). Transwomen in elite sport: scientific and ethical considerations. *Journal of Medical Ethics*, 45(6), 395–403.

Krane, V., & Barber, H. (2019). Creating a new sport culture: Reflections on queering sport. In V. Krane (Ed.), *Sex, Gender, and Sexuality in Sport: Queer Inquiries* (pp. 223–237). London: Routledge.

Lardieri, A. (2019). Women's National Soccer Team sues soccer federation for gender discrimination. *US News and World Report*, 8 March. Retrieved 16 June, 2021, from https://www.usnews.com/news/national-news/articles/2019-03-08/womens-national-soccer-team-sues-soccer-federation-for-gender-discrimination.

Leigh, M.H. (1974). The evolution of women's participation in the Summer Olympic Games, 1900–1948 (PhD thesis., Ohio State University, 1974).

Leigh, M.H., & Bonin, T.M. (1977). The pioneering role of Madame Alice Milliat and the FSFI in establishing international track and field competition for women. *Journal of Sport History*, 4(1), 72–83.

Ljungqvist, A., & Simpson, J.L. (1992). Medical examination for health of all athletes replacing the need for gender verification in international sports. *Journal of the American Medical Association*, 267(6), 850–852.

Loy, J.W., McLachlan, F., & Booth, D. (2009). Connotations of female movement and meaning. *Olympika*, XVIII, 1–23.

Lucas-Carr, B.C., & Krane, V. (2011). What is the T in LGBT? Supporting transgender athletes through sport psychology. *Sport Psychologist*, 25(4), 532–548.

Magubane, Z. (2014). Spectacles and scholarship: Caster Semenya, intersex studies, and the problem of race in feminist theory. *Signs*, 39(3), 761–785.

Martínez-Patiño, M.J. (2005). Personal account: A woman tried and tested. *Lancet*, 366, S38.

McDonagh, E., & Pappano, L. (2007). *Playing with the Boys: Why Separate Is Not Equal in Sports*. Oxford University Press.

MD tennis star's sex surgery spotlights transsexualism. (1976). *Medical and World News*, 17(19), 26–27.

Messner, M.A. (1988). Sports and male domination: The female athlete as contested ideological terrain. *Sociology of Sport Journal*, 5(3), 197–211.

Milner, A.N., & Braddock II, J.H. (2016). *Sex Segregation in Sports: Why Separate Is Not Equal*. Santa Barbara, CA: Praeger.

Mitra, P. (2014). Male/female or other: The untold stories of female athletes with intersex variation in India. In J. Hargreaves and E. Anderson (Eds.) *Routledge Handbook of Sport, Gender and Sexuality* (pp. 384–394). London: Routledge.

Mokgadi Caster Semenya v. International Association of Athletics Federations, CAS 2018/O/5794 (Court of Arbitration for Sport 2019). Retrieved 16 June, 2021, from https://www.tas-cas.org/fileadmin/user_upload/CAS_Award_-_redacted_-_Semenya_ASA_IAAF.pdf.

Moore, K.L. (1968). The sexual identity of athletes. *Journal of the American Medical Association*, 205(11), 163–164.

Munro, B. (2010). Caster Semenya: Gods and monsters. *Safundi*, 11(4), 383–396.

Nyong'o, T. (2010). The unforgivable transgression of being Caster Semenya. *Women & Performance*, 20(1), 95–100.

Olympic Games. (1936). *Time*, 10 August, 28.

Pape, M. (2020). Gender segregation and trajectories of organizational change: The underrepresentation of women in sports leadership. *Gender & Society*, 34(1), 81–105.

Pérez-Samaniego, V., Fuentes-Miguel, J., Pereira-García, S., López-Cañada, E., & Devís-Devís, J. (2019). Experiences of trans persons in physical activity and sport: A qualitative meta-synthesis. *Sport Management Review*, 22(4), 439–451.

Peters, M., with Wooldridge, I. (1974). *Mary P.: Autobiography*. London: Paul.

Preserving la difference. (1966). *Time*, 16 September, 74.

Pfister, G. (1990). The medical discourse on female physical culture in the 19th and early 20th centuries. *Journal of Sport History*, 17(2), 183–198.

Pieper, L.P. (2016). *Sex Testing: Gender Policing in Women's Sports*. Urbana: University of Illinois Press.

Pitsiladis, Y., Harper, J., Betancurt, J.O., Martinez-Patino, M., Parisi, A., Wang, G., & Pigozzi, F. (2016). Beyond fairness: the biology of inclusion for transgender and intersex athletes. *Current Sports Medicine Reports*, 15(6), 386–388.

Records of Polish girl sprinter who flunked sex test barred. (1968). *New York Times*, 26 February, 50.

Reneé Richards v. United States Tennis Association et al., 93 Misc.2d 713 (Supreme Court, Special Term, New York County 1977). Retrieved 16 June, 2021, from https://www.leagle.com/decision/197780693misc2d7131654.

Rial, C. (2012). Women's soccer in Brazil. *Revista*. Retrieved 16 June, 2021, from https://revista.drclas.harvard.edu/book/womens-soccer-brazil.

Schultz, J. (2011). Caster Semenya and the 'question of too': Sex testing in elite women's sport and the issue of advantage. *Quest*, 63(2), 228–243.

Schultz, J. (2012a). New standards, same refrain: The IAAF's regulations on hyperandrogenism. *American Journal of Bioethics*, 12(7), 32–33.

Schultz, J. (2012b). The accidental celebrisation of Caster Semenya. *Celebrity Studies*, 3 (3), 283–296.

Schultz, J. (2014). *Qualifying Times: Points of Change in U.S. Women's Sport History*. University of Illinois Press.

Schultz, J. (2018). *Women's Sports: What Everyone Needs to Know*. New York: Oxford University Press.

Schultz, J. (2021). Good enough? The 'wicked' use of testosterone for defining femaleness in women's sport. *Sport in Society*, 24(4), 607–627.

Semenya wins 800 meters. (2009). *ESPN*, 19 August. Retrieved 16 June, 2021, from https://www.espn.com/olympics/news/story?id=4409318.

Semerjian, T.Z., & Cohen, J.H. (2006). 'FTM means female to me': Transgender athletes performing gender. *Women in Sport & Physical Activity Journal*, 15(2), 28.

Serrat, A., & De Herreros, A.G. (1993). Determination of genetic sex by PCR amplification of Y-chromosome-specific sequences. *The Lancet*, 341(8860), 1593.

Sex test disqualifies athlete. (1967). *New York Times*, 16 September, 28.

Sharrow, E.A. (2017). 'Female athlete' politic: Title IX and the naturalization of sex difference in public policy. *Politics, Groups, and Identities*, 5(1), 46–66.

Simpson, J.L., Ljungqvist, A., de la Chappel, A., Ferguson-Smith, M.A., Carlson, C., Ehrhardt, A.A., & Ferris, E. (1993). Gender verification in competitive sports. *Sports Medicine*, 16(5), 305–315.

Sönksen, P.H., Bavington, L.D., Boehning, T., Cowan, D., Guha, N., Holt, R., Karkazis, K., Ferguson-Smith, M., Mircetic, J., & Böhning, D. (2018). Hyperandrogenism controversy in elite women's sport: An examination and critique of recent evidence. *British Medical Journal*, 53(23), 1481–1482.

Sosin, K. (2020). Trans athletes welcomed on teams despite hostile state bills. *Logo*, 24 February. Retrieved 16 June, 2021, from http://www.newnownext.com/transgender-athletes-welcomed-on-teams-despite-anti-trans-bills/02/2020/?fbclid=IwAR0uc0_ruvSwMcoIuNxdfjn-a8r-aUKZcM7JuxekqjmBKa8wU4_NFuPoqLg.

Spalding, A.G. (1911). *America's National Game*. New York: American Sports Publishing Company.

Spears, B. (1984). A perspective of the history of women's sport in ancient Greece. *Journal of Sport History*, 11(2), 32–47.

Stratford, T. (1988). *Guts, Tears and Glory*. Auckland: New Women's Press.

Sudai, M. (2017). The testosterone rule—constructing fairness in professional sport. *Journal of Law and the Biosciences*, 4(1), 181–193.

Tännsjö, T. (2007). Against sexual discrimination in sports. In W. Morgan (Ed.), *Ethics and Sport* (pp. 101–115). London: Taylor & Francis.

Taylor, T. (2001). Gendering sport: The development of netball in Australia. *Sporting Traditions*, 18(1), 57–74.

Tebbutt, C. (2015). The spectre of the 'man-woman athlete': Mark Weston, Zdenek Koubek, the 1936 Olympics and the uncertainty of sex. *Women's History Review*, 24 (5), 721–738.

Tests show athlete had 2 chromosome types. (1981). *New York Times*, 12 February, A2.

Theberge, N. (1989). Women's athletics and the myth of female frailty. In J. Freeman (Ed.), *Women: A Feminist Perspective* (pp. 389–402). Mountain View, CA: Mayfield.

Things seen and heard. (1936). *Sportsman*, 20, 18.

Travers, A. (2006). Queering sport: Lesbian softball leagues and the transgender challenge. *International Review for the Sociology of Sport*, 41(3–4), 431–446.

Tuchman, G. (1978). The symbolic annihilation of women by the mass media. In G. Tuchman, A.K. Daniels, & J.W. Benét (Eds.), *Hearth and Home: Images of Women in the Mass Media* (pp. 3–32). New York: Oxford University Press.

U.S. Open unit weighs sex test for applicant. (1976). *New York Times*, 12 August, 56.

USA Powerlifting. (n.d.). Transgender participation policy. Retrieved 16 June, 2021, from https://www.usapowerlifting.com/transgender-participation-policy/.

Vines, G. (1992). Last Olympics for the sex test? *New Scientist*, 153(1828), 39–42.

Wolven, E.L. (1921). College sports and motherhood. *New York Times*, 3 July, 42.

World Rugby. (n.d.). Gender identity disorder (GID) and disorders of sexual differentiation (DSD) policy document. Retrieved 16 June, 2021, from https://13248aea-16f8-fc0a-cf26-a9339dd2a3f0.filesusr.com/ugd/2bc3fc_0ae8bdf9322647dc94f7002d7dd49f87.pdf.

Chapter 3

Law and Regulatory Barriers to Increasing Inclusivity for Trans Athletes

Seema Patel

Introduction

This chapter examines gender diversity in sport through a legal lens, analysing the regulatory barriers to inclusion for trans athletes. Participation of trans athletes has been catapulted to the centre of public attention because of three connected developments that are taking place simultaneously: in sport, law and regulation, and society.

Firstly, in sport, the recent challenges made to the validity of restrictive sport gender eligibility rules by female, intersex athletes Dutee Chand and Caster Semenya have forced an evaluation of the traditional sex categories in sport. When assessing the scientific, social and regulatory implications of the participation on intersex athletes, there is an inevitable overlap with the inclusion of trans athletes. Consequently, the cases of Dutee Chand and Caster Semenya have significantly affected trans athlete sport policies, and the nuanced aspects of trans participation have become an area of key contention for sports bodies (BBC, 2019; Santos, 2020).

Secondly, in terms of law and regulation, there is increasing concern for the wellbeing of athletes, the protection of their human rights, and the duty of care in sport (Campbell et al., 2022; Grey-Thompson, 2017; Patel, 2021; Ingle, 2020b). The Semenya case went beyond sport and has taken a legal turn, with an appeal to the European Court of Human Rights (ECtHR). This signals a dissatisfaction with the ability of sport bodies to comply with human rights provisions in the treatment of athletes. As sports bodies configure guidance on the participation of trans athletes, they are struggling to balance fairly the inclusion of minority athletes with the protection of the interests of sport. Consequently, the rights of trans athletes are being compromised. This is prompting legal and regulatory scrutiny of the accountability of sports bodies and the enforceability of human rights provisions.

Thirdly, the spotlight on gender diversity in sport is also a response to the current advances and shifts in gender perspectives in society. The concepts of sex and gender have historically been used incorrectly and interchangeably in society and in law making, with the binary view taken of men and women

DOI: 10.4324/9781003050568-3

(Lembke, 2016). There are increased calls for legal gender status reforms that accurately reflect the changing nature of sex and gender and that are more inclusive in their scope (e.g., Peel & Newman, 2020). This extends to trans people and the augmentation of trans rights in legal provisions (see the UK Gender Recognition Act 2004).

This chapter investigates the intersection of the three – sport, law and regulation, and society concerns – in the context of binary trans athletes. While it is acknowledged that binary trans individuals do not represent the full spectrum of gender diverse identities, this chapter will focus on binary trans individuals only due to the current emphasis in sport on the scientific, biological evidence around performance advantage and injury risk as the driving force for trans eligibility rules. While this is the focus in sport, significantly less consideration has been given to wider legal and human rights implications of the participation of trans athletes.

This chapter shifts the debate to a legal focus and critiques the specific regulatory barriers to inclusion for trans athletes. It will begin with an outline of the current position of trans sport policies and the shortfalls in their consistency with law and recognition of human rights. An evaluation of the legal status of trans people in society will then follow, exploring the visibility of trans people within the international framework of non-discrimination and human rights legislation.

Despite a robust human rights framework, the application of those instruments to sport is complex and it will be shown that there are deficiencies in the enforcement of human rights obligations upon sports bodies, which negatively impacts upon the inclusion of trans athletes. The relationship between sport and the law and the limited trans athlete legal cases will be examined to emphasise how the autonomous private nature of sport regulation is restricting the ability of trans athletes to assert their rights and challenge derogatory treatment in sport. Proposals will be offered to achieve inclusivity through a stronger enforcement of law and human rights in sport and a refreshed renewal of gender-related human rights principles in society.

The Regulation of Trans Athletes

The constructs of sex, gender, inclusion and exclusion are intrinsically connected to competitive sport because the essence of competitive sporting activity is about testing our human differences by creating conditions which separate athletes according to these differences (Patel, 2015a). In order to defend that essence and ensure fairness in competition, sport has generally been divided into male and female categories and remains one of the few activities where sex segregation is accepted, required and controlled, despite discriminatory implications and the potential conflict with human rights. It is generally assumed that men enjoy a fundamental physiological advantage over women due to specific male traits, which dictates the division. This perspective influences the regulation of the female category and, whilst successful female athletes have been celebrated for their sport performance and ability, at the same time they are treated with caution because the physiological traits of strength, power, speed and stamina continue to be associated with masculinity and advantage in sport.

Trans people experience their gender as being different to the gender assigned to them at birth, based on their perceived sex (male or female). Trans people often experience a dysphoria as a result and may or may not alter their appearance to resolve their dysphoria, which may involve gender-affirming hormone treatment and/or surgery (Kyriacou, 2020). Trans female athletes present a regulatory dilemma for sport because it is assumed that they retain advantageous male traits which give them an unfair performance advantage over cis female athletes. Their inclusion is treated as an infraction of sport and nature (see Sharpe, 2011) because they deviate from the binary sex categories assigned at birth. In comparison, trans male athletes are not considered to possess an advantage and have not been subject to the same treatment when seeking to participate in the male sport category.

To resolve this, international sports governing bodies such as the International Olympic Committee (IOC) and World Athletics (previously the International Association of Athletics Federations, IAAF), introduced trans eligibility policies as a means of guarding the categories of sport and controlling femininity (see also Chapter 2, this volume). Early discriminatory and arbitrary forms of physical and chromosomal sex testing were mostly framed around physiological advantage and underpinned by contested scientific understandings of sex and gender (Santos, 2020). The consequences of testing and dividing sport along only some of the factors that determine sex led to the unreasonable exclusion of individuals whose sex and gender varied and could not be strictly categorised, such as athletes with intersex variations and trans people. Once it was seemingly accepted by sports bodies that legal and psychological recognition of sex must also be considered alongside biological factors, the regulations morphed into gender verification policies and were re-framed to concentrate on levels of testosterone in the pursuit of hormonally similar women in the female category. Excessive levels of testosterone were thought to provide an athlete with an unfair advantage over other competitors because testosterone is widely considered to be a key sport performance factor, although this is contested by some (Jordan-Young & Karkazis, 2019). This assertion has shaped modern regulation but has also been a key point of controversy in this area (Patel, 2021; Santos, 2020).

Sport continued to struggle to balance inclusion and exclusion in the formulation of athletes with intersex variations and trans policies, and the approaches vary across sports (Jones et al., 2017; Santos, 2020). The Stockholm Consensus on Sex Reassignment in Sport (IOC, 2004) was the first trans policy implemented by the IOC which required a trans female athlete to complete all surgical internal and external anatomical changes, legal recognition of their assigned sex, and hormonal therapy for at least two years to reduce any gender-related advantages. These requirements were inconsistent with national laws concerning legal recognition, they were discriminatory, a breach of human rights, and they lacked scientific validity. Nevertheless, they were followed in other trans sport policies (Cavanagh & Sykes, 2006, p. 92; Santos, 2020). The criticisms of the Stockholm Consensus prompted an update by the IOC Medical Commission in 2015 (IOC, 2015). In the Consensus Meeting on Sex Reassignment and Hyperandrogenism, the requirement for surgery was removed and trans female athletes were permitted to compete if they had declared that their gender identity is female for a minimum of four years; if their testosterone levels remained below 10nmol/L for at least twelve months prior to competition; and if they agreed to monitoring by testing. Trans male athletes were not subject to the same control and were eligible to compete in the male category without restriction because their hormone levels do not exceed the permitted range and they are not perceived to have an unfair advantage over cis male athletes. Other issues might have been overlooked here such as the 'potential advantage cisgender men may have over trans men athletes, creating an asymmetry in fair play priorities' (Santos, 2020, p. 273).

The conditions placed upon the eligibility of trans athletes have symbolised a barrier to inclusivity that has largely gone unchallenged until the recent cases of intersex athletes Chand and Semenya (explored on p. 00) and these have in turn prompted a review of trans policies in various sports. Whilst IOC plans to produce new guidelines were halted because of a lack of scientific consensus (Ingle, 2019), World Athletics announced the Eligibility Regulations for Transgender Athletes in 2019 (World Athletics, 2019a). In order to be eligible, the trans female athlete must provide a declaration that her gender identity is female; must demonstrate that testosterone levels are less than 5nmol/L for at least twelve months, and must maintain that for as long as she wishes to complete in the female category.

Following a World Athletics meeting on transgender eligibility, it was agreed that sports bodies should design sport specific gender rules, which are 'living documents' and that are consistent with the latest scientific knowledge (World Athletics, 2019b). To facilitate this, it was encouraged that further research should be conducted by sports bodies. This is an acknowledgement that a blanket approach is unworkable for trans athletes and instead World Athletics and the IOC appear to have granted sports bodies some autonomy when drawing up their own policies, particularly in the adoption of testosterone as the basis for any policy (Pavitt, 2020).

In response to this instruction, sports bodies across several genres have carried out a systematic review of guidelines for trans athletes (see for example British Cycling, 2021; Ingram & Thomas, 2019). Many have welcomed open consultation on how to frame their guidelines, whether by enforcing complete bans, using testosterone as a benchmark, requiring a gender declaration, or removing any gender restrictions. For example, World Rugby was one of the first international governing bodies to convene a multi-disciplinary working group in 2020, tasked with producing a rugby specific trans player guideline (World Rugby, 2020a). This signifies an attempt to shift from exclusionary to inclusionary practices in the formation of rules and some progress is evident across some sports. The consultation processes are encouraging open, multidisciplinary debate, and facilitating voices to be heard, particularly those of marginalised athletes. However, although sports bodies are trying to include trans athletes and achieve integration, there remains a battle to determine sex for the purpose of sport and include trans female athletes in the female category, whilst at the same time protecting trans rights and cis female athletes' rights and ensuring non-discrimination in sport (Patel, 2021). In the process of achieving a balance, the lens is fixated on the contested scientific attributes of performance advantage and injury risk (Harper et al., 2021) and appear to ignore human rights or law in the construction and application of eligibility rules. The over-reliance on science instead of human rights leads to barriers to inclusivity for trans athletes because it prioritises sport interests over athletes' rights and neglects the importance of balancing both values.

Whilst World Rugby intended to engage in a transparent and ground-breaking consultation, in October 2020 they introduced a ban on trans female players from competing in contact rugby at the international level on the grounds that trans female players pose a greater risk of injury for other female players (World Rugby, 2020b; Hilton & Lundberg, 2021). Consistent with the risk approach, the Rugby Football Union (RFU) is considering the implementation of height and weight eligibility assessments of trans athletes (England Rugby, n.d). Injury risk is a legitimate concern, and the welfare of all female athletes (trans female and cis female) is of equal importance when determining participation. Yet, there is an absence of conclusive evidence on whether trans female athletes present an injury risk to cis female athletes. Even if the scientific debate was settled, the exclusion of minority trans athletes is potentially incompatible with law and human rights. The treatment of trans athletes as an infraction of sport and nature persists unconsciously (Sharpe, 2011).

Sports bodies are failing to pay serious attention to minority rights in their policies (Dworkin, 2013). Mandatory legal requirements or obligations to undergo medical surgery or hormone treatment as a condition of sport participation contravenes fundamental human rights concerning human dignity, bodily integrity, self-determination, privacy and consent enshrined within human rights instruments outlined below (Davy et al., 2018). Yet it will be seen that scrutinising sport gender rules and regulations against these legal standards is not easily achievable because of regulatory limitations inherent within the complex global sports structure, and due to judicial constraints at an international, regional, and domestic level. It will be shown that sport has been afforded the freedom to regulate trans athlete participation largely without legal scrutiny.

Legal Protection of Trans People

Trans people also trouble the legal sex and gender order (Sharpe, 2011), and the barriers to inclusivity experienced by trans athletes are similar to those faced by trans people in the fight for legal recognition and human rights security. The legal status of gender-diverse individuals is gradually improving, but there is much debate around how best to ensure inclusion within legal recognition. A restrictive medicalised approach was previously taken to trans identity, which was classified as a mental disorder. In 2019, the World Health Organization (WHO) shifted this position and de-classified transgender health issues from mental and behavioural disorders to sexual health (Beek et al., 2016; Beek et al., 2017). This modification indicates a more accurate alignment with clinical practice, human rights standards, and the trans depathologisation movement (Cochran et al., 2014; Davy et al., 2018).

Domestic gender laws differ across countries but English law historically denied legal recognition of trans people, adopting the medicalised stance. The courts decided that sex was determined at birth according to chromosomes, gonads and genitals, denying trans people the right to be identified under their new sex in any aspects of their lives (*Corbett v Corbett* [1970] 2 ALL ER 33; Patel, 2008; Sharpe, 2011). This biological legal test is reflective of historic sex testing in sport and has also influenced law in other countries (Sharpe, 2011). Following continued inconsistencies between the medical field offering gender reassignment treatment to trans people, and the restriction of their civil liberties, the European Court of Human Rights (ECtHR) led in the recognition of trans rights and applied pressure to reform their legal status and consider social and psychological traits when determining gender identity (*Goodwin v UK* (2002) 35 ECtHR 18). The ECtHR found that the UK Government could no longer rely on their margin of appreciation in violating Article 8 (right to private life) and Article 12 (right to marry) of the European Convention on Human Rights 1950 (ECHR) in the exclusion of trans people from legal status.

The UK Government responded by enacting the Gender Recognition Act 2004 (GRA) which departed from the strict biological approach and grants trans people the right to change their birth certificate to their acquired gender through the process of applying for a Gender Recognition Certificate (GRC), which is ultimately determined by a Gender Recognition Panel (s. 1(3) and Schedule 1 GRA). The GRA outlines a set of evidential requirements for trans people to achieve legal recognition. It is not a requirement for an applicant to have undergone gender affirmation surgery or hormone treatment, although many applicants do so (Fairbairn, 2020). The GRA was world leading because it was the first gender-recognition legislation in the world to ostensibly abandon the requirement to undergo surgery prior to recognition of acquired gender.

However, in recent times the GRA has been referred to as outdated, overly intrusive, humiliating, expensive and administratively burdensome (Fairbairn et al., 2020). It is argued by equality and rights groups that the GRA requires significant revision since it has fallen behind newer and fairer models of legal recognition (BBC, 2020a). The medico-legal approach persists with the requirement of a medical diagnosis and a medical report. This reinforces misconceptions about trans people and conflicts with the privacy, integrity, dignity, and personal autonomy of applicants. Trans people will often have already changed their name, and other documents to confirm their acquired identity which can lead to a mismatch with their legal recognition. To resolve this, however, they must navigate the current gender recognition process (Fairbairn, 2020; House of Commons, 2016). To address these criticisms, the UK Government launched a consultation of the GRA in England and Wales, investigating how to streamline the legal recognition process for trans people. Many campaigners within the community anticipated that a non-medical, self-identification mode might be adopted, consistent with some other countries who have implemented inclusive, simpler, cheaper, and less intrusive routes (Sharpe, 2020; Fairbairn, 2020; House of Commons, 2016). In 2020 the UK Government responded to the consultation with an acknowledgement that an improvement was required but opined that the GRA strikes the correct balance between the rights of trans people and the implementation of an appropriate system (Fairbairn et al., 2020). The amendments included the move to an online paperless process and a fee reduction to £5 which demonstrates some commitment to improving the system (Gov.uk, 2021).

With mixed reaction to these changes, meaningful reform of legal gender status is ongoing (Davy et al., 2018), and formal inquiries into the GRA reform and petitions for further reform have been initiated (Fairbairn et al., 2020). Research from the UK Government consultation indicated that access to medical treatment and improved healthcare remained a key area of concern for trans people. In Scotland, a draft Gender Recognition Reform (Scotland) Bill is under consultation, which proposes significant changes to the application process and the medical evidential requirements. It is suggested that there is still some way to go to discard the notion that trans people represent a 'breach of law and nature' (Sharpe, 2011), depathologise national gender laws worldwide, and adequately protect human rights for trans people (Davy et al., 2018).

In terms of protection from discriminatory treatment, human rights and equality provisions exist to shield individuals from discrimination on the basis of sex and gender, and place obligations on signatories to take appropriate measures to ensure the protection of human rights. For instance, wider protection for trans people is located in the Equality Act 2010 (EA; see Gov.uk, 2010), which prohibits discrimination in various settings, on the basis of protected characteristics which includes sex (Section 11) and gender reassignment (Section 7). The EA protects trans people from discrimination by private companies and public organisations in the areas of provision of goods and services and employment (Sharpe, 2020). Protection under the EA also applies irrespective of whether the person has received medical or hormonal interventions, or legal gender recognition. However, in the GRA consultation, the

Government acknowledged that there are concerns about the impact of amending the GRA on the EA, particularly in relation to the EA exemption provisions related to gender reassignment discrimination, explored on p. 00.

At the regional European level, the ECHR contains fundamental civil and political human rights, such as freedom from discrimination on any ground, including sex (see Article 14 ECHR and Protocol No. 12 ECHR). The Council of Europe recognises the rights of trans people in the adoption of the Discrimination Against Transgender People in Europe Resolution (2015) which encourages Member States to bolster the protection of rights for trans people, protect individuals from discrimination arising from gender identity, and facilitate improved legal recognition processes based on the right of an individual to self-identify their gender. Rulings of the ECtHR have influenced a strengthened recognition of gender rights in the UK as evidenced above.

In the European Union (EU), equality and non-discrimination are defended through the enforcement of primary and secondary legislation, decisions of the Court of Justice of the European Union (CJEU) and informal declarations, statements, and movements that promote gender equality (Patel, 2022). The Charter of Fundamental Rights of the European Union 2009 (EU Charter) formally codifies rights and principles for EU citizens in one single document, with equality and non-discrimination represented in Title III. The CJEU has excelled in the defence of those who are not explicitly covered and has encouraged a broader interpretation of the term 'sex' to encompass other identities such as trans people (Lembke, 2016). The Gender Recast Directive (Directive 2006/54/EC) confirms this jurisprudence (Recital 3) and states that all legislation prohibiting sex discrimination and ensuring equal treatment for men and women must be extended to include gender reassignment. This places obligations on domestic courts to interpret sex discrimination consistently with the Directive and include trans people. The implementation of the Directive is in progress with many countries directly codifying gender reassignment discrimination, but not all Member States. Furthermore, the interpretation of gender reassignment and gender identity continue to cause some confusion (Fabeni & Agius, 2009). Regardless of this, human rights are universal and should apply to all gender identities through the broad interpretation of non-discrimination clauses.

Explicit references to gender identity are also debated internationally. Overarching universal values of human dignity and bodily integrity are represented at an international level and enshrined within a wide range of international instruments, most notably the Universal Declaration of Human Rights 1948 (UDHR), the International Covenant on Civil and Political Rights 1976 (ICCPR) and the International Covenant on Economic, Social and Cultural Rights 1976 (ICESCR). The Committee on Economic, Social and Cultural Rights (CESCR) has offered commentary on trans depathologisation and recognised the right to health (Article 12 ICESCR) and non-discrimination (Article 2.2 ICESCR) of trans people (explored in Theilen, 2014). The right to gender equality and freedom from sex discrimination are guaranteed within these provisions and contained within the Convention on the Elimination of All Forms of Discrimination Against Women 1979 (CEDAW) (Article 10(g)).

The Yogyakarta Principles Plus 10 (2017) (supplementing the Yogyakarta Principles 2006) provide authoritative guidance on applying international human rights law to a wider range of people of sexual orientations and gender identities who may be subject to human rights violations. The Principles aim to ensure that binding international legal standards apply broadly to those individuals and groups. Although they are not binding law, the Principles affirm the primary obligation of States to implement human rights and they provide instructions for each Principle on how to effectively achieve this. The Principles have been steadily influential at the international, regional and domestic level (see O'Flaherty, 2015).

Overall, within the existing international framework of provisions for human rights, the recognition and preservation of trans peoples' rights is emerging, whether explicitly or implicitly through references to sex and gender. That said, this does not go far enough and there is a lack of visible endorsements of broader gender identities in human rights provisions, which can restrict the inclusivity of trans people. Similarly, although progress is being made in gender recognition legislation, there are shortfalls in the system, and this requires reform and refreshing, given the shifting parameters of sex and gender. It will be shown that the enforceability of legal and human rights obligations are also problematic, particularly in the context of sport.

Extension of Legal Protection to Trans Athletes

Fundamental sources of sport obligations declare that 'the practice of sport is a human right' which preserves human dignity and should be free from discrimination (IOC Olympic Charter Principle 4, IOC, 2021). However, the intersection between sport and human rights standards is curious because these commitments are not absolute (Sailors, 2020). There is an inevitable infringement of unilateral sport gender rules and practices upon athletes' human rights that often escape legal scrutiny because of the lack of application and enforcement of human rights provisions upon non-state actors such as sports bodies (Patel, 2021). This creates a barrier to inclusion for minority athletes who suffer human rights abuses.

Application of human rights law to sport

The framework outlined above also credits the value of human rights and participation in sport within a range of provisions which reinforce the obligations of States to promote inclusivity through sport, and supports the right of athletes to seek a legal remedy when their liberties have been violated (Harmon, 2020, p. 256; see the Beijing Declaration and Platform for Action 1995; The Brighton plus Helsinki 2014 Declaration on Women and Sport). For example, at an international level the United Nations Human Rights Council (UNHRC) has been vocal in their condemnation of gender discrimination in sport, outlining the incompatibility of female eligibility regulations with equality and non-discrimination principles, in respect of athletes with variations in sex characteristics. The UNHRC has placed further obligations on States to redress human rights abuses through the application of pressure on sport (UNHRC, 2019; UNHRC, 2020).

Accompanying this, non-legally binding soft law tools are being established to encourage non-state actors to comply with human rights and to encourage states to more closely regulate non-state actors (Lane, 2018). The UN Guiding Principles on Business and Human Rights (UNGP's) introduce a universal standard for rectifying human rights violations connected to business practice (United Nations, 2011). Some sports bodies have responded positively by formally embedding the UNGP's into their policies and regulations. The IOC updated the Host City Contract (HCC) 2024, to ensure that any violation of human rights is remedied in a manner consistent with law, and with human rights standards including the UNGP's (IOC, 2017, Article 13.2). In addition, the Olympic Agenda 2020 committed everyone to gender balance (IOC, 2019). Similar UEFA and FIFA documents also include explicit obligations to comply with international provisions such as the UNGP's and CEDAW (UEFA, 2017; FIFA, 2017). Although explicit declarations of human rights recognition are a steady step in the reconciliation of sport with human rights, the soft law tools lack effective enforceability and impact as demonstrated on p. 00 (Wettstein, 2015; Naess, 2019; West, 2019; Patel, 2021).

The application of EU law to sport has strengthened over time and there is a body of case law that evaluates the compatibility of EU law with sports rules. However, despite a robust assurance of equality in the EU, sport gender rules have not been tested against these standards. In addition, the EU White Paper on Sport stipulates that the segregation of competitions for men and women is specific to sport and therefore requires a sensitive and autonomous application of law (Chappelet, 2017). This unmitigated protection of the binary categories of sport perpetuates the misconception of sex and gender and fails to address the rights and inclusion of gender-diverse athletes (Patel, 2021). Despite some gaps in the European system, a steady discourse is developing in the context of securing athletes' rights through responsible regulation (Patel, 2022).

The enforceability of domestic equality provisions upon sports bodies is reduced by the existence of exemption clauses contained within legislation such the EA and GRA. During the initial stages of its passage through Parliament, the GRA originally required both domestic and international sporting events to allow trans athletes to compete in their identified gender (Patel, 2008). This provoked a dispute around whether legal status should contribute to the eligibility of trans athletes or whether this should remain dictated by physiological traits. The GRA was subsequently enacted with an exemption clause contained in s. 19(2) GRA which permits sports bodies to exclude trans athletes from competing in gender affected sports. A sport is gender-affected if the physical strength, stamina, or physique of average persons of one sex or gender would put them at a disadvantage to average persons of the other sex or gender (s.19 (4) GRA). This was rationalised to maintain safe and fair competition, underlining the view that trans female athletes retain advantageous physiological male traits that give them an unfair advantage and potential injury risks to other female competitors. In their response to the consultation of the GRA, the UK Government confirmed the status of the exclusion of trans people from single-sex activities based on biological sex, where it is a proportionate means of achieving a legitimate aim (Fairbairn et al., 2020).

Similarly, neither is the discrimination ban absolute in the EA, with s.195 EA permitting separate categories for men and women where the physical strength, stamina or physique of an athlete are key performance factors in the sport. In addition, the EA lawfully prevents the participation of trans athletes if this is necessary to ensure safe and fair competition (Gov.uk, 2010). However, there is limited scientific data to confirm this proposition and the fallacy of the generalised strength, stamina and physique argument within legislation has been heavily criticised (Patel, 2015a).

The limitations to extending equality and human rights protection to athletes in sport form part of a much broader dialogue concerning the relationship between sport and the law generally. The social and economic significance of sporting activity places sports bodies in a dominant position, exerting significant power in their regulation of sport and influence beyond those structures. The sophistication of the internal regulation of sport has obscured the parameters of formal law and the rules of sport, leading to the notion that a unique body of law is being developed by international sports bodies and organisations, rather than by the State (Nafziger, 1999). This is evidenced by the successful internal resolution of sport disputes through the Court of Arbitration for Sport (CAS), which have a binding impact upon the participation of athletes. There is a preference for private self-regulation that is immune from government control. However, with this autonomy comes potential abuse of power and vulnerability of athletes' rights. There is increasing commentary around the transparency of CAS and its ability and capacity to appropriately balance sport interests with athletes' rights (Lenskyj, 2018).

As a result of this arrangement, there is ongoing discourse about the effective governance and accountability of sports bodies, and the role that the law and government play in this. Some countries locate sport in the public domain and therefore intervene in sport matters by enforcing legislation. In contrast, in the UK, government intervention in sport is minimised by a reluctance to trespass on the authority of sports bodies, instead preserving the special nature of sport. There is a general hesitancy to regard sports bodies as fulfilling a public function for the purpose of imposing human rights law (Boyes, 2000). In the UK, whilst the courts have deliberated that sports bodies may be hybrid public authorities, that is, private bodies that exercise public functions, the application is constricted (Boyes, 2000; Patel, 2021).

The management of sports bodies as private authorities has given them freedom to operate under their own system of virtues, at times inconsistent with the societal or legal trends (Patel, 2021). Sport rules, such as trans policies, therefore remain untested against human rights standards and act as a barrier to inclusivity for trans athletes (Grell, 2018 p. 160). The UNHRC acknowledges the autonomy of sport to govern itself but stresses that sport rules should be implemented in a manner harmonious with human rights standards (UNHRC, 2019).

Athlete Challenges

The ability of athletes to assert their rights and challenge discriminatory treatment under human rights provisions is restrained because of the autonomous regulatory power held by sports bodies. Athletes tend to be bound by forced arbitration clauses and refer any challenges to CAS rather than pursue a legal claim (Schwab, 2018). The Chand and Semenya cases (of intersex athletes) demonstrate how CAS assesses the validity of sports rules, premised upon contested and inconclusive scientific evidence around testosterone and advantage (Kidd, 2018; Savulescu, 2019), but lacks the capacity to address human rights matters.

Indian female athlete Chand successfully argued that the IAAF 2011 Hyperandrogenism Regulations (2011 Regulations) (Patel, 2015b) which prohibited her from competing based on excessive levels of testosterone, were discriminatory, scientifically flawed, and disproportionate.[1] Following the two-year suspension of the 2011 Regulations by CAS, the IAAF unveiled the Eligibility Regulations for the Female Classification (Athletes with Differences of Sex Development (DSD)) (2018 Regulations) (World Athletics, 2018). The 2018 Regulations require 'biologically male' athletes with 46 XY DSD, who have natural excessive testosterone levels, to reduce their level to a permitted female range (below 5nmol/l), through hormone treatment. The 2018 DSD Regulations were challenged by South African female sprinter Semenya who claimed that they were discriminatory and lacked scientific validity. Here, CAS applied the same yardstick to measure the legitimacy of the 2018 Regulations but concluded that although they were discriminatory, they were a necessary, reasonable, and proportionate means of achieving the aim of protecting female athletes in certain events.

The reliance on biology alone to determine sex in sport is contentious, but CAS held that biology rather than legal sex or gender identity must determine eligibility in sport, which is reflective of the historic rationale for policing sex and gender in sport. Whilst it is accepted that biology is a key factor for sport categorisation, and that physical advantage might be identifiable in some studies, participation for gender-diverse athletes becomes a question of what sport is willing to accept and what degree of difference we are willing to permit in sport, particularly as society transitions to recognise a broader range of sex and gender (Patel, 2021). Human rights harms are at stake but these issues were not examined by CAS. Both Chand and Semenya disputed that the gender regulations were incompatible with sport human rights commitments, domestic laws and broader fundamental human rights law. Potential breaches of other rights concerning consent and privacy in the medical assessment and treatment processes were also raised. Semenya emphasised that this fight reaches beyond the right to compete in sport and instead concerns the right to be human. However, CAS confirmed its limited judicial role and concluded that human rights are a subject for the courts of the various jurisdictions to decide. The Semenya case has publicly exposed the deficits in the regulation of sex and gender in sport and the deflection of human rights issues represents a further regulatory barrier to inclusivity for gender-diverse athletes. The rights of the athlete should receive pronounced attention at every stage of sport regulation, from rulemaking to dispute-resolution.

Semenya unsuccessfully appealed to the Swiss Federal Supreme Court (SFT), and she now seeks to appeal to the ECtHR (BBC, 2020b). In various recent cases the ECtHR has offered commentary on sport regulation and affirmed that sport arbitration proceedings must be compatible with human rights in that hearings must be subject to public scrutiny (Article 6 ECHR). Although it has exhibited a willingness to scrutinise sports proceedings against human rights standards, rulings on discrimination in sport is unknown territory and the outcome is likely to significantly impact future sport regulation, including gender eligibility policies.

Because of the restrictive nature of athletes' contractual obligations, only a few legal cases have appeared before the law courts on these issues. One of the early trans athlete legal cases was *Dr Renee Richards v United States Tennis Association* (USTA) (1977) 400 NYS 2d 267. Trans female tennis player Richards brought a claim against the USTA who forced her to pass a sex test in order to compete. The Court ruled in favour of Richards, deciding that the mandatory genetic test was discriminatory and a breach of s.290(3) Executive Law of the New York Human Rights Law, which declares that the State has the responsibility to act to assure that every individual within this State is afforded an equal opportunity to enjoy a full and productive life. Richards was permitted to compete in the female category in her acquired gender. This was a positive decision for Richards, but the judge did not reject the validity of the sex test entirely, implying that a case-by-case approach should be taken in the future (Pieper, 2012). Given this limitation, the case did little to alter further eligibility gender policies, such as the Stockholm Consensus, which continued to be exclusionary.

In 2016, an inclusive approach was taken by the Human Rights Tribunal of Ontario, Canada in *Worley v Ontario Cycling Association* (2016 Human Rights Tribunal of Ontario 952). Kristen Worley is a trans female Canadian cyclist who was subject to gender verification testing, under the controversial Stockholm Consensus. Worley brought a legal challenge against the Union Cycliste

Internationale (UCI), Cycling Canada (CC) and Ontario Cycling Association (OCA) claiming that she was subject to sex discrimination under the gender verification policies, and this constituted an infringement of the Ontario Human Rights Code. She reiterated that this was a human rights matter that went beyond sport. The tribunal concluded that the application had a 'reasonable prospect of success' and should not be dismissed. The sports bodies settled in 2017 and committed to use objective independent scientific research in the establishment of standards and guidelines for trans female athletes. This is a pivotal victory for athletes' rights and their autonomy to pursue a legal claim, but Worley's success is not commonplace because of the dominance of arbitration clauses.

The inclusion or exclusion of trans athletes in school and college sports has created intense legal conflict across the USA. Some states, educational institutions and high school and college associations have introduced policies permitting the participation of trans student athletes based on their gender identity (Buzuvis, 2021). In contrast, others have no formal policy or have imposed complete bans on participation (GLSEN, 2019; Associated Press, 2020; Malagrino, 2020). The rules also vary across and within states; this has created a volatile regulatory setting for the protection of trans athletes. Fuelling the debate further, state anti-transgender laws were being negotiated which seek to supress trans legal rights by banning trans student athletes from competing in sports at school in their acquired gender and blocking them from changing their birth certificates (Graham, 2021). The Trump Government in power during this period perpetuated negative treatment of trans people and reduced the protection offered to trans student athletes.

In a twist of equality and equal treatment, the inclusive policies have been subject to legal challenge by opponents who claim that permitting trans student athletes to participate gives them an unfair advantage in competition. It is argued that such policies in fact violate sex discrimination laws by restricting opportunities for cisgender female student athletes (Levenson & Vigdor, 2020), particularly if the trans athletes have not received any gender affirming hormonal intervention which would lower testosterone levels and potentially athletic advantage. A key source of equality law in the USA is Title IX of the Education Amendments Act 1972 (Title IX) which prohibits sex discrimination in educational institutions and withdraws federal funding from educational institutions if they violate the provision. Historically, Title IX generated great opportunity for women and girls in sport, but it is now being used to subject trans athletes to the same derogatory treatment that it seeks to prevent. The ambiguity of the definition of sex in Title IX and Title VII of the Civil Rights Act of 1964, has contributed to the confusion over whether protection extends to trans student athletes (Levenson & Vigdor, 2020; Buzuvis, 2021). In the absence of clarification there have been inconsistent rulings for trans student athletes (West-Sell et al., 2019).

Title IX sought to eradicate sex and gender barriers, but some courts have held that inclusive trans athlete policies violate Title IX. In 2020, a group of cisgender female student athletes filed a complaint against the Connecticut Interscholastic Athletic Conference (CIAC) policy allowing trans females to compete in high school sports in their gender identity. Although the policy complies with state laws protecting the gender identity of trans people, the complainants argued that it contravenes Title IX because by allowing two trans female athletes to compete and enjoy an unfair physical advantage, the equal opportunities for cisgender female athletes are denied (Ingle, 2020a; Malagrino, 2020). As discussed, the legitimacy of the scientific evidence supporting this argument continues to be debated, but from a human rights perspective, the rights of trans people and cisgender females have been dangerously and falsely placed in opposition to each other (Hines, 2018).

The claim was championed by the Trump administration, but the subsequent Biden presidency seeks to reverse much of the damage and has retracted government support for the case (Associated Press, 2021). Clarifying and strengthening the protection of trans people under non-discrimination law, Biden signed an executive order in January 2021 which forces federal agencies to extend the scope of sex discrimination in legislation, including Title IX, to include sexual orientation and gender identity discrimination (Graham, 2021). This is an encouraging example of increasing inclusivity through regulation and such a development is critical to eliminate pitting trans rights against cis female rights.

Conclusions: Increasing Inclusivity by Extending and Refreshing Legal Protection

Human differences such as sex and gender characterise the essence of inclusion and exclusion in competitive sport. At the same time, sex, gender, human dignity, bodily integrity, health, and privacy are human qualities that are protected by a network of equality and human rights legal and non-legal provisions. These opposing perspectives have triggered an impossible clash between sport interests and athletes' rights. The three developments in sport, law and regulation and society have created a unique dilemma for trans people, who are struggling for recognition and inclusion in each of these spaces. In the pursuit of balancing the competing interests, this chapter has identified several legal and regulatory barriers to inclusivity for trans female athletes.

The legal recognition of trans people and the legal protection of sex and gender discrimination is not universal and is outdated to some degree. The traditional absence of gender identity from the strong human rights legal framework outlined above, has led to inconsistency and confusion in the protection of trans people. Whilst this is slowly being detected and rectified at the international, regional, and domestic level, trans rights are in a state of change and review. As the nature of sex and gender in society evolves, a more inclusive agenda should be adopted by domestic governments, intergovernmental organisations and international human rights institutions to remove barriers to legal recognition, refresh valuable human rights principles, and widen the scope of sex and gender definitions in legislation to unequivocally include trans people and gender identity.

Where trans sport policies unreasonably exclude, this chapter has illustrated that the extension of legal protection for trans athletes is inadequate due to the lack of enforcement mechanisms available to impose human rights obligations upon private sports bodies. The wider friction between public and private regulatory sport spaces, and the autonomous power held by sports bodies, preclude athletes from seeking an appropriate remedy for human rights violations, which acts as a barrier to inclusivity. There are pockets of good practice emerging in the legislative landscape that prioritise the inclusion of trans athletes where appropriate and necessary. The cases examined indicate legal victories for the individual athletes concerned but are limited in their influence beyond.

Sport has dramatically departed from its past policing of female bodies, but underlying biological aspects of previous regimes continue to haunt current regulation. The consultation processes for trans athlete participation are certainly progressive but only target trans women and continue to place over-reliance on science and performance advantage, rather than equally prioritising human rights and equality. The argument for defending the level playing field and protecting the safety of cis female athletes is objectively reasonable. However, the exclusion of trans athletes pushes the test of reasonableness beyond the constraints of fairness and there must be a reflection upon what degrees of difference sport will accept in this transitional era of sex and gender. For instance, non-binary people may wish to participate in sport, but may not fit into the sex-segregated sport categories. There is limited conclusive evidence of whether trans female athletes possess an unfair performance advantage and present an injury risk to cis female athletes to justify exclusion. Even if this were to be confirmed, gender eligibility rules remain incompatible with the human rights of trans athletes. Instead, their exclusion is at odds with the gradual inclusion of trans people in law reforms.

To resolve this, human rights must be taken seriously in sport (Dworkin, 2013; O'Flaherty, 2015) and declarations to protect minority rights should be explicitly incorporated into trans sport policies. Furthermore, dedicated research into the protection of athletes' rights in their respective sports should be conducted. Instead of treating trans people as an infraction of sport, law and nature (Sharpe, 2011), it must be acknowledged that the right to be human is now a key part of this debate, as illustrated by the Semenya, Worley and Richards cases. A stronger balance between sport interests and human rights is necessary to ensure that sports bodies act in a manner consistent with their own human rights statements and with the wider legal framework. We are beyond theoretical assurances around human rights recognition by sports bodies and it is time to re-align sport boundaries with the changing nature of sex and gender by actively engaging in the trans rights movement.

Where sports bodies fail to do so, regulatory recommendations have been made to overcome deficiencies in the protection of athletes' rights, which are framed around holding sports bodies accountable for human rights violations and enforcing compliance with the law. This could be achieved through the formation of an independent body such as an International Anti- Discrimination in Sport Unit (IADSU) (Patel, 2021). In the context of trans sport policies, the IADSU could perform an audit of the sports rules to measure human rights consistency. An anti-discrimination in sport charter could be introduced to reconcile the gulf between the legal protection of trans people and the extension of those rights to trans athletes, by binding sports bodies to human rights. Furthermore, an international tribunal for the resolution of human rights disputes in sport would provide trans athletes with an independent route of appeal for human rights violations, and potentially correct limitations to the existing legal and regulatory mechanisms (Patel, 2021).

As athletes begin to assert their human rights and confront discriminatory treatment, increasing inclusivity for trans athletes can be achieved by prioritising the athlete and providing a supportive platform for their voices to be heard. Consistent with proposals for the launch of an athlete-focused Sports Ombudsman, an independent Athlete Advice Service (AAS) could improve athlete wellbeing by assisting trans athletes with legal guidance when negotiating the complex sport and legal regulatory framework (Patel, 2021; Grey-Thompson, 2017; Campbell et al., 2022; Anderson & Partington, 2018). Law and regulatory barriers to inclusivity for trans athletes can be eased through a stronger enforcement of human rights obligations, and a refreshed renewal of human rights principles.

Note

1 CAS 2014/A/3759 Dutee Chand v. Athletics Federation of India (AFI) and The International Association of Athletics Federation (IAAF).
2 CAS 2018/O/5794 Mokgadi Caster Semenya v. The International Association of Athletics Federation (IAAF) and CAS 2018/O/5798 Athletics South Africa v. The International Association of Athletics Federation (IAAF).
3 *Mutu and Pechstein v Switzerland* [ECtHR 2 October 2018] App no 40575/10 and 67474/10; Ali Riza and Others v. Turkey [2020] App. No. 30226/10 Unreported.

References

Anderson, J., & Partington, N. (2018). Duty of Care in Sport: Time for a sports ombudsman? *International Sports Law Review*, 1, 3–10. ISSN 1467–6680.

Associated Press. (2020, April 15). Civil rights groups file suit against Idaho ban on trans athletes in women's sports. *The Guardian*. https://www.theguardian.com/sport/2020/apr/15/idaho-transgender-ban-womens-sports-lawsuit.

Associated Press. (2021, February 24). Biden administration withdraws from transgender athlete case. *NBC News*. https://www.nbcnews.com/feature/nbc-out/biden-administration-withdraws-transgender-athlete-case-n1258723.

BBC. (2019, June 26). *The Trans Woman Athlete Dispute with Martina Navratilova*. [Documentary]. BBC. https://www.bbc.co.uk/programmes/m00069nr.

BBC. (2020a, September 22). Changes to gender recognition laws ruled out. BBC. https://www.bbc.co.uk/news/uk-politics-54246686.

BBC. (2020b, November 17). Caster Semenya takes appeal to European Court of Human Rights. BBC. https://www.bbc.co.uk/sport/athletics/54973244.

Beek, T., Cohen-Kettenis, P., Bouman, W.P., de Vries, A., Steensma, T., Witcomb, G.L., Arcelus, J., Richards, C., & Kreukels, B. (2016). Gender incongruence of adolescence and adulthood: Acceptability and clinical utility of the World Health Organization's proposed ICD-11 criteria. *PLoS One*, 11 (10). https://doi.org/10.1371/journal.pone.0160066.

Beek, T., Cohen-Kettenis, P., Bouman, W.P., de Vries, A., Steensma, T., Witcomb, G.L., Arcelus, J., Richards, C., & Kreukels, B. (2017). Gender incongruence of childhood: Clinical utility and stakeholder agreement with the World Health Organization's proposed ICD-11 criteria. *PLoS One*, 12 (1). https://doi.org/10.1371/journal.pone.0168522.

Beijing Declaration and Platform for Action. (1995). https://www.unwomen.org/en/digital-library/publications/2015/01/beijing-declaration.

Boyes, S. (2000). The regulation of sport and the impact of the Human Rights Act 1998. *European Public Law*, 6(4), 517–530. ISSN 1354-3725.

Brighton plus Helsinki 2014 Declaration on Women and Sport. https://iwgwomenandsport.org/brighton-declaration/.

British Cycling. (2021, March 25). British Cycling launches consultation on Transgender participation policy. British Cycling. https://www.britishcycling.org.uk/about/article/20210325-about-bc-news-British-Cycling-launches-consultation-on-Transgender-participation-policy-0.

Buzuvis, E. (2021). Law, policy, and the participation of transgender athletes in the United States. *Sport Management Review*. https://doi.org/10.1080/14413523.2021.1880757.

Campbell, N., Brady, A., & Tincknell-Smith, A. (2022). *Holistic Athlete Development and Wellbeing: Person first, athlete second*. Routledge.

Cavanagh S.L, & Sykes, H. (2006). Transsexual bodies at the Olympics: The International Olympic Committee's Policy on transsexual athletes at the 2004 Athens Summer Games. *Body & Society*, 12(3), 75–102. https://doi.org/10.1177/1357034X06067157.

Chappelet, J-L. (2017). Beyond governance: The need to improve the regulation of international sport. *Sport in Society*, 21(5), 724–734. https://doi.org/10.1080/17430437.2018.1401355.

Charter of Fundamental Rights of the European Union. (2009). https://eur-lex.europa.eu/legal-content/EN/TXT/?uri=CELEX:12012P/TXT.

Cochran, S.D., Drescher, J., Kismödi, E., Giami, A., García-Moreno, C., Atalla, E., Marais, A., Vieira, E.M., & Reed. G.M. (2014). Proposed declassification of disease categories related to sexual orientation in the International Statistical Classification of Diseases and Related Health Problems (ICD-11). *Bulletin of the World Health Organization*, 92, 672–679. http://dx.doi.org/10.2471/BLT.14.135541.

Convention on the Elimination of All Forms of Discrimination Against Women. (1979). https://www.ohchr.org/en/hrbodies/cedaw/pages/cedawindex.aspx.

Davy, Z., Sørlie, A., & Schwend, A.S. (2018). Democratising diagnoses? The role of the depathologisation perspective in constructing corporeal trans citizenship. *Critical Social Policy*, 38(1): 13–34. https://doi.org/10.1177/0261018317731716.

Discrimination Against Transgender People in Europe Resolution. (2015). http://assembly.coe.int/nw/xml/xref/xref-xml2html-en.asp?fileid=21736.

Dworkin, D. (2013). *Taking Rights Seriously*. Bloomsbury Academic.
ECHR (European Conventions on Human Rights). (1950). https://www.echr.coe.int/Documents/Convention_ENG.pdf.
England Rugby. (n.d). Transgender and non-binary players current policy. https://www.englandrugby.com/about-rfu/rfu-policies/transgender-policy.
Fabeni, S., & Agius, S. (2009). *Transgender People and the Gender Recast Directive: Implementation guidelines*. The European Region of the International Lesbian, Gay, Bisexual, Trans & Intersex Association (ILGA) Europe. https://www.ilga-europe.org/sites/default/files/Attachments/transgenderpeople_and_the_gender_recast_directive_guidelines_dec2009.pdf.
Fairbairn, C. (2020, January 8). The gender recognition process. House of Commons Library. https://commonslibrary.parliament.uk/research-briefings/cbp-8746/.
Fairbairn, C., Gheera, M., & Pyper, D. (2020, December 10). Gender Recognition Reform: Consultation and outcome. House of Commons Library. https://commonslibrary.parliament.uk/research-briefings/cbp-9079/.
FIFA (Fédération Internationale de Football Association). (2017, May). *FIFA's Human Rights Policy*. FIFA. https://img.fifa.com/image/upload/kr05dqyhwr1uhqy2lh6r.pdf.
GLSEN. (2019). Policy brief: Transgender inclusion in high school athletics. GLSEN. https://www.glsen.org/sites/default/files/2019-10/GLSEN-Transgender-Inclusion-High-School-Athletics.pdf.
Gov.UK. (2010). Equality act explanatory notes. https://www.legislation.gov.uk/ukpga/2010/15/pdfs/ukpgaen_20100015_en.pdf.
Gov.UK. (2021, May 4). Press release: Gender recognition certificate fee reduced. https://www.gov.uk/government/news/gender-recognition-certificate-fee-reduced.
Graham, B.A. (2021, January 22). Joe Biden's gender discrimination order offers hope for young trans athletes. *The Guardian*. https://www.theguardian.com/sport/2021/jan/22/transgender-athletes-joe-biden-executive-order.
Grell, T. (2018). The International Olympic Committee and Human Rights Reforms: Game changer or mere window dressing? *The International Sports Law Journal*, 17 (3), 160–169. https://doi.org/10.1007/s40318-018-0127-x.
Grey-Thompson, T. (2017). Duty of care in sport: Independent Report to the Government. https://assets.publishing.service.gov.uk/government/uploads/system/uploads/attachment_data/file/610130/Duty_of_Care_Review_-_April_2017__2.pdf.
Harper, J., O'Donnell, E., Sorouri Khorashad, B., McDermott, H., & Witcomb, G.L. (2021). How does hormone transition in transgender women change body composition, muscle strength and haemoglobin? Systematic review with a focus on the implications for sport participation. *British Journal of Sports Medicine*. https://doi.org/10.1136/bjsports-2020-103106.
Hilton, E.N., & Lundberg, T.R. (2021). Transgender women in the female category of sport: Perspectives on testosterone suppression and performance advantage. *Sports Medicine*, 51(2), 199–214. https://doi.org/10.1007/s40279-020-01389-3.
Hines, S. (2018, July 13). Trans and feminist rights have been falsely cast in opposition. *The Economist*. https://www.economist.com/open-future/2018/07/13/trans-and-feminist-rights-have-been-falsely-cast-in-opposition.
House of Commons. (2016). *Transgender Equality. First Report of Session 2015–16*. https://publications.parliament.uk/pa/cm201516/cmselect/cmwomeq/390/390.pdf.

Ingle, S. (2019, September 24). IOC delays new transgender guidelines after scientists fail to agree. *The Guardian*. https://www.theguardian.com/sport/2019/sep/24/ioc-delays-new-transgender-guidelines-2020-olympics?CMP=Share_iOSApp_Other.

Ingle, S. (2020a, May 28). Policy allowing transgender athletes to compete as girls found to violate US law. *The Guardian*. https://www.theguardian.com/sport/2020/may/28/connecticut-transgender-federal-civil-rights-lawsuit.

Ingle, S. (2020b, December 13). Rugby players' claim for brain injury has 'less than 50/50' chance, say experts. *The Guardian*. https://www.theguardian.com/sport/2020/dec/13/rugby-union-players-claim-for-brain-injury-dementia-world-rugby.

Ingram, B.J., & Thomas, C.L. (2019). Transgender policy in sport: A review of current policy and commentary of the challenges of policy creation. *Current Sports Medicine Reports*, 18(6), 239–247. https://doi.org/10.1249/JSR.0000000000000605.

International Covenant on Civil and Political Rights. (1976). https://www.ohchr.org/en/professionalinterest/pages/ccpr.aspx.

International Covenant on Economic, Social and Cultural Rights. (1976). https://www.ohchr.org/en/professionalinterest/pages/cescr.aspx.

IOC (International Olympic Committee). (2004, May 17). IOC approves consensus with regard to athletes who have changed sex. https://olympics.com/ioc/news/ioc-approves-consensus-with-regard-to-athletes-who-have-changed-sex.

IOC (International Olympic Committee). (2015). IOC Consensus Meeting on sex reassignment and hyperandrogenism. https://stillmed.olympic.org/Documents/Commissions_PDFfiles/Medical_commission/2015-11_ioc_consensus_meeting_on_sex_reassignment_and_hyperandrogenism-en.pdf.

IOC (International Olympic Committee). (2017). Host City Contract-Principles. Games of the XXXIII Olympiad in 2024. https://stillmed.olympic.org/media/Document%20Library/OlympicOrg/Documents/Host-City-Elections/XXXIII-Olympiad-2024/Host-City-Contract-2024-Principles.pdf.

IOC (International Olympic Committee). (2019). *The Olympic Agenda 2020*. https://www.olympic.org/olympic-agenda-2020.

IOC (International Olympic Committee). (2021). *The Olympic Charter*. https://stillmed.olympics.com/media/Document%20Library/OlympicOrg/General/EN-Olympic-Charter.pdf?_ga=2.187257832.1531765840.1638952189-1245824087.1638952188.

Jones, B.A., Arcelus, J., Bouman, W.P., & Haycraft, E. (2017). Sport and transgender people: A systematic review of the literature relating to sport participation and competitive sport policies. *Sports Medicine*, 47, 701–716. https://doi.org/10.1007/s40279-016-0621-y.

Jordan-Young, R. M., & Karkazis, K. (2019). *Testosterone: An Unauthorized Biography*. Harvard University Press.

Kidd, B. (2018). Towards responsible policy-making in international sport: Reforming the medical-scientific commissions. *Sport in Society*, 21(5), 773–787. https://doi.org/10.1080/17430437.2018.1401357.

Kyriacou, S. (2020). What is gender dysphoria? *Pink News*. https://www.pinknews.co.uk/2020/04/20/what-is-gender-dysphoria-meaning-definition/.

Lane, L. (2018). The horizontal effect of International Human Rights Law in practice: A comparative analysis of the general comments and jurisprudence of selected United Nations Human Rights Treaty monitoring bodies. *European Journal of Comparative Law and Governance*. https://doi.org/10.1163/22134514-00501001.

Lenskyj, H.J. (2018). *Gender, Athletes' Rights, and the Court of Arbitration for Sport*. Emerald Publishing.

Lembke, U. (2016). Tackling sex discrimination to achieve gender equality? Conceptions of sex and gender in EU non-discrimination law and policies. *European Equality Law Review*, 2. https://www.equalitylaw.eu/downloads/3938-european-equality-law-review-2-2016.

Levenson, M. & Vigdor, N. (2020, May 29). Inclusion of transgender student athletes violates Title IX, Trump Administration says. *The New York Times*. https://www.nytimes.com/2020/05/29/us/connecticut-transgender-student-athletes.html.

Malagrino, D.O. (2020). May They Play: *Soule v. Connecticut Association of Schools, Inc.*, Title IX, and a policy of inclusion for high school transgender athletes without prerequiring hormone therapy or puberty blockers. *Marquette Sports Law Review*, 31 (1), 35–84.

Naess, H.E. (2019). Good intentions, vague policies: A thematic analysis of recommendations by the United Nations, the European Commission and the OECD on sporting events and human rights. *Journal of Global Sport Management*, 4(1), 25–37. https://doi.org/10.1080/24704067.2018.1531245.

Nafziger, J.A.R. (1999). Globalising Sports Law. *Marquette Sports Law Journal*, 9(2), 225–238.

O'Flaherty, M. (2015). The Yogyakarta Principles at Ten. *Nordic Journal of Human Rights*, 33(4), 280–298. https://doi.org/10.1080/18918131.2015.1127009.

Patel, S. (2008). Transsexuals in sport: Inclusiveness and the level playing field. Papers in Law Series, Anglia Ruskin University.

Patel, S. (2015a). *Inclusion and Exclusion in Competitive Sport*. Routledge.

Patel, S. (2015b). Feature article: The IAAF's hyperandrogenism regulations suspended. *World Sports Law Report*. https://core.ac.uk/download/pdf/30649813.pdf.

Patel, S. (2021). Gaps in the protection of athletes gender rights in sport: A regulatory riddle. *International Sports Law Journal*. https://doi.org/10.1007/s40318-021-00182-2.

Patel, S. (2022). Athletes' sex and gender rights. In J. Kornbeck (Ed.) *Sport and Brexit: Regulatory challenges and legacies*. Routledge.

Pavitt, M. (2020, March 3). IOC confirms existing guidelines on transgender athlete eligibility to remain for Tokyo 2020. *Inside the Games*. https://www.insidethegames.biz/articles/1091417/ioc-guidelines-transgender-tokyo-2020.

Peel, E., & Newman, H.J.H. (2020). Gender's wider stakes: Lay attitudes to legal gender reform. *Feminists@Law*, 10(2). https://doi.org/10.22024/UniKent/03/fal.953.

Pieper, L.P. (2012). Gender regulation: Renée Richards revisited. *The International Journal of the History of Sport*, 29(5), 675–690. https://doi.org/10.1080/09523367.2012.675202.

Sailors, P.R. (2020). Transgender and intersex athletes and the women's category in sport. *Sport, Ethics and Philosophy*. https://doi.org/10.1080/17511321.2020.1756904.

Santos, A.L. (2020). Trans athletes and the posthuman: A critical analysis of trans policies in sports. In Z. Davy, A.C. Santos, C. Bertone, R. Thoreson, & S.E. Wieringa (Eds.), *The SAGE Handbook of Global Sexualities* (pp. 267–290). SAGE Publications.

Savulescu, J. (2019, May 9). Ten ethical flaws in the Caster Semenya decision on intersex in sport. *The Conversation*. https://theconversation.com/ten-ethical-flaws-in-the-caster-semenya-decision-on-intersex-in-sport-116448.

Schwab, B. (2018). Embedding the human rights of players in world sport. *The International Sports Law Journal*, 17, 214–232. https://doi.org/10.1007/s40318-018-0128-9.

Sharpe, A.N. (2011). Changing sex: The problem of transsexuality. In A.N. Sharpe, *Foucault's Monsters and the Challenge of Law* (Chapter 5). Routledge.

Sharpe, A. (2020). Will gender self-declaration undermine women's rights and lead to an increase in harms? *Modern Law Review*, 83(3), 539–557. https://doi.org/10.1111/1468-2230.12507.

The Gender Recast Directive (2006/54/EC). https://eur-lex.europa.eu/legal-content/EN/TXT/?uri=celex%3A32006L0054.

Theilen, J.T. (2014). Depathologisation of transgenderism and International Human Rights Law. *Human Rights Law Review*, 14, 327–342. https://doi.org/10.1093/hrlr/ngu010.

Title IX of the Education Amendments Act. (1972). https://www.justice.gov/crt/title-ix-education-amendments-1972

UEFA (Union of European Football Associations). (2017). UEFA Euro 2024 Tournament Requirements. https://www.uefa.com/MultimediaFiles/Download/OfficialDocument/uefaorg/Regulations/02/46/30/61/2463061_DOWNLOAD.pdf.

United Nations. (2011). *Guiding Principles on Business and Human Rights*. https://www.ohchr.org/Documents/Publications/GuidingPrinciplesBusinessHR_EN.pdf.

Universal Declaration of Human Rights. (1948). https://www.un.org/en/about-us/universal-declaration-of-human-rights.

UNHRC (United Nations Human Rights Council). (2019). The elimination of discrimination against women and girls in sport, Resolution 40/5. United Nations Human Rights Council. https://ilga.org/downloads/Elimination_of_discrimination_against_women_and_girls_in_sport.pdf.

UNHRC (United Nations Human Rights Council). (2020). *Report of the United Nations High Commissioner for Human Rights, Intersection of race and gender discrimination in sport, A/HRC/44/26*. United Nations High Commissioner for Human Rights https://www.ohchr.org/EN/HRBodies/HRC/RegularSessions/Session44/_layouts/15/WopiFrame.aspx?sourcedoc=/EN/HRBodies/HRC/RegularSessions/Session44/Documents/A_HRC_44_26_AEV.docx&action=default&DefaultItemOpen=1.

West, D. (2019). Revitalising a phantom regime: The adjudication of human rights complaints in sport. *The International Sports Law Journal*, 19, 2–17. https://doi.org/10.1007/s40318-019-00147-6.

West-Sell, S.A., Van Ness, J.M., & Ciccolella, M.E. (2019). Law, policy, and physiology as determinants of fairness for transgender athletes. *Professionalization of Exercise Physiology*, 22(2).

Wettstein, F. (2015). Normativity, ethics, and the UN Guiding Principles on business and human rights: A critical assessment. *Journal of Human Rights*, 14(2), 162–182. https://doi.org/10.1080/14754835.2015.1005733.

World Athletics. (2018). IAAF introduces new eligibility regulations for female classification. https://www.worldathletics.org/news/press-release/eligibility-regulations-for-female-classifica.

World Athletics. (2019a). *The World Athletics Eligibility Regulations for Transgender Athletes (Transgender Regulations)*. http://www.athletics.org.tw/Upload/Web_Page/WA/Eligibility%20Regulations%20for%20Transgender%20Athletes,%20.pdf.

World Athletics. (2019b). *Report of the International Meeting on Transgender Eligibility in Competitive Sports*. https://www.worldathletics.org/news/press-release/international-federations-rules-transgender-a.

World Rugby. (2020a, February 27). Press release: Landmark World Rugby Transgender Workshop important step towards appropriate rugby-specific policy. https://www.world.rugby/news/563437?lang=en.

World Rugby. (2020b, October 9). World Rugby approves updated transgender participation guidelines. https://www.world.rugby/news/591776/world-rugby-approves-updated-transgender-participation-guidelines.

Yogyakarta Principles Plus 10. (2017). https://yogyakartaprinciples.org/principles-en/yp10/.

Chapter 4

'For Some People they'd Never Be Able to Tick all those Boxes'

Exclusion of Trans and Non-binary Identities in University Sport Policy

Catherine Phipps

Introduction

Within UK university settings, sport is often considered an important part of the student experience. For example, an article in *Times Higher Education* (Mayne & Diamond, 2016) suggests that involvement in university sport can help ease the transition into university life, assisting students in overcoming social isolation. Mayne and Diamond (2016) also suggest that the higher education setting is an important environment to support elite sport within the UK. There are arguably a variety of further benefits; an employability report, using mixed-methods research with graduates, employers and senior university executives, indicates regular sport participation is considered by employers to develop leadership, management, problem-solving and teamwork skills. In turn, this may have a positive impact on developing employability (Griffiths et al., 2017). This potentially leads to fewer periods of unemployment and increased earning potential after graduation for those who participate in university sport. Finally, recreational sport participation has been linked to social connectedness, higher levels of self-esteem, reduced stress levels, and protection against depression later in life; all important factors for improved mental health (Jewett et al., 2019).

Sport England data also demonstrates the prominence of university sport in the UK. Within their most recent (2013–2014) survey of over 36,000 students, 67% of those surveyed participated in a sport activity, with the majority (57%) taking part at least once a week (Sport England, 2014). Furthermore, 39% of those surveyed took part in some form of organised sport, with 24% stating they were involved in organised competition. However, it was also found that participation varied according to factors such as gender, age, ethnicity and disability. Considering the potential positive benefits of sport participation, alongside notions of fairness and inclusivity, it is clearly important that university sport is inclusive for all.

Within UK universities, student unions are usually in control of the organisation of university sport, including competitive fixtures and recreational sport and physical activity opportunities (Phipps, 2020). They usually consist of a

DOI: 10.4324/9781003050568-4

range of full-time permanent staff, alongside full-time and part-time 'sabbatical' officers. These sabbatical officers are often elected students, chosen by the wider student body, who may take time out of their studies to undertake the role. A range of sabbatical officer roles exist across different institutions, with common full-time roles including President, Activities/Sport Officer, and Education/Welfare Officer. Many student unions also include roles for the representation of specific groups of students, for example postgraduate students, students from diverse ethnic backgrounds, and LGBT+[1] students. However, it must be noted that the structure of student unions across the UK do vary, with different full-time and part-time roles evident.

Although student unions usually control sport at a local level, since 2008 most university-based competitive sport in the UK has been governed overall by British Universities and Colleges Sport (BUCS). Their mission is to provide the best university sport experience globally, aiming for an inclusive sport experience for all students (BUCS, 2017). This includes widening access to existing opportunities and ensuring inclusive practice is embedded into all BUCS' policies, strategies and practices (BUCS, 2017). Therefore, although university sport clubs are usually run through the student union at their institution – who may (or may not) have clear inclusion policies for students – these clubs are governed by BUCS policy when participating in competitive sport. In other words, regardless of an individual student union's policy on trans inclusion, they are constrained by wider policies and practices. In relation to this chapter, the main policies relevant are the guidelines for trans and non-binary athletes competing in BUCS competition.

BUCS Regulations for Trans and Non-binary Athletes

BUCS regulations regarding trans and non-binary athletes fall under their 'individual eligibility' guidelines and were last updated in October 2019. Within their regulations, BUCS state that they support 'equal opportunities in sport for all, to include transgender athletes on the basis of the gender with which they identify' (BUCS, 2021. Despite this, the regulations state that trans women not taking testosterone suppressants may only compete in male competition – that is, in line with the sex that they were assigned at birth and not with which they identify. A less restrictive regulation is in place for trans men not taking any gender-affirming hormones, who can participate in either male or female competition without restriction. These regulations are based upon arguments related to testosterone exposure – a hormone which may increase muscular size and physical performance, and which would otherwise be considered a doping drug when not medically prescribed (Mazzeo, 2018). Thus, it follows that those trans men who are receiving gender-affirming testosterone supplementation are immediately excluded from female competition. This exclusion from female competition does align with trans men's affirmed gender and therefore may not be considered entirely exclusionary. For trans women who are taking testosterone suppressants, they are allowed to participate in female competition only after one calendar year of taking these gender-affirming hormones. Prior to this, they are still eligible to participate in male competition. For mixed events, trans people may compete as their affirmed gender, subject to the regulations above; if they do not meet these, they may compete as the gender they were assigned at birth. Finally, BUCS state that they may request medical evidence to confirm any medical intervention, which is treated confidentially; however, the costs of obtaining medical information cannot be covered by them (BUCS, 2019).

A comparison can be made to the United States' National Collegiate Athletic Association (NCAA) transgender student-athlete policy of 2011. While the university sport system in the United States, managed largely by the NCAA, is significantly different to the UK BUCS system in terms of larger athletic budgets, scholarships for talented athletes, higher quality facilities and higher-profile media coverage of some events (NCAA, 2020), the trans inclusion policies of BUCS (2019) and NCAA (2011) are largely similar. To summarise, it is stated for the purpose of NCAA competition that trans men taking testosterone may compete on men's teams but are no longer eligible to compete on women's teams unless the team's status is changed to mixed gender (NCAA, 2011). Trans women taking testosterone suppressants may continue to compete in men's teams but may not compete on women's teams unless their status is changed to a mixed team or they have completed one calendar year of testosterone suppressant treatment. For those not taking gender-affirming hormones, trans men may compete on men's or women's teams, and trans women may only compete on men's teams (NCAA, 2011). These regulations therefore require trans and non-binary students to reveal their gender identity openly to others. This was evident in a study by Klein et al. (2018), whereby a trans male student athlete had to disclose their gender identity to many athletic personnel, apply for a medical exemption, and share their medical records detailing their testosterone levels in order to continue competing, with the responsibility being on the athlete to initiate this process. Both BUCS and NCAA policies therefore demonstrate a necessary and multi-layered process of students being open about their gender identity, involving multiple people such as teammates, coaches, national governing bodies, and others working in sport teams.

Considering these regulations, policies such as BUCS (2019) and NCAA (2011) do not entirely exclude those who are trans or non-binary, as they allow any athlete, regardless of birth-assigned gender, to compete in the male categories when they are not eligible to compete with or against females. However, the guidelines may restrict trans women's sport participation in accordance with their gender identity. Although the reasons for this are unclear, based on previous studies and reports on physiological differences between males and females (e.g., Hilton & Lundberg, 2020), this is presumably with safe and fair female competition in mind. Furthermore, the reliance on binary gender categories may also be exclusionary for non-binary people, who must fit into binary structures to be accepted. However, in practice, the above guidelines are only followed when sport-specific regulations for trans and non-binary athletes, taken from the international or national governing body for each particular sport, are either not in existence or have not been updated in the past three years (BUCS, 2019). This creates further complexities; sport-specific policies may vary and are not always underpinned by evidence (Jones et al., 2017), with some based upon inclusion (Segrave, 2016) and others overly stringent and focussed on elite-level sport (Jones et al., 2017).

To elaborate, the 2004 policy of the International Olympic Committee (IOC), stated that any trans athletes should have fully medically transitioned, including the completion of gender-affirming surgery and a minimum of two years of gender-affirming hormones. This has since been updated to a newer, less restrictive policy in place from the Tokyo Games onwards, whereby trans men can compete without restriction, and for trans women total testosterone level in serum should be below 10 nmol/L for at least 12 months prior to, and during, competition;[2] furthermore, the need for surgery has been removed for all (IOC, 2015). However, according to Jones et al. (2017), many sport organisation's policies have been heavily influenced by the original 2004 IOC regulations. With these issues and complexities in mind, this chapter aims to explore the realities of current BUCS rules, considering the views of student union officers who implement the policy at a local level, alongside those of trans and non-binary students who may have been directly impacted by these regulations in the UK university sport context. The research questions which guided this study, therefore, are:

1 How accessible are university sports for trans and non-binary students?
2 To what extent do student unions and BUCS reinforce and/or challenge binary models of gender through policy and practice?

Methodology

To answer the above research questions, case-studies at four student unions in the UK were conducted, as part of a wider study on LGBT+ inclusion in university sport. The case-studies involved focus groups and questionnaires with LGBT+ students alongside separate focus groups with student union officers. The rationale for the case-studies was to gain detailed and in-depth data on a specific context. All student unions were based in the South and Midlands of England,[3] with data collection initially taking place at a post-1992[4] university in the South West of England in December 2015 (Student Union A), followed by a red-brick university in the East Midlands in January 2016 (Student Union B). Next, data were collected at a red-brick university in the South West of England in February 2016 (Student Union C) and a post-1992 university in the South East of England in April 2016 (Student Union D). In terms of the focus groups, eight LGBT+ students shared their views across four focus groups, one of whom, Ben, identified as trans. At the time of the focus group, Ben was 20 years old and identified as a trans man. He had been active in the women's university rugby team but had stopped playing a short time before the focus groups took place. In conjunction with Ben's experiences, several student union officers also shared their views on trans and non-binary inclusion in university sport (see Table 4.1).

As a lower-than-anticipated number of LGBT+ students had taken part in the focus groups, to increase their engagement an online questionnaire was created using *Qualtrics*. This was produced using predominantly open-ended questions which replicated those which would have been asked across the focus groups. For example, those students who indicated from a closed question that they had observed or experienced LGBT+ discrimination in the university sport context were asked 'Can you explain what sort of discrimination you witnessed/experienced?' and those who indicated they had experienced barriers to participation were asked 'Can you explain what particular barriers or factors you have faced or had to overcome in order to take part?' Other questions centred around students' experiences of 'lad culture'[5] (Jackson & Sundaram, 2018; Phipps & Young, 2015), LGBT+ sport clubs, student union campaigns and initiatives, and what could be improved or changed about university sport to encourage participation.

The questionnaire was therefore used to gather a broader range of perspectives from LGBT+ students, albeit through a different (more limited) format, whereby follow-up questions could not be used. Once created, the questionnaire was then disseminated to LGBT+ students at the four student unions. To do this, LGBT+ societies and student union officers were contacted to promote the questionnaire, alongside various social media posts. Responses were collected between March 2016 and October 2016 and in total, 27 LGBT+ students responded to the questionnaire, with seven respondents identifying under the trans and non-binary 'umbrella', demonstrating there are multiple ways in which someone can be trans or non-binary (see Table 4.2). Across the data sets, qualitative data was prominent, and thematic analysis was used to analyse this

Table 4.1 Student Union Officers

Pseudonym	*Student Union*	*Job Area*	*Time in Job Role*
John	A	Student Experience	12 months
Luke	A	LGBT+ Officer	7 months
Zoe	B	Student Union President	6 months
Charlotte	C	Sport Officer	7 months
Robbie	C	LGBT+ Officer	7 months
Joe	D	Student Union President	9 months

Table 4.2 Questionnaire and Focus Group Respondents

Pseudonym	*Student Union*	*Identity (in respondent's own words)*	*Involvement in Sport (at the time of their response)*
Alfie	A	Trans man, homosexual	No
Jasmine	A	Gender-fluid,[6] homo-romantic pansexual	Yes
Dale	A	Bisexual, transman	Yes
Laura	B	Lesbian demi-gender[7] female	Yes
Claire	B	Lesbian androgynous[8] woman	Yes
Stacie	B	Pansexual transwoman	No
Ben	B	Trans man	No
Imogen	C	Agender,[9] attracted to women but not 'out'	Yes

data. This is a widely used qualitative data analysis method to identify, organise, describe, and report themes evident in a data set (Nowell et al., 2017).

Initially, prior to data collection, a provisional list of potential codes was created that were based on the research questions and research problems (Miles & Huberman, 1994). These provisional codes were created with previous literature and theories in mind and included those that were descriptive (for example 'lack of inclusive facilities in student unions'), but predominantly interpretative and exploratory codes were used (for example 'hegemonic power structures between LGBT+ students and others'; 'cultural problems evident in sport'). Additional codes included 'evidence of inclusive practice' and 'evidence of gender binaries', amongst others. All the preliminary codes were kept on a separate sheet for reference and clear operational definitions were outlined to ensure consistency as the coding took place (Lincoln & Guba, 1985).

In terms of the focus groups, these were recorded using a Dictaphone and transcribed verbatim shortly afterwards. After each transcription was produced, these were read and re-read to gain familiarity with the data, to begin to recognise and interpret themes across the data set, a method recommended by Bryman (2012). After the focus groups and questionnaires were complete, codes from the provisional list were then applied to the data, using a deductive approach. To do this, any data considered interesting or relevant was extracted and placed into tables, while keeping the initials of the respondent and their student union next to each quote. Following this, the meanings of the quotations and responses were interpreted and inspected for what they revealed about the phenomena (Nowell et al., 2017), and each were given a code to capture their respective meanings (Grbich, 2007). However, the provisional list of codes was adapted and refined throughout the ongoing data analysis process. Through this process, a number of themes were created. The findings relevant to trans and non-binary inclusion are presented below, starting with BUCS policy and its restrictions, followed by suggestions for more inclusive practices in university sport.

Findings

BUCS Policy: Restrictions for Trans and Non-binary Students

Most sports are organised along binary gender lines, in terms of both societal perception of appropriately 'masculine' and 'feminine' sports, and in terms of policies which segregate male and female sport. With boys/men generally playing more contact team sport using force/power (such as football and rugby) and girls playing non-contact, 'female-appropriate' team sport (such as hockey or netball), or activities centred on gracefulness (such as gymnastics or dance), this emphasises sport as a binary, heteronormative space (Plaza et al., 2017). Clearly, this can cause barriers and restrictions for anyone, regardless of their gender identity. These concerns were raised by Charlotte (*Sport Officer, Student Union C*), who discussed how a male student wanted to play netball – a female sport not currently offered to men as part of BUCS competition: 'They (*BUCS*) were just flat out no, or you can if you have your hormone levels tested'. BUCS' response therefore reinforces gender binaries and reduces gender to simply hormone levels, which may be overly simplistic (see Sailors, 2020). To expand, Klein et al., (2018) have critiqued the common discourse that people with higher testosterone levels are automatically better athletes, with the impact of testosterone potentially varying between different sports. Charlotte's quote also highlights the lack of opportunity for men and women who want to be involved in sports lying outside of gender norms. Similar restricted opportunities were later outlined by Alfie who argued:

> 'Growing up I played a lot of "female-appropriate sports" (for example in PE) and I now don't have a lot of experience playing 'male sports' due to mis-gendering in my youth'. *Alfie, Trans Man, Student Union A*

Although the vast majority of sports in BUCS competition are offered to both men and women – with notable exceptions including netball (only women) and rugby league (only men) – gendered teams and practices are commonplace, potentially leading to restricted sporting opportunities in BUCS structures, particularly for trans and non-binary people. These restrictions are often in place due to presumed strength and physiological differences between male and female athletes (Krech, 2017). Nevertheless, these sport policies – including BUCS regulations for trans students, outlined previously in this chapter – consequently reinforce gender binaries, failing to accommodate all trans and non-binary identities. For instance, Zoe argued:

> 'The fact that there are distinctive gender splits is a clear barrier. The fact that there's no clear guidance if you are gender fluid or you don't necessarily

> identify with one gender then what are your options? And as that's not clear then I think it's an automatic barrier…you might be automatically putting yourself in a position you're not comfortable with'. *Zoe, President, Student Union B*

Gender binaries are prominent, taken-for-granted and normalised, and remain a major way in which we distinguish between different groups of people in society; their status in sport consequently means trans people's participation in accordance with their gender identity – when they identify within binary gender categories – is relatively rare (Jones et al., 2017). As Zoe notes, without a trans identity that 'fits' into the binary system, it may be exceptionally difficult to participate in university sport under BUCS regulations, unless that identity is compromised in an attempt to conform. However, even for those trans students whose identities correspond with binary gender categories (for example, those who identify outright as 'men' or 'women'), issues may still exist if these students are unclear on the eligibility criteria within that particular sport. As stated previously in this chapter, this is particularly problematic when BUCS often rely on sport-specific national or international governing body guidelines, and it is unclear how clearly these are advertised. Within the focus groups, it was revealed that BUCS policy had restricted participation for Ben, a trans man, who had checked the England Rugby guidelines, which at the time[10] had one of the strictest policies regarding trans participation. In 2017, the policy outlined a requirement for surgical anatomical changes (two years prior to applying for approval to participate in rugby), legal recognition of the trans person's acquired gender, and confirmation from a medical professional that gender-affirming hormones had been administered for a sufficient length of time to minimise gender-related advantages (England Rugby, 2017). This policy was in place for all trans and non-binary people, at all levels of rugby.

National governing body guidance such as the policy by England Rugby (2017) may be more relevant to elite level competition, as opposed to UK university sport, which is usually (although not always) played recreationally and/or at a lower standard. Particularly problematic in the 2017 policy is the requirement for gender-affirming surgery. Historically, gender-affirming surgery was considered a normal part of a trans persons' transition, reinforcing the idea that gender identities are binary and should correlate with a person's physical characteristics, emphasising appearance expectations for trans people (Krane, 2014). However, many trans people do not desire to have such surgical interventions. Regarding some sport policies, this requirement may be in place due to ideas that men may otherwise pretend to be trans in order to compete with women, under the presumption they have more chance of success (Carroll, 2014). This is also reflected in historical accounts; according to Reeser (2005), reports and suspicions of men masquerading as women in sport date back to the early cold war era. Regardless of this justification, gender-affirming surgery has no bearing on sport performance and cannot be conducted in the UK prior to age 18. Furthermore, requiring surgery in order to participate in sport forces people to undergo medical procedures, potentially against their will. Forced medical intervention has also been explored in relation to the case of Caster Semenya, an intersex athlete who has been required to medically reduce her testosterone levels in order to compete in athletics, which is deemed both unethical and invasive (Farham, 2019).

It is also important to highlight that many trans students are unlikely to have undergone gender-affirming surgery before attending university, particularly if they start university at the age of 18 (Gibson, 2013). This is because waiting lists for National Health Service (NHS) procedures in the UK are often several years long due to increasing demands for these services. To elaborate, Westcott (2018) states that some trans people may wait up to two and a half years for an initial consultation. Thus, requiring gender-affirming surgery in policies may be exclusionary, enforcing binary models of gender despite not being necessary to preserve fair competition (IOC, 2015). This would effectively exclude many trans students, such as those who may be part way through transitioning or who are pre-medical transition. In addition, there is an assumption within many of these policies that all trans people's identities align with the gender binary, when in reality some identities fall outside of binary structures. Differences in experience between trans people who identify within and outside of binary structures has been evidenced in several areas, including social support (Thorne et al., 2019), mental health (Rimes et al., 2017) and access to health care (Clark et al., 2018), although little research has explored this within the sport context.

Ben (*Trans Man, Student Union B*) had checked the England Rugby (2017) regulations, arguing the policy was only inclusive to those who wanted and were able to undergo gender-affirming surgery and hormones. Ben was hoping to start taking gender-affirming hormones soon after the focus group took place but had no intention of undergoing gender-affirming surgery, similar to many trans men (Gleaves & Lehrbach, 2016). The policy outlined by England Rugby may be considered an attempt to 'fit' trans participants into the gender binary, without considering the fluidity of their gender and identity, emphasising binary gender models as a potentially flawed system. Rules such as these may also emphasise trans people as 'outsiders', who are separated from the normalised binary framework of male/female (Ingrey, 2012). Ben used the focus group to critique this policy:

> 'It was all about after transitioning and you need to have all your hormones, all your surgery, everything. And it all must have been completed two years ago. For some people they'd never be able to tick all those boxes'. *Ben, Trans Man, Student Union B*

These issues were also reiterated by a questionnaire respondent who did not participate in university sport due to the barriers she had faced:

> 'BUCS have guidelines that I consider prohibitive for trans competitors. For example, the current guidelines for my sport state that trans competitors must have: HRT,[11] sexual reassignment surgery (but must be two years post-op to compete as own gender), and a gender recognition certificate'. *Stacie, Trans Woman, Student Union B*

The restrictions outlined for Ben and Stacie (as well as other trans and non-binary students) highlight sex-segregation as an unjust and unethical system for some; gender arguably cannot be separated into two discrete categories and many trans people may simply not want to undergo these medical procedures. Evidently, deciding if someone is male or female does not always lead to a binary answer, and other means of categorising people may need to be considered to segregate sport with fairness and inclusion in mind (Foddy & Savulescu, 2010). However, to play sport currently, trans and non-binary people need to conform to the norms and structures that are available to them, which are highlighted in policies. Although Ben had not yet begun undertaking any sort of medical transition at the time of the focus groups and was therefore still eligible to compete in women's rugby, he further outlined the reasons why he had chosen to cease participation – at least temporarily – in this sport. The quote provides evidence that people who are trans and non-binary may socialise out of sport to avoid potential abuse and harassment, contributing to their perceived lower sport participation rates compared to cisgender people (Jones et al., 2017):

> 'Partly I didn't really want to start the season without knowing when I wouldn't be allowed to play anymore and even though the teams I've been playing for are really accepting of gay people, although I knew a lot of people would have my back, I wasn't really sure if everyone would. I knew it would probably cause quite a bit of gossip at the start and I just didn't want to be around that'. *Ben, Trans Man, Student Union B*

It is evident from Ben's quote that trans and non-binary students need support from a wide range of people, including coaches, teammates and wider sport departments to feel accepted and comfortable to continue playing after 'coming out'. This was also reinforced in a previous study by Klein et al. (2018), whereby a trans male athlete competing in NCAA competition received overwhelming support from coaches, teammates, and the wider athletic department, making the transition an easier process. However, it was acknowledged that not all university athletic departments provide this level of support and inclusion, and several may not adhere to policy disallowing discrimination (Klein et al., 2018). As UK university sport teams tend to have fewer support systems in place compared to NCAA provision, this could also prove an issue in the UK context.

Ben then went on to explain his concerns with joining the men's rugby team at his university once he began his medical transition:

> 'I've been looking into gay men's rugby teams because I think they may be better to play for than a regular rugby team. I want to play men's rugby when I'm big enough to compete with the guys but it's putting me off with lad culture, homophobia and transphobia with men's rugby and the reputation that they've got. Although I've found women's rugby is quite welcoming, even though it's the same sport, it's like a different atmosphere'. *Ben, Trans Man, Student Union B*

As can be seen from Ben's quote, he had temporarily stopped playing sport and appeared to be in limbo, not feeling able to compete with either the men's or the women's rugby teams. A similar scenario was evident in the study by Klein et al. (2018); after starting gender-affirming hormones, the trans male cross country and track and field athlete was no longer able to continue competing with the women's team under the NCAA (2011) policy. However, this athlete also felt unable to join the men's team immediately, due to his body being 'in-flux' and unaccustomed in a short period of time. Similar to Ben, the same athlete also witnessed sexism, misogyny and sexualisation of women by the men's team when he started training with them (Klein et al., 2019). Thus, policies for trans people may need to be re-visited in sport, allowing a transition period to train and compete with both the men's and women's teams. Although this would still promote binary models of gender in sport, a transition period would help support trans athletes and sport teams to include trans students and provide support systems to increase inclusion and equitable treatment (Klein et al., 2018).

Evidently, the experiences of trans and non-binary people (in sport and elsewhere) challenge orthodox ideas about gender roles and identities by destabilising gender binaries (Nagoshi et al., 2012). However, many sport bodies reinforce adherence to gender expectations through policy and practice. Underpinning some policies including BUCS (2019) regulations are essentialist, binary ideas about gender, supporting beliefs about the superiority and hegemony of men in sport, despite the fact that ability is situated on a continuum that arguably transcends gender (Fink et al., 2016). Gender identity is fluid, but most sport organisations do not account for identities that fall outside of the binary and ask people who transition from one gender to another to meet particular (often complex) criteria. It is arguably problematic to consider male/female and man/woman as mutually exclusive and oppositional categories (McPhail, 2004), yet this is clearly taking place within contemporary university sport policies in the UK.

Suggestions for Inclusive Practice

When asked to identify ways in which to increase inclusion and accessibility of university sport, some student union officers suggested this was difficult under the current BUCS system, and were critical of the dualistic approach to gender identity evident in BUCS policy. For instance, Charlotte stated:

> 'It's quite difficult working within a system that we have little control over and making any change. BUCS is responsible as well, as they're just following national governing body guidelines. I do think they're looking at it, we did try and push them to say you could actually do something that's sector leading. Yes, it might have to get more complicated at national or at international level but at university it really shouldn't be this complicated'. *Charlotte, Sport Officer, Student Union C*

Thus, as demonstrated in previous literature (Klein et al., 2018), even when athletic departments are trans inclusive, they must follow wider guidelines which may prove exclusionary for some athletes. In the UK system, it is clear that student unions are only able to create their own guidelines and policies for trans and non-binary inclusion if that sport or activity lies outside of BUCS structures. Therefore, inclusive, all-gender sport may be more evident in recreational and intramural leagues – not controlled by BUCS – whereby trans and non-binary inclusion policies can be developed by student unions. This was highlighted by Joe:

> 'Yeah we have a lot of mixed sport and we have a lot of capacity for casual sport as well because we have a programme called [programme name] which is where you can just turn up and have a go. That's been good for inclusive participation because they're all just mixed, they're all like just turn up and play sport'. *Joe, President, Student Union D*

Despite this, it was evident that in relation to BUCS sports teams and competitions, they were unable to make sporting practices more inclusive within the context of their student union officer roles. However, other officers argued that little change is required as the current system can be accessible for all, particularly emphasising mixed-gender sport teams as inclusive alternatives to the usual gendered sporting structures. In other words, mixed teams may be considered a potential solution to the 'problem' of gendered sport, and a viable alternative for many trans and non-binary students. For example, several officers in the focus groups discussed the prominence of sports such as mixed-badminton, American football, Korfball (a sport consisting of four male and four female players per game), and mixed hockey at their student unions. Furthermore, two questionnaire respondents suggested further provision for mixed sport would prove to be less restrictive for trans and non-binary students, with Laura (*Demi-Gender Woman, Student Union B*) stating 'one of the main problems for trans people are gender-based teams so more mixed teams would be good' and Imogen (*Agender Student, Student Union C*) suggesting 'all gender teams rather than binary teams'.

Despite the arguments in favour of more mixed sport, these structures should not automatically be considered suitable alternatives. As an example, American football is mixed under the BUCS system, but Joe (*President, Student Union D*), argued that 'they have rules but they play practically slightly different when a guy's going up against someone they perceive to be a woman at least'. Thus, although it is a mixed sport, it still poses problems for trans and non-binary students due to rules surrounding gender; it 'matters' if you are a man or a woman while playing the sport. To expand, those trans students who do not meet the eligibility criteria to compete as their affirmed gender may be excluded, alongside those whose identities lie outside of binary gender structures. Krech (2017) develops this critique, suggesting most mixed gender sports require a certain number of male and female athletes on each team, effectively presenting the same restrictions for trans athletes. This was further reiterated by John in relation to both mixed hockey and mixed badminton.

> 'Hockey and badminton for example, there are clearly defined rules for each gender in those sports. Badminton for example, even in mixed badminton it has to be one woman, one man and they have different roles so the woman stands at the front more often and the man stands at the back more often'. *John, Student Experience Officer, Student Union A*

Robbie expanded on this with a focus on students whose identities lie outside of the gender binary, explaining:

> 'Not everyone who identifies as transgender identifies as a man or a woman and there's a significant amount in-between. If you don't identify as either a man or a woman, where do you fit on that mixed lacrosse team? It's then almost more awkward to then play for that mixed team than to blend in potentially and play on a gendered team. I think there are very few sports where women and men compete together where it doesn't matter if you're a man or a woman'. *Robbie, LGBT+ Officer, Student Union C*

The perceptions of cisgender people may also pose a barrier to mixed-gender sport. In the focus groups with student union officers, Luke suggested mixed sport could pose injury risks:

> 'There are obviously some medical reasons or health reasons...we have some big rugby players and some quite small girls, and it can be dangerous. That was certainly the reason when we were at school that we couldn't have mixed teams'. *Luke, LGBT+ Officer, Student Union A*

Injury risk is something that has been considered (and critiqued) in wider literature. Alongside differences in sporting ability related to gender discrimination (see Travers, 2008), after puberty, males tend to have physiological advantages which equate to increased sporting performances over females in many sports (Sailors, 2020). Hence, separate 'protected' women's categories may promote fairness and reduce any injury risks associated with mixed-gender competitions. This was recently presented as a rationale for not allowing transwomen to play women's rugby at international level (World Rugby, 2020). However, it is worth noting that this may vary between sports and the level played; thus, blanket approaches and generalisations may not be useful when considering trans and non-binary inclusion policies. Pennington et al., (2017) explored injuries in Quidditch, a mixed-gender full-contact sport considered trans and non-binary inclusive as the rules allow players to self-identify regarding their gender identity. Using self-reporting questionnaires with 348 respondents, there was found to be no difference in superficial injuries between males and females, although females had a higher rate of concussion. Thus, despite being mixed, it appears from this preliminary research that there is no significant difference in injury risk for females, although further research is required to consider females' higher rates of concussion in greater depth (Pennington et al., 2017), especially as concussion can have long-term impacts on brain health and mortality.

Perceptions about mixed-gender youth football have also been gathered by Hills et al. (2020). Several coaches and parents in this study perceived physical disparities to be greater *within* the sexes, rather than between them. In other words, it was argued there were significant physical disparities *between* males, and several parents resented the idea that their daughters were at greater injury risk than male players in mixed teams (Hills et al., 2020). Finally, Pieper (2016, p. 1151) has also argued that even if sex-segregated sport is a requirement, this is scientifically impossible, as there is no 'neat categorical divide between the sexes' revealing biological sex as a spectrum, an argument previously explored by Fausto-Sterling (2000). Thus, the arguments both for and against mixed competition may need to be acknowledged to create more inclusive environments for trans and non-binary students.

To summarise, in most mixed-gender sports (as well as university sport provision in general) gender still matters and this is often reflected in the rules and regulations of each activity. Trans and non-binary students may be unsure of the eligibility criteria to participate/compete in sport (regardless of whether the activity is gender-segregated or mixed) or may not feel comfortable revealing their gender identity to others in order to ask for clarification. By not fitting neatly into binary gender categories, trans and non-binary people disrupt the notion of stable and concrete (gender) identities (McPhail, 2004). However, this may create tension and conflict; binary gender categories remain the norm in sport, with the views of scholars such as Pieper (2016) and others – who argue sex-segregation in sport is flawed – largely marginalised (McPhail, 2004) both in policy and practice.

Conclusion

The aim of this chapter was to consider BUCS policies in the context of trans and non-binary inclusion in university sport. This involved exploring the perceptions of student union officers – who implement the policy at their respective institutions – alongside trans and non-binary students who may be directly affected by these restrictions. Through a combination of focus groups and questionnaires, findings suggest BUCS reinforce binary gender structures through their policies. Although most sports under BUCS structure have opportunities for males and females, these regulations do not account for those students who may be non-binary alongside those who cannot meet eligibility criteria such as hormone level requirements in order to participate as their affirmed gender. This is particularly problematic given the reliance on national and international governing body guidelines, notably how much evidence is available to determine their suitability, how well advertised they are, and if they are more suited to elite levels of competition as opposed to university sport. The focus groups also revealed that some policies may be geared towards those who are post-medical transition, posing problems for those who are pre or mid-medical transition, those who have no intention of undergoing gender-affirming surgery/hormones, and those whose identities are not aligned with dualistic structures. These practices may result in some trans students suspending or delaying their sport participation, or simply not participating at all due to perceptions that sports are exclusive and unwelcoming environments.

Despite these key findings, this study had several limitations. Firstly, due to the reliance on student unions agreeing to take part in the study, the aim of achieving variance in terms of location and type of institution was not achieved within the sample. Therefore, future research may aim to gather the perceptions and experiences of student union officers and students at a wider variety of student unions, including those in the north of England and Russell Group universities. In addition, student recruitment for the study took place through LGBT+ societies and it must be noted that they may potentially foster an environment of politics and activism (Brooks et al., 2015). Thus, in future studies, researchers may wish to recruit trans and non-binary students through numerous sources where possible. Finally, this study did not explore the perceptions and viewpoints of BUCS, national governing bodies, or cisgender students, all of which may be useful to further consider the constraints and challenges of implementing trans and non-binary inclusive policies.

Notwithstanding these weaknesses, the study has several practical implications. Firstly, it is argued that wider sport bodies may need to re-think their guidelines before change can occur in the university sport context, and thus they may wish to consider reviewing their policies. Policies which reduce the policing of trans and non-binary bodies and allow athletes to compete in the category aligned with their identified gender have been recommended by Klein et al. (2018) in the US university sport context, and could also be considered in the UK. In addition, more mixed-gender sporting options which support individual gender autonomy and reduce binary thinking may be considered. As an alternative, sport bodies may also wish to provide evidence that their current requirements are necessary. However, it is also acknowledged that further research is needed to provide this evidence base. As an example, World Rugby recently recommended that trans women do not play women's contact rugby, based on the current available physiological evidence, but recognised that these guidelines may need to be reviewed as studies develop and evolve (World Rugby, 2020). Alternatively, sport bodies could also include university-specific or casual sport guidelines. By doing so, this would highlight that elite sport practices should not be mimicked in (non-elite) university sport, acknowledging the restrictions of gendered sport practices.

Student unions may also wish to challenge the specifics of BUCS policy directly to BUCS, particularly if they are aware of students who are unable to participate due to the apparent restrictions. At present, the reliance on wider national and international governing body policies by BUCS arguably shifts the blame for trans and non-binary exclusion onto others. Until BUCS and other sport policies are adapted, it is recommended that student unions clearly advertise the current guidelines to students. Ensuring students are aware of BUCS policy would minimise any eligibility questions, as some may not feel comfortable 'coming out' about their gender identity to ask for clarification.

Finally, one of the key weaknesses of BUCS policy may be the fact it fails to acknowledge the education and resources that are needed to support trans and non-binary athletes, instead focussing on the physical transition of trans students. This was also evidenced in a critique of NCAA policy by Klein et al., (2019), whereby it was argued that a further policy is needed to create an inclusive foundation to support trans athletes, in order to find solutions regarding changing rooms, gendered uniforms and the transitions between male and female sport teams. Furthermore, having a specialist in trans inclusion at each member institution was recommended (Klein et al., 2019). Despite the structure of UK and US university sport differing significantly, these recommendations could also be considered in the UK university context.

Notes

1 LGBT+ stands for lesbian, gay, bisexual and trans (Stonewall, 2017). An increasing number of different identities, including non-binary, queer, questioning and asexual, are included in the '+' sign for both consistency and simplicity.
2 It is worth noting that this policy has been critiqued for not meeting its objective of fair and safe female competition. For instance, Hilton and Lundberg (2021) suggest that male physical performance advantages are not removed by the current requirements.
3 Although diversity was aimed for in terms of type and location of the institution, reliance on student unions' agreement to take part in the study meant that convenience sampling was employed. This resulted in an absence of student unions in the north of England and from Russell Group universities.
4 See *The Student Room* (2021) for a description of different types of UK universities.
5 Phipps and Young (2015) describe 'lad culture' as a template masculinity for young British men that includes integral elements of UK university life such as drinking, sport, and sex. Jackson and Sundaram (2018) add that 'lad culture' often includes a wide range of practices from drunkenness and rowdiness to sexist, harassing, and homophobic practices.
6 Gender-fluid is a term used to describe someone whose gender identity is fluid between two or more genders (LGBTQIA Resource Center, 2020).

7 Those who are demi-gender feel a partial connection to both male and female genders. A demi-gender woman is someone who feels more feminine than masculine, whereas a demi-gender man feels more masculine than feminine (Moon, 2019).
8 Someone who is androgynous has traits which are usually ascribed to both men and women; androgyny can be physical, presentational or a combination of both (LGBTQIA Resource Center, 2020).
9 Agender refers to someone who does not have a gender or describes their gender as neutral (Pulice-Farrow et al., 2020).
10 Effective from May 2019, the policy has changed and is now more in-depth, differentiating between non-contact and contact rugby, the latter of which is still 'gender affected'. Trans male players can participate without restriction after signing a declaration, and trans female players still have restrictions in terms of their testosterone levels. In addition, non-binary players are also acknowledged. For more detail, the policy can be found here: https://www.englandrugby.com/dxdam/26/26de38f3-d82f-4816-8be3-b582f6a9f757/TransgenderPolicy.pdf.
11 HRT stands for hormone replacement therapy.

References

Brooks, R., Byford, K., & Sela, K. (2015). Inequalities in students' union leadership: The role of social networks. *Journal of Youth Studies*, 18(9), 1204–1218.

BUCS (British Universities and Colleges Sport). (2017). *BUCS Strategy 2017–2021*. https://www.bucs.org.uk/static/d5bd6b20-fca8-4e2d-b13769a84aae0cfa/bucsstrategy-2017-21.pdf.

BUCS (British Universities and Colleges Sport). (2021, January 4). Reg 4 individual eligibility. BUCS. https://www.bucs.org.uk/rules-and-regulations/general-regulations/reg-4-individual-eligibility.html.

Bryman, A. (2012). *Social Research Methods*. Oxford University Press.

Carroll, H.J. (2014). Joining the team: The inclusion of transgender students in United States school-based athletics. In J. Hargreaves & E. Anderson (Eds.), *Routledge Handbook of Sport, Gender and Sexuality* (pp. 367–375). Routledge.

Clark, B.A., Veale, J.F., Townsend, M., Frohard-Dourlent, H., & Saewyc, E. (2018). Non-binary youth: Access to gender-affirming primary health care. *International Journal of Transgenderism*, 19(2), 158–169.

England Rugby. (2017). RFU transgender and transsexual policy. England Rugby. http://www.englandrugby.com/mm/Document/General/General/01/30/69/64/RFUTransgenderandTranssexualPolicy_Neutral.pdf.

Farham, B. (2019). Caster Semenya – the questionable practice of gender verification. *South African Medical Journal*, 109(8), 543.

Fausto-Sterling, A. (2000). *Sexing the Body: Gender politics and the construction of sexuality*. Basic Books.

Fink, J.S., LaVoi, N.M., & Newhall, K.E. (2016). Challenging the gender binary? Male basketball practice players' views of female athletes and women's sports. *Sport in Society*, 19(8–9), 1316–1331.

Foddy, B., & Savulescu, J. (2010). Time to re-evaluate gender segregation in athletics. *British Journal of Sports Medicine*, 45(15), 1184–1188.

Gibson, S. (2013). Transgender and intersex sports provision at the University of Cambridge. https://www.lgbt.cusu.cam.ac.uk/wp-content/uploads/2013/04/Transgender-and-Intersex-Sports-Provision.pdf.

Gleaves, J., & Lehrbach, T. (2016). Beyond fairness: The ethics of inclusion for transgender and intersex athletes. *Journal of the Philosophy of Sport*, 43(2), 311–326.

Grbich, C. (2007). *Qualitative Data Analysis: An introduction*. Sage.

Griffiths, K., Bullough, S., Shibli, S., & Wilson, J. (2017). The impact of engagement in sport on graduate employability: Implications for higher education policy and practice. *International Journal of Sport Policy and Politics*, 9(3), 431–451.

Hills, L.A., Maitland, A., Croston, A., & Horne, S. (2020). 'It's not like she's from another planet': Undoing gender/redoing policy in mixed football. *International Review for the Sociology of Sport*, 56(5), 658–676.

Hilton, E.N., & Lundberg, T.R. (2021). Transgender women in the female category of sport: Is the male performance advantage removed by testosterone suppression? *Sports Medicine*, 51(2), 199–214.

Ingrey, J.C. (2012). The public school washroom as analytic space for troubling gender: Investigating the spatiality of gender through students' self-knowledge. *Gender and Education*, 24(7), 799–817.

IOC (International Olympic Committee). (2015). IOC consensus meeting on sex reassignment and hyperandrogenism. https://stillmed.olympic.org/Documents/Commissions_PDFfiles/Medical_commission/2015-11_ioc_consensus_meeting_on_sex_reassignment_and_hyperandrogenism-en.pdf.

Jackson, C., & Sundaram, V. (2018). "I have a sense that it's probably quite bad … but because I don't see it, I don't know:" Staff perspectives on "lad culture" in higher education. *Gender and Education*, 33(4), 435–450.

Jewett, R., Kerr, G., & Tamminen, K. (2019). University sport retirement and athlete mental health: A narrative analysis. *Qualitative Research in Sport, Exercise and Health*, 11(3), 416–433.

Jones, B.A., Arcelus, J., Bouman, W.P., & Haycraft, E. (2017). Sport and transgender people: A systematic review of the literature relating to sport participation and competitive sport policies. *Sports Medicine*, 47(4), 701–716.

Klein, A., Krane, V., & Paule-Koba, A.L. (2018). Bodily changes and performance effects in a transitioning transgender college athlete. *Qualitative Research in Sport, Exercise and Health*, 10(5), 555–569.

Klein, A., Paule-Koba, A.L., & Krane, V. (2019). The journey of transitioning: Being a trans male athlete in college sport. *Sport Management Review*, 22, 626–639.

Krane, V. (2014). Gender nonconformity, sex variation, and sport. In T.J. Schinke & K. R. McGannon (Eds.), *The Psychology of Sub-culture in Sport and Physical Activity* (pp. 48–63). Routledge.

Krech, M. (2017). To be a woman in the world of sport: Global regulation of the gender binary in elite athletics. *Berkeley Journal of International Law*, 35(2), 262–294.

LGBTQIA Resource Center. (2020, January 14). LGBTQIA resource center glossary. LGBTQIA Resource Center. https://lgbtqia.ucdavis.edu/educated/glossary.

Lincoln, Y., & Guba, E.G. (1985). *Naturalistic Inquiry*. Sage.

Mayne, V., & Diamond, I. (2016, April 14). Campus sport is alive and kicking in the UK. *Times Higher Education*. https://www.timeshighereducation.com/blog/campus-sport-alive-and-kicking-uk.

Mazzeo, F. (2018). Anabolic steroid use in sports and in physical activity: Overview and analysis. *Sport Mont*, 16(3), 113–118.

McPhail, B.A. (2004). Questioning gender and sexuality binaries. *Journal of Gay and Lesbian Social Services*, 17(1), 3–21.

Miles, M.B., & Huberman, A.M. (1994). *Qualitative Data Analysis*. Sage.
Moon, I. (2019). 'Boying' the boy and 'girling' the girl: From affective interpellation to trans-emotionality. *Sexualities*, 22(1–2),65–79.
Nagoshi, J.L., Brzuzy, S., & Terrell, H.K. (2012). Deconstructing the complex perceptions of gender roles, gender identity, and sexual orientation among transgender individuals. *Feminism and Psychology*, 22(4), 405–422.
NCAA (National Collegiate Athletic Association). (2011). NCAA inclusion of transgender student athletes. https://www.ncaa.org/sites/default/files/Transgender_Handbook_2011_Final.pdf.
NCAA (National Collegiate Athletic Association). (2020). About the NCAA. NCAA. http://www.ncaa.org/about.
Nowell, L.S., Norris, J.M., White, D.E., & Moules, N.J. (2017). Thematic analysis: Striving to meet the trustworthiness criteria. *International Journal of Qualitative Methods*, 16, 1–13.
Pennington, R., Cooper, A., Edmond, E., Faulkner, A., Reidy, M.J., & Davies, P.S.E. (2017). Injuries in quidditch: A descriptive epidemiological study. *The International Journal of Sports Physical Therapy*, 12(5), 833–839.
Phipps, C. (2020). 'We already do enough around equality and diversity': Action taken by student union officers to promote LGBT+ inclusion in university sport. *Sociology of Sport Journal*, 37(4), 310–318.
Phipps, A., & Young, I. (2015). Neoliberalisation and 'lad cultures' in higher education. *Sociology*, 49(2), 305–322.
Pieper, L.P. (2016). 'Preserving la difference': The elusiveness of sex-segregated sport. *Sport in Society*, 19(8–9),1138–1155.
Plaza, M., Boiche, J., Brunel, L., & Ruchaud, F. (2017). Sport=male…but not all sports: Investigating the gender stereotypes of sport activities at the explicit and implicit levels. *Sex Roles*, 76, 202–217.
Pulice-Farrow, L., McNary, S.B., & Galupo, M.P. (2020). 'Bigender is just a Tumblr thing': Microaggressions in the romantic relationships of gender nonconforming and agender transgender individuals. *Sexual and Relationship Therapy*, 35(3), 362–381.
Reeser, J.C. (2005). Gender identity and sport: Is the playing field level? *British Journal of Sports Medicine*, 39, 695–699.
Rimes, K.A., Goodship, N., Ussher, G., Baker, D., & West, E. (2017). Non-binary and binary transgender youth: Comparison of mental health, self-harm, suicidality, substance use and victimization experiences. *International Journal of Transgenderism*, 20(2–3), 1–11.
Sailors, P.R. (2020). Transgender and intersex athletes and the women's category in sport. *Sport, Ethics and Philosophy*, 14(4), 419–431.
Segrave, J.O. (2016). Challenging the gender binary: The fictive and real world of quidditch. *Sport in Society*, 19(8–9), 1299–1315.
Sport England. (2014). Higher education sport participation and satisfaction survey. https://sportengland-production-files.s3.eu-west-2.amazonaws.com/s3fs-public/he-sport-survey-national-summary-year-3.pdf.
Stonewall. (2017). *Glossary of terms*. Stonewall. https://www.stonewall.org.uk/help-advice/glossary-terms#l.
The Student Room. (2021, February 27). Types of university. The Student Room. https://www.thestudentroom.co.uk/wiki/Types_of_University.
Thorne, N., Witcomb, G.L., Nieder, T., Nixon, E., Yip, A., & Arcelus, J. (2019). A comparison of mental health symptomatology and levels of social support in young

treatment seeking transgender individuals who identify as binary and non-binary. *International Journal of Transgenderism*, 20(2–3), 241–250.

Travers, A. (2008). The sport nexus and gender injustice. *Studies in Social Justice*, 2(1), 79–101.

Westcott, H. (2018, January 30). Transgender people face two-year wait for NHS appointment. BBC. https://www.bbc.co.uk/news/uk-england-42774750.

World Rugby. (2020, October 9). World rugby approves updated transgender participation guidelines. World Rugby. https://www.world.rugby/news/591776/world-rugby-approves-updated-transgender-participation-guidelines.

Chapter 5

The Navigation of Non-binary Expression through Sports Kit

L. Whitehouse, C. Armstrong and J. Cooke

Introduction

The gender binary, which is the assumption that there are only two genders (male and female) and only two associated gendered behaviours (masculine and feminine), governs the structure and culture of most Western sport. For example, most opportunities to participate in sport are divided into the gender binary categories of male and female and there are expectations around how individuals should look when participating within these binary categories. Williams (2015, p.1) comments how 'sports kit is ubiquitous and a significant marker of identity'. While research has been conducted exploring the presentations of femininity and clothing/kits/equipment in sports spaces (Comber & Sprake, 2018), no research has explored the presentations of those who are gender non-conforming and how these individuals navigate the often-strict sports uniforms and/or kit requirements.

This chapter explores the significance of the role of sports, and sports kit, in the lives of non-binary individuals. The experiences of non-binary individuals within this chapter stems from the reflexive thematic analyses of oral history interviews from a wider project on the life histories of the non-binary sporting community. Specifically, this section follows how non-binary people have negotiated sports apparel in line with their gender expression over the course of their lives. We consider how puberty and body image contributes to intense experiences of gender dysphoria for non-binary people when wearing sports kits. Then the chapter examines how coming out and seeking specific sports spaces helped some of the participants to express their gender identity, which positively impacted upon their articulations and confidence in everyday life. The chapter also delves into how this assurance can increase positive body image, alleviate gender dysphoria, and facilitate experiences of gender euphoria benefitting these individuals physically and mentally. To conclude we argue that gendered sports clothing requirements are frequently unnecessary, and that flexibility and choice can be easily accommodated to avoid provoking distress amongst non-binary individuals.

Transfeminist, poststructural, and queer conceptual perspectives frame our discussion. Transfeminism seeks to disrupt the binary assumptions surrounding

DOI: 10.4324/9781003050568-5

sex and gender, thus opening up the possibilities for them to be seen as fluid. How such terms are defined is therefore crucial within this research area. In this chapter gender is understood to be socially constructed (Butler, 1990, 1993, 2004). Gender is often presented as binary and there are corresponding systems of rules, social characteristics, and expectations of how people should be and how they should behave that are gender specific. Therefore, according to Butler (2004, p. 48) gender at a social level is understood as a system of regulatory power: 'If gender is a norm, it is not the same as a model that individuals seek to approximate. On the contrary, it is a form of social power that produces the intelligible field of subjects, and an apparatus by which the gender binary is instituted'.

At an individual level, gender consists of two meanings; gender identity and gender expression. Gender identity is a person's innate sense of their gender and could be female/woman/girl or male/man/boy or other gender(s), such as non-binary. Gender expression is how a person outwardly chooses to express their gender: feminine, masculine, or other, such as androgenous or gender non-conforming. A person's gender identity is often presumed through a person's gender expression, which can be assessed by their visible presentation, such as their clothing, demeanour or hairstyle. For the purpose of this chapter, non-binary 'broadly covers any gender identity which lies outside the one-or-the-other binary of "man" and "woman", "he"' and "she", "male" and "female"' (Young, 2020, p.18). Richards et al. (2016) highlight how, under the non-binary umbrella, identities are diverse and can result in individuals identifying with multiple terms or labels. Some persons may identify as neither male nor female through not associating themselves with either of the binary genders; others may identify as a combination of both masculine and feminine characteristics rather than one fixed binary identity (Young, 2020). They may also identify as transgender too (Barker & Iantaffi, 2019). There is not a singular way to be transgender or non-binary.

This chapter will also draw upon a Foucauldian model of power when discussing gender identities.

> Foucault argued, power is widely dispersed, and operates intimately and diffusely. Especially it operates discursively, through the ways we talk and categorise people. It impacts directly on people's bodies as 'discipline', as well as on their identities, constituting subject positions that people take up. And it is productive not just repressive: it generates forms of life.
>
> (Connell, 2009, p. 77)

According to Foucault (1991), power is not exclusively owned by individuals but is distributed throughout society. Rather than viewing power as solely top-down and repressive, Foucault suggested that it operates through complex capillary-like networks. However, Foucault (1991) acknowledged that power is not without resistance. Foucault (1993) recognised that he was limited in his thinking and that in his earlier work he had insisted 'too much on the techniques of domination' (p. 204). As a result of this reflection, Foucault (1988) suggested a new line of inquiry, focusing on

> [T]echnologies of the self, which permit individuals to effect by their own means or with the help of others a certain number of operations on their own bodies and souls, thoughts, conduct, and way of being, so as to transform themselves in order to attain a certain state of happiness, purity, wisdom, perfection or immortality.
>
> (p.18)

Foucault's (2000) theory of technologies of the self implies that individuals do not passively accept discourses and therefore can resist technologies of power (Markula, 2003). For example, this chapter will show how non-binary people have been subjected to cisgenderism through sports kit requirements which seek to control their expression, but they are able to challenge such controls. Foucault's (1988) theorisation of 'technologies of the self' will guide the analysis of the role of sports clothing in enhancing experiences of non-binary gender. Furthermore, within the technologies of the self, individuals can question normality through processes of critical awareness (Markula, 2003). This questioning will be seen throughout this chapter to show how non-binary individuals are not passive recipients of gender policing and normative sports attire but rather can use sports kits to acquire bodily and self-awareness and facilitate gender identity development.

Gender Non-conformity and Expression in Sport

There is a misconception that non-binary people do not participate in sport due to the emphasis on polarised gender, especially evident through competition structures and participation avenues. Additionally, non-binary individuals already face a lack of legal recognition and protection in UK law through the Equality Act (2010) as there is no explicit outline of what constitutes discrimination against gender diverse individuals. There is also a lack of visibility, inclusion, and validation of non-binary people within public services, employment, and general health and wellbeing spaces and practices (Scottish Trans Alliance, 2016). It was therefore unsurprising that 76 per cent of non-binary people surveyed in the national LGBT survey in 2018 indicated that they would avoid expressing their gender identity openly in institutions such as work or sport due to fear of prejudice (Government Equalities Office, 2018).

Despite the recognition of significant impediments, there has been limited research into the experiences of non-binary individuals in sport. Instead, increasing focus has been given to binary transgender individuals and their engagements with sport, especially those who are medically transitioning (Jones et al., 2017). Some trans and non-binary athletes will fit into binary sport structures and participation avenues whereas others will not and completely withdraw themselves from participation (Caudwell, 2014). Studies such as that by Jones et al. (2017) have noted binary transgender experiences, including the inadequacy of changing facilities and clothing, body dissatisfaction, fear of non-acceptance and surveillance by others, and issues negotiating team sports settings. Specifically, Jones et al. (2017) commented that binary transgender people encounter issues finding clothes that fit with societal gender roles that are comfortable to wear and that are not revealing of both themselves and to others. However, no non-binary individuals were recruited as part of the study sample. A later study by Jones et al. (2019a) found that, in comparison to binary transgender individuals, non-binary people experienced similar levels of gender congruence[1] and poorer levels of body satisfaction. Despite sport being identified as helping to boost body gratification amongst binary transgender persons waiting for gender affirming surgeries (Jones et al., 2017), limited research has sought out non-binary people to assess whether sport has or would be able to help them with their body confidence and non-binary expression.

Research into trans and non-binary engagements with recreational sports is beginning to grow as a field of inquiry, especially in terms of reviewing examples of good practice. A recent qualitative study has demonstrated how access to trans inclusive 'participation-driven' spaces is of pivotal importance to enable trans people to partake safely and present their embodied self. Caudwell (2020) has found that in public swimming spaces trans and non-binary people have to navigate constant surveillance of their bodies by others due to the revealing nature of swimming attire. However, the creation of trans and non-binary exclusive swimming sessions meant that the embodied gender dysphoria previously experienced in relation to clothing and the stages of their medical (if applicable) and social transitions, was shown to reduce when they were participating. Caudwell's (2020) analysis was restricted to one sport, swimming, therefore the findings are context specific. Also, the study included both transgender and non-binary participants and therefore there was no separate analysis of solely non-binary experiences. The conflation of 'non-binary' with 'transgender' is a key issue when combining identities under an umbrella due to the incorrect assumption of homogeneity (Darwin, 2020). Despite some non-binary individuals also identifying with transgender terminology – often due to previous, current or future engagements with gender affirming surgeries or treatments (e.g., hormone therapy) – there are significant disparities between the lives of non-binary individuals and those who are binary transgender.

Even the government is apt to make misleading statements about non-binary people. In response to an online petition by Ashley Reed in 2015 asking that the United Kingdom join other countries where gender self-identification is permissible, the response from the Ministry of Justice (2015) was:

> The Equality Act 2010 protects people from discrimination if it arises from their being perceived as either male or female. We recognise that a very small number of people consider themselves to be of neither gender. We are not aware that that results in any specific detriment.
>
> (p. 25)

Non-binary people contested this response and paved the way for evidence gathering of the specific detriments experienced by non-binary people (see Scottish Trans Alliance, 2016). In 2020 the only study solely focusing on non-binary identities to date by Erikainen et al. was published. It highlighted that non-binary individuals do in fact face significant barriers when accessing sports spaces, communities, and competitions, contradicting the Ministry of Justice's statement. Again, similarly to Caudwell's (2020) findings, swimming as a space presented numerous impediments for the non-binary participants, who pointed out the restrictions surrounding clothing and bodily exposure. Erikainen et al. (2020, p. 13) also concluded how more inclusive access could be better facilitated, an example of such steps being the removal of 'unnecessary gendered and other dress codes'. However, the study sample was primarily comprised of members of major activist and sports organisations in Scotland who exclusively engaged in non-binary and trans sports. Therefore, this constrained the findings' applicability to a wider audience and those non-binary people who are not involved in activist circles or have an organisational sporting role. But Erikainen et al. (2020, p.23) recognise that their paper acts as 'a starting point for further research in this area'. To date, then, there have been no studies of solely non-binary sporting experiences that have taken an oral history approach. With the intention of expanding upon and addressing the reach of previous literature in this area, this chapter not only explores non-binary expression through sports clothing of non-binary participants but also considers their experiences before coming out. The above approach has remained nascent both in studies of binary transgender and non-binary individuals, but this chapter seeks to showcase the benefits of the oral history methodology in understanding the depth of identity and expression for those who establish themselves outside of the gender binary.

Method

The analysis in this chapter focuses on 15 interviews from a wider project on the sporting histories of non-binary individuals which sought to investigate the main research question: 'How do non-binary individuals engage with and experience sport or physical activity?' Oral history was identified as the ideal research method for the aforementioned research due to its emphasis on understanding the past in order to move forward (Abrams, 2016). As the analysis shows, the oral history method was appropriate for eliciting reflections on clothing, expression, and identity. No specific questions were asked about sports kit during the interview, instead the focus of the interviews was to amplify the participants' voices by giving them the opportunities to discuss their experiences at their own pace, in their own words with minimal interviewer input. People need to be able to describe their identity and experiences in their own words, as using the words of others would detract from their own individual authenticity and this is what the oral history method enables participants to do. Gender is plural: there is no single story to tell about it. Therefore, there is the need to embrace the multiplicity of stories that occur outside of binaries. Undertaking deep readings of individual personal gender stories is more revealing at the early stages of a research field and this is especially the case with non-binary identities in both general life and in sport.

The participants' experiences discussed within this chapter, show evidence of their reflections on how sporting attire affected them and how they were able to overcome discomforts through adaption and seeking out specific inclusive sporting environments. Many non-binary people remain deeply closeted in their mainstream sports and have to compromise their gender non-conforming identities because if they do come out, there is the fear that they could get 'locked out' or excluded from these spaces. For recruitment purposes, this therefore meant that, initially, LGBT+ organisations and sports groups were contacted. Contact was made directly via email to ask whether they would circulate project information and recruitment materials amongst their memberships. This was not, however, a particularly fruitful approach due to these spaces tending to be dominated by cis gender individuals with gay and lesbian identities. Instead, social media platforms, namely Facebook and Twitter, were used and these proved to be the best recruitment grounds. Research by Byron et al. (2019) and Vivienne (2017) has identified how social media spaces offer non-binary individuals a space to socialise with each other and explore and reaffirm their identities. These interconnections of non-binary people on such platforms therefore aided the recruitment process significantly. It also facilitated snowball sampling, whereby the individuals the first author interviewed reposted the recruitment call which gave access to friendship networks and/or sporting links.

Video interviews were used for all but one (which took place face-to-face) due to the COVID-19 pandemic and the suspension of face-to-face in person interviewing as advised by the University and the Oral History Society. This method proved to be advantageous as it allowed the sample to be unrestricted by geographical location. Additionally, non-binary individuals are often the only gender diverse people they know within their sports space, so the video interviewing allowed access to dispersed participant groups. Online interviews are also convenient especially with regards to the time taken to conduct them. The interviews lasted an average of 69 minutes (range 46 to 91 minutes) which due to the online format meant that the participants could be involved from the comfort of their own home.

Overall, 15 participants took part in the study. The mean age of participants was 29.4 years (range 19–45). This project departed from standard ethical guidance on anonymity because of the nature of the project's aims to amplify the voices of non-binary people. Instead of the anonymisation usually advised and practiced, the participants were given the choice to be anonymous or to be referred to by their first names. Previous research guidance by Vincent (2018) stipulates how anonymisation can remove the agency of non-binary people to own their voices, presence, and experiences. Nine participants chose to be identifiable and six chose to be anonymous, illustrating that having the anonymous/identifiable option was well-received. When asked to describe their gender identity the participants named eight different identities under the non-binary umbrella, but non-binary was used and preferred by 14 of the 15 participants, alongside the gender-neutral pronouns they/them.

To analyse the interviews thematic analysis was used. When investigating an under-researched area, thematic analysis has been highlighted as advantageous in that it provides a loose structure and order of analysis (Braun et al., 2016). The six phases outlined by Braun and Clarke (2006) were followed. Firstly, the lead author familiarised themselves with the data and identified items of potential interest related to items of sports dress across the entire data set. Next, codes were generated which became grouped into themes. For example, codes of gender attire, gender dysphoria and sports kit, and body dissatisfaction were placed under an overarching barrier of gendered kit theme. The themes were then reviewed for the purpose of writing this chapter to ensure the data present within each theme followed a narrative progression.

Findings

The analytical process generated two overarching themes: barriers, and pathways to change. The *barriers* theme highlights the various difficulties that the participants experienced when wearing (or attempting to wear) gendered sportswear. They discussed how their personal insider awareness of expression was heightened when dressed in highly feminine or masculine uniform which led to dissonance between their outward appearance and their innate sense of gender (e.g., struggles with gender dysphoria). These experiences were also aggravated by the external or outsider policing of expression (e.g., gendered expectations imposed and regulated by others). Following on from barriers, the theme of *pathways to change* highlights the various ways suggested by the participants that gendered sports clothing could be changed or adapted, and requirements could be challenged to enable non-binary expression. The participants discussed how individuality should be addressed rather than the formality of polarised gender attire. This would then complement non-binary identity within sporting spaces and provide an outlet for expression. The themes that follow also present the experiences of the participants in chronological order which complements the oral history methodological approach.

Barriers

One of the main personal barriers discussed by participants was how sports clothes significantly contributed to experiences of gender dysphoria – removing autonomy of external expression which is often achieved through wearing clothes that can be read by others as contributing to their gender non-conforming. Casey (1), a 23-year-old footballer and dodgeball player, commented how this has been the case for themselves as a non-binary person and amongst their transgender peers:

> We tell a lot of the stories of ourselves through like demeanour and the clothes we wear and the accessories but obviously when you're playing sports a lot of that by necessity has to be stripped away, I've found it a common theme with myself and other trans people who play sport that you can feel at your most dysphoric when you're playing sport because, you don't have the clothes that you wanna wear that make you feel a certain way. *Casey (1)*

Unlike previous studies (Jones et al., 2017), the oral history approach allowed the participants to directly reflect on when these feelings of dysphoria and discomfort first started occurring. For Jesse, a 19-year-old ex-ballet dancer, they did not realise they were non-binary until they engaged with platforms such as Pinterest and Tumblr where they were able to connect with others who shared their gender non-conforming experiences and feelings. However, upon reflection, within the interview Jesse acknowledged how their engagements with ballet throughout their childhood and adolescence helped them to realise how gender dysphoria had been a continuous battle throughout their life:

> I can look back on it and kind of use it [to identify] significant points in me kind of discovering who I am and points where I'm coming out cause they tend to sort of overlap and big changes… when I stopped ballet and was able to stop shaving my legs the time I was able to wear my binder for the show, the point I started feeling uncomfortable wearing the leotard, all of that kind of stuff you can pinpoint when things are happening. *Jesse*

For Frankie a 28-year-old powerlifter, their bodily dysphoria was not immediately attributed to their gender but was as a result of being uncomfortable with the bodily exposure that some sports clothing entails:

> Putting a swimming costume on to just go in the garden to play in the paddling pool and crying to my mom because I didn't want to wear it so there was a body consciousness from probably around nine or ten but that particularly started to spark as I went into secondary school and around the age 12, 13 puberty starts to hit. *Frankie*

This discomfort surrounding the bodily exposure entailed by swimwear featured prominently in the participants' sporting oral histories. Anna, a 25-year-old netballer, echoed Frankie's experiences surrounding bodily dysphoria but also expanded on how for them there was a gendered element to this discomfort:

> I kinda stopped doing swimming cos my body was changing and it was too much for me and I remember the swimming people saying that I needed to be

> thinner and fitter …swimming you have to be there in a swimming costume and you have to look a certain way in a swimming costume and you also have to look a certain gender in a swimming costume and it's all too much. *Frankie*

Al, a 40-year-old runner, also acknowledged how uncomfortable going swimming was for them:

> In swimming it's probably the single most exposed sport there is in terms of exposing your body and I have dysphoria about my body cause I don't like those bits of it so as much as I enjoy swimming you have to shove those down for the duration of the swim. *Al*

Here Al adds to the previous remarks by Frankie and Anna, by commenting on how they have just accepted that to participate they have to fight off the intense feelings of gender and bodily dysphoria. For Al, this suppression could also lead to exhaustion and eventual avoidance and, as Anna commented above, the battle between identity suppression and participation could get 'all too much'. Their experiences of swimming and its clothing requirements solidify the importance of transgender and gender diverse swimming groups and initiatives such as TAGS and the community swimming group included in Caudwell's (2020) study. Although such groups are unlikely to remove gender dysphoria completely, they can provide spaces where solidarity and awareness of experiences are shared and there can be reductions in anxieties over being stared at by others.

Previous studies (e.g., McGuire et al., 2016) have documented how puberty is especially distressing for binary transgender people. However, limited discussions have presented the experiences of non-binary people (Jones et al., 2019a). It is evident from the participants' narratives following this study that puberty, coupled with gendered sports kits, can result in difficult and traumatic experiences for non-binary individuals too. Frankie formerly commented how their body consciousness 'started to spark' as they went to secondary school. Leo a 34-year-old triathlete and weightlifter comments on how when they were at school in the 1990s, they felt the girls' PE kit at their secondary school was highly inappropriate and unnecessarily exposed bodies:

> The red knickers…and you wore them over your existing underwear and that's what you played sport in…so for the athletics you would just literally be in an airtex shirt and a pair of red knickers… I mean the majority of the time you were like overwhelmingly undressed, it was not a fun environment where you didn't feel like you weren't just on display constantly which was terrible. Not a great environment for anyone. No one feels good in that environment. *Leo*

Previous studies have documented how PE kits for secondary-aged pupils in particular are unnecessarily gendered and can result in uncomfortable experiences of bodily exposure, especially for those required to wear the 'girls' PE kits (Mills & Cooling, 2019, see also Chapter 6). The requirements for PE kits often allow boys to wear a t-shirt and shorts and girls a t-shirt and skirt/skort. PE kits such as the one Leo is describing also contribute towards the male gaze; presenting such individuals in an exposed way draws attention away from their sporting abilities and instead towards their perceived physical feminine attributes (Clark, 2021). This adds an additional layer of complexity to those who are questioning their gender non-conforming identity.

The notions of being judged especially for their gender and physical appearance and being gazed upon by others contributed to lifelong experiences of discomfort amongst the participants when wearing sports clothing. Jesse commented how, as their life progressed, they became 'more uncomfortable with it throughout the years'. When Jesse says 'it' they are referring to the items of clothing they were required to wear for ballet and how such clothing fitted and looked on their body. Jesse described how their ballet was often split into binary gendered dance schools and clothing requirements reflect this. Jesse was often required to wear a dress to enhance the uniformity of a dance piece. Furthermore, men and women are required to perform set roles and routines within ballet, making it difficult for non-binary individuals to find their place within the space physically through costumes and structurally through performance roles.

The participants had all gone through puberty associated with a binary gender and by necessity often wanted to conceal elements of their bodies which made them feel dysphoric and/or disconnected from their non-binary identity. Jem, a 27-year-old softball player, reiterated this by commenting on how 'sports clothing is not the most concealing clothing ever so it wasn't very easy to just look kind've androgynous'. Quinn, a 31-year-old weightlifter and Crossfit enthusiast, also expanded on Jem's point:

> I just felt really uncomfortable in them [leotards] and always were, it wasn't what I wanted to wear, it's really tight, it sort of shows off every bit of your body which was not necessarily what I was comfortable with. *Quinn*

The development of performance fabrics that emphasise sleek bodies made sportwear more tailored to polarised gender bodies. Many non-binary individuals prefer to dress androgynously which often entails neutral coloured loose-fitting clothing. For Jem and Quinn, a shift to accommodating gender non-conforming attire would mean they could avoid drawing unnecessary attention to their bodies while facilitating their expression in line with wider understandings of androgyny.

Gendered sports kit requirements also focus on archaic gender norms and stereotypes about feminine dress codes. Anna comments upon this through their experiences of having to wear netball dresses:

> [I] hated hated hated wearing the [netball] dresses. I hated it so much cos I thought I was too fat and I thought that I didn't look good in it and I just wanted to wear my tracksuits under my dress and I remember crying at the finals because they said 'this time you can't wear your tracksuits you have to just have your bare legs out'. I was crying in the toilet and I was like 'I'm just not gonna play', but I wanted to play so badly, so I ended up doing it. But I just remember feeling so conscious of my legs that whole time which is probably quite a common thing for any teenager but especially when when you feel so different from everyone else. *Anna*

Above, Anna comments upon key intersectional issues around body dysmorphia and fatphobia. It has been documented that LGBT+ youth in particular suffer from distorted views of body image (McClain & Peebles, 2016). For Anna, wearing a netball dress was not just about tackling experiences of bodily discomfort at the expense of puberty and gender dysphoria, but this took a mental toll on them too. It has been previously documented (see Jones et al., 2017) that binary transgender people often suppress their experiences of gender dysphoria in order to continue playing sport, and for Anna as a non-binary person they also had to contend with these intense discomforts. However, unlike previous research focusing on binary transgender people, as a non-binary individual Anna had to endure this mental torment due to limited sports spaces being available where they could openly express and play under their non-binary identity. This mental anguish was also experienced by Jesse when wearing a ballet costume consisting of a dress which exhibited binary bodily attributes.

> I tried it on one time in the lesson like 'this is gonna be fine' 'I can do this' and then I tried it on for five minutes or something and went home and cried to my mum quite a lot and was like 'I can't do this' 'I can't wear it'. *Jesse*

It is important to reiterate here Jesse's use of language when describing their experiences of the mental implications gendered sports clothing has on them. Jesse says they 'can't do this' and they 'can't wear it'. They are describing how they have a lack of choice, knowing that their gender dysphoria will dominate if they proceed to wear the required costume. Non-binary people are often presented negatively by the media and are portrayed as being part of the millennial generation through the derogatory and demeaning term 'snowflake' (Barker & Scheele, 2019). This is based on the premise that young people are 'rebelling' against the binary gender categorisation by identifying as non-binary or gender non-conforming. This uprising is presented as toxic and as young people just being 'picky'. However, Jesse is contradicting these assumptions and indicates that dismissing their identity and experiences has both physical and mental implications. This concurs with research by Thorne et al. (2019) and Jones et al. (2019b) that non-binary individuals are more prone than binary transgender individuals to develop depression, anxiety, and low self-esteem.

Another barrier discussed by the participants was related to the policing of gender expression by others that has stemmed from the reliance on archaic gender norms and stereotypes to determine gendered clothing requirements and expectations. A prime example of this reliance was discussed by Nat, a 42-year-old cyclist and runner, and specific colours being attributed to binary gendered clothes: 'there's an endless frustration with running clothes for females which is always pink it's a bit like it doesn't have to be pink?!'. Nat also highlights how binary gender norms and stereotypes do not just impact the production of gender specific clothing but also the sports equipment that is needed in order to participate. For example, Nat discusses how bicycles are produced according to the gender binary:

> They are sold as male and female bikes…I know it's ridiculous. Female bikes originally didn't have a crossbar and the only reason for that was because it was unseemly for a lady to cock her leg in public. *Nat*

Nat alludes to bike manufacturers in particular reproducing the gender binary through their reliance on historical design factors which have not been challenged. The assumption that only two binary genders exist makes purchasing a bike for non-binary individuals difficult to navigate due to there being limited gender-neutral bike frames on offer and non-binary individuals often want to deviate away from binary gender choices. This also implies that binary individuals are two biologically homogenous groups, which they are not.

Regulation of binary gender by others through clothing can also be dictated by the individuals that physically occupy sports spaces. Previous research (Caudwell, 2020; Jones et al., 2017) has commented on how binary transgender individuals are often concerned about others negatively evaluating their gender expression. The participants in this chapter reported similar anxieties. Quinn's experiences of gymnastics throughout childhood and early adolescence highlight how other people police gender within these spaces.

> I did team gymnastics, and it's a very specific kind of culture. It includes all sorts of things that are to do with, for example, how you're supposed to present yourself in the unified way as a team; so you're supposed to do your hair a certain way, you're supposed to have your outfit in a certain way, but I always had short hair for example. So [it] was constantly 'oh but your hair is wrong', 'oh what are we gonna do with your hair, it's just wrong, it just doesn't fit'; it was the kinds of make-up that was supposed to come with it and I didn't want to [wear] really bright make up…I was never particularly drawn to those things. *Quinn*

For Quinn the unified presentation of their gymnastics team illustrates the operation of disciplinary power within the space to mould others according to gender norms. According to Foucault (1991, pp.137–138), disciplinary power is having hold 'over other's bodies, not only so that they may do what one wishes, but so that they may operate as one wishes, with the techniques, the speed, and the efficiency that one determines. Thus, discipline produces subjected and practised bodies, 'docile' bodies'. Disciplinary power presents significant physical and mental safety issues for non-binary individuals because their gender identities challenge binary understandings. Jodi, a 28-year-old cyclist and runner, has experienced these safety worries frequently when choosing what to wear to participate in sport.

> I have to either conform to the expectations of what a male bodied person looks like and the kind of sportswear style that they're supposed to have, or I wear what I wanna wear, but that's gonna bring up questions and funny looks and all of that scary stuff, and like at the moment it's kinda safer to go with the first option, to go with just like conforming. *Jodi*

On the other hand, it could be argued that non-binary people are undocile bodies. Jodi may have to be conforming due to safety reasons for now, but society and the continuous shifts in understandings of gender identity and expression could mean that non-binary bodies are not tamed and disciplined in the long term.

This section has shown how gendered sports kit requirements remove the autonomy of non-binary expression. The reinforcement of binary gendered styles of sports dress coupled with puberty is highly distressing for non-binary individuals and results in experiences of gender dysphoria that becomes more prominent especially post coming out. The policing of gender by other cisgender and binary gender people, and their passive compliance to gender normative sports kits within sports spaces that non-binary people occupy, illustrates how disciplinary power is instilled to mould gender non-conforming individuals into submission to the gender binary. However, the analysis and discussion that follows shows how the non-binary sporting community can fight for and create their own bodily autonomy within sports spaces through sports clothing.

Pathways to Change

The participants all reiterated that when it came to sports, the gender binary needs to be re-addressed. They wanted to see more questioning of the requirements of gendered clothing for sports, exercises, and physical activities. Nat frames this questioning when discussing the marketing of bikes according to binary genders: 'you can get bikes where they've got like pretty little patterns on it for the girls and go faster stripes for the guys, but at the end of the day you need a bike that does the job'. While gender stereotyping is challenged in relation to children's toys (Davis & Hines, 2021), sportwear and sports equipment receive limited scrutiny. Nat's comments indicate how a move towards a focus on functionality over formality to combat gender labelling could be advantageous. This emphasis has been suggested by researchers and academics when increasing the inclusion of transgender and gender diverse individuals in sport as a way of categorising competition. For example, Kerr and Obel (2018) have discussed changing sports categorisation from a medical system to a functional system, concentrating on bodily attributes and skills in order to classify competition and participation, similar to that used when grouping disability sport athletes. However, this notion has not yet been applied to challenge binary sports clothing.

In wider research on transgender and gender diverse inclusion in sport, there have been calls to remove the need for categorisation methods in sport in their entirety, regardless of gender identity (Segrave, 2016). For the non-binary individuals that the lead author interviewed, the removal of specific clothing requirements also mirrored the erosion of barriers in sport, and was seen as a necessary step to improve inclusion and expression for non-binary people. Anna discussed how their queer netball club/team has operated to achieve such inclusion.

> There's no dress code. We have bibs and we use the bibs and we were thinking of getting patches with our logo on that you can iron onto any clothing so we might pick a colour or we might just say put it on any kind of clothing so that it's kind of a team look, but it's not too prescriptive. *Anna*

Flexibility over sports clothing can give non-binary people the freedom of choice which is so often eradicated by the strict uniformity of team kits. Another way to give non-binary individuals autonomy when choosing sports kit is to remove gender labelling on items of clothing. Nat explains how the removal of gendered language in this way has impacted them when purchasing sports clothing.

> I've just bought some new running socks and it was really annoying me that it was male and female socks and I found a few brands where it's like these are socks in these sizes and they're good for running, they're not necessarily male they're not necessarily female, they're just socks in this size. So I found it much more freeing to be able to do that. *Nat*

The removal of gendered language and design for items of sports clothing is an important first step, however the participants also reiterated that there needs to be a shift or complete removal of gendered expectations to make non-binary individuals feel comfortable in their clothing choices. Jem discusses how they try to 'queer', in their words, the clothing used to participate in swimming.

> There would be quite specific rules around what you could wear in the pool and so what I tend to do now is wear like boardshorts. Well I don't

> know if I mean boardshorts but like boy's swimming trunks and a sports bra or something. So again, I'm trying to like queer the uniform and I'm more comfortable wearing like those shorts than I am wearing a one piece. *Jem*

The allowance of individuality evidenced through how Jem subverted the swimwear requirements can enable non-binary people to avoid the initial concerns over how to present. While individuality can be easily incorporated to solo sports and solitary physical activities, there are also examples of best practice from team sports too. Casey (2) is 25-years-old and plays for an LGBT + field hockey team. Rather than their club adopting gendered kit requirements, such as wearing a hockey skort for league matches, team members have flexibility over what they feel comfortable wearing as Casey (2) goes on to comment.

> We can wear shorts or skirt or skorts, whatever you want to wear really, but I would say the majority of us wear shorts and I don't know if I could wear a skort [laughs]. No I definitely couldn't wear a skort... I don't like dresses I don't like skirts [or] anything like that I am not interested in one bit and it doesn't feel great at all. I hate it, it's definitely not me. *Casey (2)*

While all of the non-binary people interviewed acknowledged the challenges that participating in sport brings when navigating binary gendered clothing requirements, through change and negotiation, sports spaces and the clothing used within them can provide non-binary individuals with a unique avenue for the outlet of gender non-conforming expression. Casey (1) commented upon this rareness and how engaging with sport has allowed them to develop their understandings of non-binary expression.

> It doesn't change who you are fundamentally. Y'know I'm as non-binary as when I'm looking very androgynous as when I am looking like a dude and playing sports and that's something that I wouldn't really have gotten without sport and that sort of forcible stripping down of the aesthetic elements of gender. *Casey (1)*

The fluidity of gender diverse identities means that there is no 'right' way for anyone to experience or express their gender (Fiani & Han, 2018). Butler (1990, p. 9) reiterates this, describing gender as 'a free-floating artifice, with the consequence that man and masculine might just as easily signify a female body as a male one, and woman and feminine a male body as easily as a female one'. Certain sports spaces are more accommodating than others when stretching binary gender expressions. For Jamie, a 37-year-old ex-roller derby player, this specific team sport allowed them to break out of binary gender norms and embrace gender non-conformity through the style and clothing choices available.

> A part of the appeal of roller derby to me was that the sort of style of it and that I am quite unashamed about, you can see there I'm wearing some fairly snazzy leggings ...a lot of people are really into makeup, like really heavy makeup and really bright colours and that was a perfect kind've confluence with what I was enjoying about breaking out of male gender norms and things. I would do my make-up colours to match our teams colours and stuff. It was all great fun. *Jamie*

In this instance Jamie was able to choose their sporting community and this shows how their experiences of freedom of expression had changed significantly since their school days. For Jamie, gender euphoria came through an overt challenging of binary gender norms, especially through make-up, which was an optional extra within this sporting context. Unlike the experiences outlined earlier on in this chapter by Quinn and their requirement to put on make-up as a part of their sporting uniform, here make-up is used more affirmatively and as a choice. Non-binary expression and identity is complex and, as the above examples show, there are multifaceted interactions between identity, personality, and the activity.

As Casey (1) discussed, there are also subtle methods in which non-binary individuals can wear affirming items to express their identity and accentuate their non-conformity in other ways.

> A lot of dodgeball players wear like compression sleeves on their throwing arms... so what I did was I got a black fish net sleeve to wear on my non-throwing arm because I think it looks cooler... it's just kind of like dumb things like that, y'know, that are kind of like, affirmative appearance based things, that fit within the quite tightly, constrained world of sport and what you can wear in sport. *Casey (1)*

Ideally, non-binary individuals should be able to participate and feel that their identity and expressions are included and visible when participating in sport, whether this is through overt engagements with gender non-conformity or 'quiet' androgyny. There are also further alternative avenues of engagement free from negotiations of expression that are outside of being competitors or on a team. For example, when in a coaching and umpiring role there is limited regulation over the sports-related clothing to be worn to fulfil the position. Anna discusses how being a netball coach, rather than a player, helped them avoid the experiences of gender and bodily dysphoria they experienced when playing in a netball dress: 'The clothes are like it's your own choice what you wear and they've got masc and fem versions of what you want to wear'. Without the strict clothing requirements, individuals like Anna can have power over their gender expression, through having a choice of what to wear that is not detrimental to their non-binary identity. For non-binary individuals, having access to spaces where they can openly express their identities is limited, even in wider spheres, due to the gender binary that governs Western societies and results in the domineering presence of discrimination and transphobia. Jamie reiterates this in their discussion of why they got involved in roller derby:

> It gave me a very different context in which to do it. It gave me a sort of daytime context; it gave me an excuse to leave the house looking like that [and] not on my way to a club or whatever. That was really nice in terms of coming out as non-binary and wanting to experiment more with clothes in the daytime and in a work context. That sort of thing was a really helpful bridge in terms of giving me a reason to be looking pretty unusual in the daytime... we would go to the pub after practice and that sort of stuff. It was quite a helpful steppingstone in terms of y'know having the confidence to go out and look different. *Jamie*

The freedom of expression which can be created through LGBTQI+ inclusive spaces can also contribute towards experiences of unity, despite perceived individuality. For example, within Jamie's roller derby space, everyone's desire to express themselves within agreed boundaries was accommodated regardless of their gender identity. This meant that Jamie did not stand out on their own within that space, as others around them were also diversifying their expressions. This illustrates how unity can be achieved despite sportwear formalities being stretched and adapted in comparison to polarised gender norms.

Conclusion

Despite the prevalence of the gender binary and strict dress codes in sport, non-binary individuals are contributing to challenging sports attire and encouraging change and revisions. From an early age, the inflexibility over gendered sportwear, especially within secondary school PE, resulted in physical and emotional discomfort amongst the participants, especially during and post puberty. Additionally, these experiences were/are exacerbated by other people's gender policing stemming from historical understandings of gender norms. The creation of a toxic insider/outsider culture follows, whereby non-binary people find themselves fearing for their emotional/mental safety if they do not conform. However, if there could be a focus on individuality and how this can be incorporated into apparel requirements, then the anxieties about other people's perceptions and some of the dysphoria it instils for non-binary people could be reduced. Avoiding stringent kit regulations by enabling choice, flexibility, and adjustment of sportswear will be key for non-binary people to feel comfortable, supported, and recognised. Furthermore, taking into account differing forms of expression through clothing can contribute to the personal development of non-binary individuals to grow in body satisfaction (gender euphoria) and transfer this newfound confidence to enrich other avenues of their lives.

Overall, adopting flexibility regarding sports dress, especially at recreational level, will not only contribute towards improved levels of self- and body-confidence amongst the non-binary persons already involved within sport and physical activity, but will be one less barrier to negotiate and overcome for those non-binary individuals wanting to partake. Additionally, it would be advantageous for future research to utilise, combine and expand upon the novel findings presented in this chapter, with the calls from women to challenge the sexist, sexualised and degrading kit requirements, based upon outdated gender norms, and work towards sports kits that are inclusive to all.

Note

1 Gender (in)congruence can be used as another word for gender dysphoria. Therefore, it means incongruence (discomfort/unpleasant feelings) between sex assigned at birth and gender identity.

References

Abrams, L. (2016). *Oral History Theory*. Oxon: Routledge. Second Edition.

Barker, M.J., & Iantaffi, A. (2019). *Life Isn't Binary: On Being Both, Beyond, and In-between*. London: Jessica Kingsley.

Barker, M.J., & Scheele, J. (2019). *Gender: A graphic guide*. London: Icon.

Braun, V., & Clarke, V. (2006). Using thematic analysis in psychology. *Qualitative Research in Psychology*, 3(2), 77–101.

Braun, V., Clarke, V., & Weate, P. (2016). Using thematic analysis in sport and exercise research. In B. Smith & A. Sparkes (Eds.), *Routledge Handbook of Qualitative Research Methods in Sport and Exercise* (pp. 191–205). London: Routledge.

Butler, J. (1990). *Gender Trouble: Feminism and the Subversion of Identity*. Oxon: Routledge.

Butler, J. (1993). *Bodies that Matter: On the Discursive Limits of 'Sex'*. Oxon: Routledge.

Butler, J. (2004). *Undoing Gender*. Oxon: Routledge.

Byron, P., Robards, B. J., Hanckel, B., Vivienne, S., & Churchill, B. (2019). 'Hey, I'm having these experiences': Tumblr use and young people's queer (dis)connections. *International Journal of Communication*, 13(1), 2239–2259.

Caudwell, J. (2014). [Transgender] young men: Gendered subjectivities and the physically active body. Sport. *Education and Society*, 19(4), 398–414.

Caudwell, J. (2020). Transgender and non-binary swimming in the UK: Indoor public pool spaces and un/safety. *Frontiers in Sociology*, 5(64), 1–12.

Clark, S. (2021). Embodying sporty girlhood: Exploring perspectives on girls' sporting participation through postfeminism. In S. Clark (Ed.) *Sporty Girls: Gender, Health and Achievement in a Postfeminist Era* (pp. 21–51). London: Palgrave Macmillan.

Comber, A., & Sprake, A. (2018). Pink whistles and pocket mirrors: Why is the FA reproducing gender stereotypes? *Journal of Qualitative Research in Sports Studies*, 12 (1), 305–310.

Connell, R. (2009). *Gender: In World Perspective* (2nd ed.). Cambridge: Polity.

Darwin, H. (2020). Challenging the cisgender/transgender binary: Non-binary people and the transgender label. *Gender & Society*, 1–24. https://doi.org/10.1177/0891243220912256.

Davis, J.T., & Hines, M. (2021). The magnitude of children's gender-related toy interests has remained stable over 50 years of research. *Archives of Sexual Behavior*, 50(3), 749–751.

Erikainen, S., Vincent, B., & Hopkins, A. (2020). Specific detriment: barriers and opportunities for non-binary inclusive sports in Scotland. *Journal of Sport and Social Issues*, 1–28. https://doi.org/10.1177/0193723520962937.

Fiani, C.N., & Han, H.J. (2018). Navigating identity: Experiences of binary and non-binary transgender and gender non-conforming (TGNC) adults. *International Journal of Transgenderism*, 1–14. https://doi.org/10.1080/15532739.2018.1426074.

Foucault, M. (1988). Technologies of the self. In L.H. Martin, H. Gutman, & P.H. Hutton (Eds.). *Technologies of the Self: A Seminar with Michel Foucault* (pp. 16–49). London: Tavistock.

Foucault, M. (1991). *Discipline and Punishment: The Birth of the Prison*. London: Penguin.

Foucault, M. (1993).About the Beginning of the Hermeneutics of the Self: Two Lectures at Dartmouth. *Political Theory*, 21(2), 198–227.

Foucault, M. (2000). Technologies of the self. In P. Rabinow (Eds.) *Michel Foucault: Essential Works of Foucault 1954–1984, Volume 1* (pp. 223–251). London: Penguin.

Government Equalities Office. (2018). *National LGBT Survey: Research Report*. Retrieved from: https://assets.publishing.service.gov.uk/government/uploads/system/uploads/attachment_data/file/721704/LGBT-survey-research-report.pdf.

Jones, B.A., Arcelus, J., Bouman, W.P., & Haycraft, E. (2017). Barriers and facilitators of physical activity and sport participation among young transgender adults who are medically transitioning. *International Journal of Transgenderism*, 18(2), 227–238.

Jones, B.A., Bouman, W.P., Haycraft, E., & Arcelus, J. (2019a). Gender congruence and body satisfaction in nonbinary transgender people: A case control study. *International Journal of Transgenderism*, 1–12. https://doi.org/10.1080/15532739.2018.1538840.

Jones, B.A., Bouman, W.P., Haycraft, E., & Arcelus, J. (2019b). Mental health and quality of life in non-binary transgender adults: A case control study. *International Journal of Transgenderism*, 20(2–3), 251–262.

Kerr, R., & Obel, C. (2018). Reassembling sex: Reconsidering sex segregation policies in sport. *International Journal of Sport Policy and Politics*, 10(1), 1–16.

Markula, P. (2003). The technologies of the self: Sport, feminism, and Foucault. *Sociology of Sport Journal*, 20(1), 87–107.

McClain, Z., & Peebles, R. (2016). Body image and eating disorders among lesbian, gay, bisexual, and transgender youth. *Pediatric Clinics*, 63(6), 1079–1090.

McGuire, J.K., Doty, J.L., Catalpa, J.M., & Ola, C. (2016). Body image in transgender young people: Findings from a qualitative, community based study. *Body Image*, 18, 96–107.

Mills, C.D., & Cooling, K.E. (2019). The 'ideal' PE Kit to help reduce body image concerns within adolescent girls. *Obesity Weight Management and Therapy*, 2(1), 1–8.

Ministry of Justice. (2015). *Transgender Equality: First Report of Session 2015–16*. Retrieved from: https://publications.parliament.uk/pa/cm201516/cmselect/cmwomeq/390/390.pdf.

Richards, C., Bouman, W.P., Seal, L., Barker, M.J., Nieder, T.O., & T'Sjoen, G. (2016). Non-binary or genderqueer genders. *International Review of Psychiatry*, 28(1), 95–102.

Scottish Trans Alliance. (2016). *Non-binary People's Experiences in the UK*. Edinburgh: Scottish Trans Alliance, Equality Network.

Segrave, J.O. (2016). Challenging the gender binary: the fictive and real world of quidditch. *Sport in Society*, 19(8–9), 1299–1315.

Thorne, N., Witcomb, G.L., Nieder, T., Nixon, E., Yip, A., & Arcelus, J. (2019). A comparison of mental health symptomatology and levels of social support in young treatment seeking transgender individuals who identify as binary and non-binary. *International Journal of Transgenderism*, 20(2–3), 241–250.

Vincent, B.W. (2018). Studying trans: Recommendations for ethical recruitment and collaboration with transgender participants in academic research. *Psychology & Sexuality*, 9(2), 102–116.

Vivienne, S. (2017). 'I will not hate myself because you cannot accept me': Problematizing empowerment and gender-diverse selfies. *Popular Communication*, 15(2), 126–140.

Williams, J. (2015). Kit: Fashioning the sporting body – Introduction to the Special Issue. *Sport in History*, 35(1), 1–18.

Young, E. (2020). *They/Them/Their: A Guide to Non-binary and Genderqueer Identities*. London: Jessica Kingsley.

Chapter 6

Negotiating Gender Performances in Physical Education and School Sport

Gender Diversity and Inclusive Practices

H. Kettley-Linsell, R. Sandford and J. Coates

Introduction

Schools act as institutions which both operate and regulate gendered social practices (Gerdin, 2016; Devís-Devís et al., 2018). Within this context, Physical Education (PE) and school sport play a significant role in how gender is socially constructed. Indeed, unlike other environments, PE is said to produce a somewhat 'heightened' expression of gender (Paechter, 2006; Hills, 2007), due to its focus on physicality and the centrality of the body within the field (Dismore, 2007). Moreover, PE is organised according to a gender binary which reflects traditional heteronormative ideals and stereotypical gender norms that mirror the biological sexed body. Here, *sex* refers to the biological aspects which distinguish male from female, whereas *gender* refers to the social construction of norms and expectations of masculinity and femininity (Metcalfe, 2018). Previous studies have explored the gendered nature of these settings and how they contribute to a knowledge of gender identity which, in turn, influences the way in which young people view their own physical capabilities (Azzarito & Solomon, 2005; Fisette, 2011; Fagrell et al., 2012). Such influences can be seen to effectively train young people to 'perform' in gender appropriate ways (Cahn, 1994; Hargreaves, 1994; Theberge, 2000).

The (gendered) organisation and provision of PE and school sport (PESS) reinforces the cultural assumption that all people can be classified as either male or female, which creates problems for those who do not easily align with these categories. This includes those who are transgender (i.e., whose gender is not the same as the sex they were assigned at birth; Stonewall, 2020) and non-binary (i.e., whose gender identity does not sit comfortably with either 'man' or 'woman'; Sykes, 2011). Neither side of the binary feels 'right' for some individuals and this produces a sense of crisis (Hargie et al., 2015; 2017), as they learn that transgressing normative gender boundaries and acting differently to prescriptive gender norms is unacceptable, shameful, and to be avoided (Butler, 1996; Tejada, 2016; Barron & Capous-Desyllas, 2017; Broussard & Warner, 2019). For transgender and non-binary young people, this means either choosing to remain invisible within PE contexts – so they do not risk facing consequences

DOI: 10.4324/9781003050568-6

of gender non-conformity (Hellen, 2009; Trujillo, 2015) – or performing their chosen gender identity through abiding by gender norms which are grounded in cisnormativity.

Although transgender issues have not traditionally been a specific focus in PESS contexts, an increasing recognition of transgender and non-binary identities in recent times has led to increased attention being given to this area of practice (Hills & Croston, 2012; Caudwell, 2014; Pahlke et al., 2014; Devís-Devís et al., 2018). While it is difficult to track the size of the UK population of transgender and non-binary young people, the Gender Identity Development Service (GIDS) in London, which specialises in the counselling of children and young people who are questioning their gender, records their referral numbers each year. In 2011–2012, GIDS had 210 referrals, by 2015–2016 referrals were at 1,409, having doubled since the previous year. The most recent referral report, for 2020–2021, shows 2,383 referrals (GIDS, 2021). Whilst not all gender-questioning young people who are referred to GIDS later identify as transgender or non-binary, the increase in referrals over the last decade reveals transgender and non-binary identities to be an emergent phenomena, and coincides with an increase in the visibility of these young people within PESS settings.

The considerations and discussions within this chapter stem from a wider project comprised of three studies which investigated: i) the reflective experiences of transgender and non-binary individuals; ii) the attitudes of teachers towards transgender and non-binary students; and iii) the perspectives of parents towards gender diversity in PE. Specifically, this chapter follows how transgender and non-binary individuals constructed and performed gender in PESS contexts and the implications that this had on their experiences in this area.

In this chapter, we first examine the literature surrounding gender performativity and the construction of gender in PESS before we consider how the organisation of PE classes, curricular and spaces impacted participants' gender performances, and examine how peers and teachers were felt to respond to and discipline non-conforming behaviours. We then consider practices that could potentially be adopted within PESS to facilitate transgender and non-binary students' inclusivity, drawing upon the recommendations from participants in our study, along with examples from wider research. To conclude, we contend that PESS contexts typically construct and enforce gender practices and performances which regulate cisgenderism and the gender binary – potentially causing distress for transgender and non-binary students. We suggest that implementing a gender inclusive approach to PESS is necessary to deconstruct traditional gender norms and stereotypes and provide transgender and non-binary students a sense of belonging within this environment.

Gender Performativity and the Construction of Gender in PESS

During our daily lives we consistently assign gender to the individuals we interact with, based on established cultural ideologies associated with different behaviours and characteristics perceived as 'normal' (Kessler & McKenna, 1978). For example, western societies attribute gender-based meanings with visible characteristics, behaviours and traits (Garfinkel, 1967; Kessler & McKenna, 1978; Beemyn & Rankin, 2011; Serano, 2016). Through cultural socialisation we learn the meanings behind gender and unconsciously reproduce these meanings through committing to normative gender performances. In this way, gender is understood here as a 'doing', not a 'being'. It does not refer to a single, coherent or stable identity category, but instead can be understood as *performative* (Butler, 1999). The understanding of gender as performative is common within academic discussions on the topic, informing the work in a range of disciplines (see, for example, Cameron, 1996; Campbell, 2000; Plumridge et al., 2002).

Judith Butler's (1999) theorisation of gender performativity in her book *Gender Trouble* is particularly influential in this respect and introduces the notion that the appearance of a 'gendered self' is produced via the 'regulation of attributes along culturally established lines of coherence' (Butler, 1999, pp. 32–33). By this she means that gendered behaviours and attributes – those we commonly associate with femininity and masculinity – are imposed upon us by socio-cultural regulations. In this way Butler suggests that gender is socially constructed through speech acts and nonverbal communication. She contends that gender identity is an *effect*, rather than the *cause, of our performances*, arguing that 'there is no gender identity behind expressions of gender…[gender] is performatively constituted by the very "expressions" that are said to be its results' (1999, p. 33). For Butler, identity is retroactively constructed and comes into being through these expressions. Through bodily gestures, movements, and enactments of various kinds we establish the 'illusion of an abiding gendered self' (1988, p. 519), bringing into being categories of male and female, man and women. This performativity of gender is not merely a single act, but 'a set of repeated acts within a highly rigid regulatory frame that congeal over time to produce the appearance of substance, of a natural sort of being' (Butler, 1999, p. 44). Hence, Butler suggests that gender involves the performative repetition of acts in a pre-determined social context over time, in such a way that it appears to be natural and innate. In this way, Butler does not view the expression of gender as a 'performance', rather, she views gender as the process that constitutes subjectivity as opposed to an active choice and performance on the part of the subject. Put simply, gender is not something you 'put on' in the morning and discard at will, rather we are constrained into gender.

Within social interaction, the notion of 'gender performance' encompasses both behaviours and physical attributes. Kessler and McKenna's (1978) gender attribution theory explores the way that we, as a society, create and reproduce gender-based meanings around physical attributes and behaviours in order to assign gender to bodies. In this way, we understand and interpret bodies based on a collection of meanings which are reproduced within society. For example, within western societies, facial hair and a deep voice mean a body is male, whilst no facial hair and a higher pitched voice signify female. They argued that the display and interpretation of bodies is guided by such social rules for attributing gendered bodies (Kessler & McKenna, 1978, p.157). They posit that men and women engage in different gendered practices and performances in order to convince others that a person is one gender and not another. Moreover, they contend that one must sustain others' sense that their gender is 'natural', rather than sustaining one's gender in social interaction. In other words, others must be convinced not that one is a particular gender, but rather that one has always been that gender. All behaviours are thus filtered through the gender attributions and made sense of in that context (Kessler & McKenna, 1978).

It is argued that the internalisation of gender practices and performance takes place before a child starts school, though its manifestation and development are further negotiated once they enter the school environment (Parker, 1996; Berkowitz & Ryan, 2011). In particular, gender norms and expectations permeate young people's experiences of PE (Wright & Laverty, 2010), whereby there are subtle gender dimensions which can be potentially damaging to a student's own gender identity, especially if they do not fit within the rigid gender dimensions prevalent in physical culture. Kirk (1999) refers to physical culture as a 'range of practices concerned with the maintenance, representation and regulation of the body centred on three highly codified, institutionalised forms of physical activity – sport, physical recreation and exercise', suggesting that it serves to produce and reproduce corporeal discourses concerned with 'meaning-making' (pp. 65–66). It is certainly argued that dominant notions of the 'ideal' feminine body (slender, athletic and toned) and the 'ideal' masculine body (strong, aggressive and muscular) are deeply embedded; reinforced through physical culture discourses and reproduced by social practice (Fisette, 2011; lisahunter et al., 2014). Moreover, within the context of physical education and school sport, much attention has been focused on the impact of physical culture discourses on young people's constructions of embodied identities and perceptions of gender-appropriate activities (e.g., Azzarito, 2009). Thus, physical culture is significant in PESS as it acts to regulate and reproduce the meanings surrounding gendered practices and bodily performances – each of which is significant when considering the experience of transgender and non-binary pupils.

Methods

As noted, the data presented in this chapter stem from one study within a broader research project which focuses on transgender issues in physical education and school sport. The project was granted ethical approval by Loughborough University's Ethics Committee, and appropriate protocols for ensuring safeguarding, consent and anonymity were followed throughout. The specific study drawn on here utilised a mixed-methods approach to generate data via an online survey and semi-structured telephone interviews. An online survey was developed for transgender and non-binary young adults (aged 18–25) in the UK and was designed to capture reflections on their experiences of PE in secondary school (ages 11–16 years). The survey consisted primarily of open-response questions, deemed essential to capture participant voices. Questions acted as prompts for participants to share details of their own lived experiences of PE, capturing what is important to participants, accessing their personal language and terminology (Frith, 2000), essential to understanding participants' narratives and the barriers and facilitators to their participation. The online survey was promoted on social media by the researchers and multiple UK-based LGBT organisations (including sports clubs and university societies), entailing a degree of participant self-selection (Andrews et al., 2003).

Following completion of the survey, participants were also invited to take part in a semi-structured telephone interview to further discuss their experiences. These interviews were conducted via mobile or video call, lasting between 45 minutes and one hour. A broad schedule was prepared before the interview, with questions such as: 'What comes to mind when you think about your experience of PE? Did you enjoy it?' 'Were your PE classes mixed sex or single sex?' 'What activities did you participate in? Were activities divided by gender?' 'Were you aware of your gender identity?' and 'Did you feel safe within PE spaces?' However, question wording and order were contextual and there was scope to be responsive to the participants' developing account. Interviews were all audio-recorded and then transcribed verbatim.

In total, 30 individuals completed the online survey: 12 participants identified as transgender men, four as transgender women, 11 as non-binary and three as gender questioning. The mean age of the participants was 21 years. Of this sample, 22 participants attended a coeducational secondary school, with seven participants attending a single-sex secondary school. Three of this sample went on to participate in a semi-structured interview, comprising of one non-binary participant and two transgender men. All participants engaged in PE classes as/with their assigned gender.

Data Analysis

Discourse analysis was used to analyse all qualitative data collected during the study (Sutherland, 2015). Due to the focal point of the study being on transgender and non-binary individuals' narratives, an analysis tool was required which centred on spoken and written language, as well as discourse. Thus, the discourse analysis utilised here aimed to understand the 'discursive worlds' that people inhabit, and to interrogate and theorise these in relation to the possibilities for subjectivity and practice(s) they enable or constrain. A key element of discourse analysis is identifying discourses that shape people's realities (Taylor, 2013). A discourse provides culturally available and shared ways of talking and thinking about objects, with the language we use situated within these meanings. Discourses also act to both enable and constrain the ways individuals can understand themselves; their subjectivity, and the things individuals can see as possible, want to do, and do; their desires and practices. In this way discourse analysis was well suited to make sense of one's experiences (Sutherland, 2015).

The process of analysing the data was not linear but exploratory and iterative. It was assisted using NVivo 12, which helped to store, organise, categorise, retrieve and export data more efficiently. The analysis then focused on identifying connections between different pieces of material and assembling subsets and collections, essentially coding the data using NVivo 12's node system (Bazeley, 2007). Consequently, the data could be read by node to look for patterns. As the codebook grew, some categories shifted with reading and clarification of concepts becoming more detailed. Similar or overlapping codes were amended and re-evaluated to avoid duplication. This helped to make sense of what was being said on, for example, barriers and facilitators to participation including peer support, teacher relationship, instances of bullying and class organisation; and how it was said including coping strategies and gender performance. From this, more connections and questions arose from the data, which led to revisiting the datasets again with this new connection or question in mind. In this way, the analysis process took an interpretative analytic approach grounded in the data (Taylor, 2013). In the following section, we draw upon this analysis to highlight some of the key issues identified by transgender and non-binary participants, which align with broader debates within the literature. All participant names are pseudonyms allocated by the research team.

Transgender and Non-binary Experiences of PESS

With the discourse of binary gender being central to PESS (Sykes, 2011), transgender and non-binary young people are frequently excluded within this context. For young people who wish to identify with a gender which is different to their biological sex, they must embark on the performative repetition of bodily gestures, movements and enactments in order to produce the appearance of substance, of a natural sort of being. This concept is known as 'passing', whereby transgender individuals who show no signs of their birth assigned gender are accepted as the gender they identify with, whilst those who do show signs fail to 'pass' (Billard, 2019). This is highlighted by the gender performance theories discussed earlier. The predominantly single-sex organisation of PE in many countries means that the pressure to meet the expectations set for males and females can be the difference between being a member of the class or being an 'outcast'.

Peer Discipline and the Homosexual Assumption

Transgender and non-binary young people face ample pressure to enact gender in culturally accepted ways in order to avoid the risk of negative assessment by those around them (Devís-Devís et al., 2018). Within school settings, transgender and non-binary individuals may enact their chosen gender, but they may also enact their given gender to avoid being deemed as non-conforming. For transgender and non-binary young people it has long been argued that facing 'wrong' gender attributions can lead to continued self-consciousness about their behaviours and movements, believing that not passing is potentially devastating (Kessler & McKenna, 1978; Schilt & Westbrook, 2009; Westbrook & Schilt, 2014). The work of West and Zimmerman (1991) took this further, suggesting that we 'do' gender in the presence of others and engage in self-regulating processes to ensure we are doing it 'correctly'. This essentially means that we perform gender under the surveillance of others as well as our own self-surveillance, considering the presence of the self within a disciplinary society (Foucault, 1977).

In our study, transgender and non-binary participants were asked to reflect on their experiences of PE. When asked 'Were you aware of your gender identity during your time in secondary education?', 23 participants (76.6%) responded that they were aware of their gender identity during this time. Despite this awareness, none of the participants socially transitioned to their chosen gender during their time participating in PE, with many enacting their given gender so that their peers did not question their gender identity, or their place within the class. In fact, participants held it of great importance that their peers did not suspect their identities. When asked whether her peers had been aware of her gender identity, Hayley, an 18-year-old transgender woman who attended a single-sex secondary school stated: 'I probably would have gotten beaten up if they had'. The possibility of peer bullying drove many participants to enact their given gender within these spaces, with the possibility of peers noticing any non-conforming behaviour deemed a potentially devastating scenario. Indeed, Charlie, a 25-year-old non-binary participant who attended a coeducational school, described an incident they remembered vividly. They recall being laughed at in the boys' changing room for taking off their shirt in a way that was deemed 'too girly'. Instances like this were regularly described by participants and often led to them surveying and disciplining their gendered enactments so as not to face the discipline of their peers again.

Similarly, peers were often observed to discipline those who did not conform to accepted gender norms and behaviours via bullying and harassment. Within broader discussions of boys' single-sex PESS settings, peers have been shown to enforce male dominance and hegemonic masculinity (Alonso & Zurbriggen, 2014). Participants in our study who experienced this setting articulated feelings of unease and isolation, describing how the constant need to enact masculinity in accepted ways dominated their experience of PE. Claire, a 23-year-old trans woman who attended a coeducational school, reflected on her experience of boys' PE, stating: 'it reinforces harmful traditional gender roles and opens up channels of abuse for individuals who either "underperformed" or failed to fit gendered expectations'. School fitness suites (or gyms) were depicted as particularly traumatic for participants, where the focus on possessing a body type that fit the standard for the 'ideal' masculine body was essential. Thus, being slight and non-muscular within this setting was deemed as non-conforming. For Charlie, the gym space perpetuated their belief that they did not align with the gender expectations that the setting demanded. Charlie reflected on how they were made fun of for not being particularly 'buff'. They went on to explain how they utilised the gym outside of lesson hours, but would only use the space when they were alone, so that they were not seen to be 'weak' in front of their peers, stating 'I didn't want people to be there seeing the weights that I would be lifting that were a third of the size that they would'. In this way, the participant tried to change their body in order to adhere to the expectations of the setting but was also fearful of the boys observing the lighter weights that they were using to build their strength. These instances highlight how the presence of hegemonic masculinity acts as a cultural control mechanism, with those who do not conform seen as dissidents of this mechanism.

For some participants who did not meet gender expectations, and/or did not try to, it was evident that peers often tried to enforce their conformity. Tony, an 18-year-old transgender man who attended a coeducational school, described how they were 'bulky' and outwardly masculine presenting, and that this led peers to often comment on how they could/should align more with gender expectations. This was further elaborated by Sam, a 21-year-old transgender man who attended a single-sex school, when reflecting on their experiences at an all-girls school. Sam described the way gender expectations were enforced, stating 'the environment…my year group created was exclusively like "You will dress like this, you will look like this, you will not be queer" all of that was incredibly toxic'. Sam further described an instance where a girl, positioned high in the school's social hierarchy, 'encouraged the entire sixth-form common room to shout "dyke" at me as I walked past'. In fact, this discourse of assumed homosexuality was widespread across the study sample, with many participants describing instances where they were called 'gay', 'dyke' or 'queer' by their peers and were mocked and isolated during PESS. In this way, peers were seen as working to regulate heteronormative systems by utilising their own language and behaviour to enact a form of discipline upon participants who portrayed any sign of gender non-conformity (see also Alonso & Zurbriggen, 2014). When participants reflected upon these instances, they articulated that their peers' treatment of them was a primary factor for their negative experience of PESS.

Hostility, Harassment and the Changing Room

It is well documented that peers' perceptions of transgender and non-binary students in schools can induce different types of discrimination and harassment, in some cases leading to negative outcomes, including mental health issues and suicide (Sausa, 2005; Grossman & D'Augelli, 2007; Grant et al., 2011; Puche et al., 2013; Johnson, et al., 2014; Devís-Devís et al., 2017). Devís-Devís et al. (2018) in their study of transgender students' experiences of secondary school

PE found that transgender students, especially those who did not perform gender conforming practices (e.g., performing skipping exercises in a 'girlish' way), were objectified in PE classes. Our study yielded similar findings, with instances of harassment and bullying present within participants' reflections. Many participants described feeling apprehensive during PESS, where their treatment by their peers often entailed micro-aggressions. Max, a 20-year-old transgender man who attended a coeducational school, reflected on his experience with his peers, stating:

> 'People, especially girls, were micro-aggressively discriminative. Whispering about me, laughing at me, staring at me. Someone once asked me why I don't shave my legs, putting me on the spot in front of the rest of the class'. *Max*

Instances such as this were common amongst our sample and worked to perpetuate participants' feelings of social exclusion. One such practice which was particularly excluding for participants was the act of 'picking teams'. Nick, a 20-year-old transgender man who attended a coeducational school, described how the practice of 'picking teams' during PE was utilised to bully him. He stated, 'students would often target me for bullying, picking me last for team games and would physically assault me during class under the guise of just "rough sport"'. In this way, the nature of PESS was not only utilised by Nick's peers to exclude him, but also to physically assault him without fear of repercussion. When asked whether he felt safe within PE, Nick reflected 'discrimination, harassment and abuse from other students made PE a nightmare'. In this way, by not fitting into cisgender and/or heteronormative gender norms, transgender and non-binary students faced social exclusion, micro-aggressions and physical assaults.

One of the most hostile spaces described by participants in our study was that of the changing room. Ample research has explored the experiences of transgender and non-binary individuals within changing rooms, finding that they are embarrassing and unsafe places that hinder participation and generate fear of social rejection (Semerjian & Cohen, 2006; Hargie et al., 2017; Jones et al., 2017; Devís-Devís et al., 2018). Sykes (2011) argues that changing spaces are 'one of the most traumatic spaces within the built environment of schools for queer and trans students' (p.45). The findings from our study support this narrative, with some participants describing the emotional turmoil they faced within the changing space. Clarke, a 23-year-old non-binary participant who attended a coeducational school, reflected 'my anxiety in changing rooms alone was overbearing and caused panic attacks'. In fact, intense emotional responses were common in participants' accounts of changing rooms. For instance, Jo, a 21-year-old non-binary participant who attended a coeducational school, described feelings of 'dread' stating: 'I hated getting changed in a room full of girls and having to expose myself. I knew I wasn't a girl, but I wasn't out, and it was incredibly dysphoric'. Many participants' accounts highlighted how the changing room was a space which accentuated their feelings of gender dysphoria (discomfort between sex assigned at birth and their gender identity), due to both the focus upon, and exposure of, the body as well as their gender segregated nature. In order to negotiate their gender within the space, along with their feelings about their bodies, participants tactically managed their practice. For instance, Craig, a 23-year-old transgender man who attended a coeducational school, described how 'it was a habit to lock oneself in the bathroom and change in there'. Others also described how they sought private spaces away from other students within the changing rooms, communicating a discourse of 'hiding'. Billie, a 25-year-old non-binary participant who attended a coeducational school, discussed how the girls changing room was a site for bullying, where girls 'often looked for weakness in other students' which led them to 'desperately trying to hide my body from them'. In this way, seeking privacy was not only to help participants with their own feelings towards their bodies, but also to avoid the gaze of other students. Sam described how he sought alternative changing spaces: 'going behind the shower wall so no one could see me or going into a toilet cubical'. However, when these spaces weren't available, participants deemed non-conforming by their peers described being mocked (Sam, Jordan, Phoebe, Charlie, Karl) or threatened (Charlie, Sam, Hayley, Nick, Claire), rendering changing rooms a hostile space which perpetuated gender dysphoria and vulnerability.

The discourse of assumed homosexuality was brought to the fore within changing room spaces for many participants in our study. It was reported that peers often accused participants of being predatory, making threats of violence if participants were caught looking in the direction of other students. For instance, Sam described how he was mocked by his peers and told 'Don't you dare be looking at me, we all know you're a lesbian'. Similarly, Karl, a 22-year-old transgender man who attended a coeducational school, described how his peers stated that 'queer people shouldn't be in the changing rooms because they would "perv on" other students'. These instances worked to further exclude participants from their peers, increasing participants' need for privacy. In this way, changing rooms were recounted as being highly charged spaces and were often the primary site for physical violence for participants (Sam, Claire), aligning with broader research in the field (Sykes, 2011; Caudwell, 2014; O'Donovan et al., 2014). In this way, other students dictated where non-conforming students could and could not get changed, and participants were told that they were not allowed to get changed with other students. For those who sought privacy, this was not always an issue. As Sam outlined: 'I was told by other students, in no uncertain terms, I wasn't allowed to get changed with them, but I also didn't want to get changed with them. I was very dysphoric'. In fact, many participants shared similar thoughts suggesting that being around other students perpetuated their gender dysphoria, causing them to seek to avoid being around their peers within changing spaces. Whilst this was the case for some, peers dictating their movements within the changing space still worked to accentuate participants' division from their peers. Their experiences illustrate how heteronormative gender binarism generated multiple forms of exclusion and rejection within changing room spaces, becoming a subtle form of violence in itself, but for many accompanying acts of physical violence as well.

Sex Segregation and the Gender Typing of Activities

As noted, the structure of PESS in gender segregated ways brings significant barriers to the participation of transgender and non-binary young people, due to pressures surrounding gender expectations and performances. In particular, it creates issues for those whose gender identity does not match their assigned gender or for non-binary individuals who do not identify with either side of the binary, meaning they must participate in a class with those they do not necessarily identify with or relate to. Participants within our study, for example, highlighted their discomfort at having to participate in lessons with those of their assigned gender, describing how they felt out of place. Jordan, a 20-year-old transgender man who attended a coeducational school, described his experience of single-gender classes as being like 'putting a puzzle piece in the wrong spot and like it's being shoved in, but it's not in the right place'. When participants participated in mixed (coeducational) lessons, this sense of displacement was alleviated somewhat, as the focus on gender was seen to dissipate. However, Tony described his experience during a 'boys vs girls' dodgeball game and having to go over to his assigned gender's side of the hall, despite personal preferences, in order to not 'out' himself or get in trouble with his teachers. This illustrates something of the conflict and discomfort that transgender and non-binary students can face during PE when it is organised based on birth assigned gender.

Furthermore, gender is typically attributed to activities in PESS based on their ability to elicit 'appropriate' gender behaviours, categorising activities as either masculine or feminine. A study conducted by Plaza et al. (2017) investigated the gender stereotyping linked to sports activities with a group of secondary school students. They highlighted how students identify aesthetic sports (e.g., dance and gymnastics) as feminine activities, whilst fighting sports and contact team sports (e.g., soccer and ice hockey) are categorised as masculine activities. In schools providing activities based on gender expectations, students are channelled away from certain activities and into others. In England, this is illustrated by the traditional provision of netball to girls and basketball to boys. For participants in our study, the provision of activities based on gender created more feelings of conflict. Many participants did not want to socially transition or 'come out' whilst taking part in compulsory PE, which meant that they had to adhere to gender expectations and performances regarding the activities they were perceived to enjoy. In respect to this, Jamie, a 20-year-old transgender man who attended a single-sex school, expressed his frustration at not being able to participate in his preferred sports and commented that he felt intense pressure at having to effectively 'perform gender' in other activities. This illustrates the tension that is present within these gender segregated and differentiated environments for transgender and non-binary individuals and the perceived pressure to abide by gender expectations. It also highlights participants' feelings of longing to participate in sporting activities that align with their chosen gender. The role that the provision and structure of PE plays on constructions of gender is brought into question here. For example, it could be argued that a change in traditional gender segregated organisation may offer the possibility to deconstruct gender expectations and performativity, thereby making PESS environments more inclusive for transgender and non-binary individuals to enact gender in multiple ways.

Gender Inclusive PE

There is, to date, little research that highlights the impact of gender inclusive spaces within PESS, which perhaps reflects the identification of transgender and non-binary identities as an emerging phenomena. For this reason, our study sought to not only reflect on the barriers and facilitators of transgender and non-binary people's participation within PE, but also to provide a space where they could articulate the practices that could/would have made PE more inclusive and positive for them. This section will outline the recommendations made by the participants, highlighting discussions around mixed gender spaces, deconstructing the gendered curriculum, and the importance of privacy and safe spaces. It closes with a reflection on the possibilities of inclusive sport spaces by examining examples of gender inclusive sports from broader recreational contexts.

Mixed Gender Spaces and the Deconstruction of the Curriculum

Previous research around transgender and non-binary inclusion in PESS has highlighted the need for 'queering' and 'deconstructing' the curricula and educational contexts which enforce and reproduce cisgenderism, heteronormativity and the two-sex binary (Planella & Pié, 2015). Participants in our study also articulated the need for a change in PE structure to facilitate mixed gender classes. Primarily, the arguments for mixed-gender classes came from participants' positive experiences of these spaces. However, ideas regarding the implementation of this varied between participants. Many participants shared the belief that mixed gender classes should be 'the norm', eradicating the provision of PE in single gender classes entirely. Claire, for example, stated that she found single-sex PE 'utterly repulsive' and that 'gender segregation needs to be destroyed entirely'. Participants' reasoning for the removal of single-sex PE classes in schools commonly focused on the way that they reinforce traditional gender roles and gender expectations that are harmful for transgender and non-binary students. Participants often incorporated reflections on their experiences of coeducational PE classes and how these spaces were more inclusive of them.

As Max reflected, 'I am against it [single-sex PE] quite intently, but that comes from my own experiences and knowing that if I'd had more mixed-sex sporting experiences through school I would've felt a lot more included, less alienated'. Whilst some believed that coeducational classes should be the norm, others advised for single-gender classes to be an option alongside mixed gender classes, reflecting broader arguments for girls to be able to access single gender classes (Azzarito & Hill, 2013; Lentillon-Kaestner & Roure, 2019; Wallace et al., 2020). Charlie, for instance, reflected on how coeducational PE works to break down gender stereotyping, but also noted:

> 'I also kind of am aware, particularly for a lot of school aged girls they might not be comfortable being in a mixed environment…there are some legitimate reasons that students would want to be in a single-sex class for PE…it would be good if schools had some kind of option where you could be in a single or mixed class.' *Charlie*

Literature around coeducational PE often focuses on the impact that these environments have on the participation of girls, reporting on how boys can dominate the environment, impact girls' participation levels, and the impact of the male gaze (Wallace et al., 2020). Interestingly, participants in this study suggested that the deconstruction of the gendered curriculum could enhance inclusion in general, granting equal opportunities for *all* students to participate in activities they previously may have missed out on due to the rigid gender attributes associated with them (Ahmed, 2020). For instance, Jamie stated that PE would be more inclusive by 'giving all students, regardless of gender, opportunity to take part in all sports…just letting people take part in sports they want to, outside of the typical sport stereotypes'. In this way, mixed gender spaces can allow students to belong within an environment where multiple gender performances take place and there is no strict enforcement or disciplining of these performances. Therefore, non-conformity does not equal discrimination.

To achieve such an inclusive environment, studies have also identified a need for change in teacher education. The work of Williamson and Sandford (2018) has highlighted how PE teachers have limited knowledge of/about transgender students and the challenges they face, emphasising a need for introductory and ongoing training for staff. Work by Walton-Fisette et al. (2018) on PE teacher education programs further supports this. Their findings suggest that issues of social justice (such as gender diversity) struggle to have an explicit presence within PE teacher education programmes and that education of trainee teachers on sociocultural issues and social justice is significantly lacking. These findings were supported by participants in this study, who highlighted their teachers' lack of knowledge and understanding of transgender or non-binary identities and perceived reinforcement of heteronormative ideals. As Jordan reflected, 'I feel like a lot of teachers weren't aware of it [the fact of different gender identities], or worse, not attuned to it…there was definitely a huge lack of awareness and a gap in knowledge and sensitivity'. Furthermore, participants describe how teachers' lack of knowledge on gender diversity meant that they often did not know how to address transphobia. In this respect, Sam argued that more teachers need to know 'what homophobic and transphobic discrimination is and what forms it takes'. Essentially, participants highlighted that, to shift the current culture of PE, further training around gender diversity is required for teachers so that they have the knowledge and tools needed to create a welcoming and inclusive environment for transgender and non-binary students.

The Importance of Privacy and Safe Spaces

With regard to the issue of privacy, our participants highlighted that PESS changing spaces would be more inclusive of them if they provided gender-neutral spaces. For instance, Charlie stated that schools should be 'providing non-binary or gender-neutral facilities for anyone who doesn't want to get changed in a single-sex changing room or an environment of their assigned gender. I think that's a right that trans students should have.' Some participants also articulated that providing more cubicles within gender segregated changing spaces (allowing them privacy and safety whilst getting changed) would also be welcome. However, they acknowledged that creating such spaces could prove difficult for some schools if they lack the necessary funding. Interestingly, Max described his conflicting thoughts regarding gender-neutral spaces. On the one hand, he acknowledged that these spaces can be positive in providing a safe space for transgender and non-binary people, increasing their participation as they do not have to negotiate open, gender segregated, changing rooms (see also Jones et al., 2017). However, on the other, and drawing on his own experience of a gender-neutral changing room, he articulated the way that these spaces could be isolating and 'single out' transgender and non-binary people. This links to the work of Lucas-Carr and Krane (2012) who describe the experiences of a transgender male who liked the safety of the gender-neutral changing room for swimming lessons at a private college, but who felt that it removed instances of social interaction that are usually present within a locker room. The participant felt it highlighted that 'one person in the class was really, really different' (Lucas-Carr & Krane, 2012, p. 36). Whilst this illuminates the difficulties faced in providing safe spaces that do not highlight differences, it also indicates the need for options to be available to meet the needs of each individual and that the sole provision of gender segregated changing rooms based on binary assumptions of gender is not enough.

The Possibilities of Gender Inclusive Sport

Whilst there is little research that highlights the impact of gender inclusive spaces within PESS, there have been several examples of the positive impact of sex-integrated recreational sports contexts with transgender and non-binary youth and adults (Buzuvis, 2011; National Union of Students, 2012). Integrated sport has the potential to offer inclusive spaces for transgender and non-binary individuals, as they do not require people to classify themselves with one of only two distinct gender categories. This provides transgender and non-binary individuals the opportunity to perform their gender in the way they feel comfortable, without the typical gender boundaries in place within traditional sporting environments. This has been evidenced by, for example, Tagg's research on mixed netball (2012, 2014), Travers' discussion of softball and baseball (2013, see also Travers & Deri, 2011) and Pavlidis and Connor's (2015) account of the controversies over inclusion policies in roller derby.

The most notable space for gender inclusion is Muggle Quidditch. One of the International Quidditch Association's (IQA) core values is 'to be a leader in gender inclusivity for all age groups' (IQA, 2013). Quidditch adheres to a 'two-minimum rule' which dictates that 'each team must have at least two players in play who identify with a different gender than at least two other players. The gender a player identifies with is considered to be that player's gender' (p. 12). A study by Segrave (2016) on Quidditch highlights the ways that an inclusive and respectful gender inclusive sport environment enhances self-confidence and feelings of safety and comfort for all gender identities. Indeed, participant testimonies showed that 'virtually every player acknowledged that they benefit from the opportunity to meet and interact with a diverse array of gendered peers' (p. 198). This highlights the positive impact that gender inclusive spaces could have on transgender and non-binary individuals, hinting towards possibilities for more equitable and socially just PESS practice.

Concluding Comments

Overall, it is evident from the discussion here that PESS contexts currently work to construct and enforce gender expectations and performances that regulate heteronormativity and the gender binary. Within these contexts, students are expected to abide by rigid gender expectations. For those who wish to identify with a gender which differs from that assigned to them, they must embark on a performative repetition of bodily gestures and enactments in order to 'pass'. In this way, transgender and non-binary young people can face significant pressure from their peers (and, perhaps, teachers) to enact gender in culturally accepted ways, often experiencing harassment, bullying and isolation in PESS contexts. Participant reflections highlighted in this chapter evidence, in particular, the hostility of changing rooms as spaces where bodies are subject to the gaze of others and where established systems and practices perpetuate a sense of gender dysphoria and vulnerability. Moreover, they confirm that the structure of PESS in gender segregated and differentiated ways is a significant barrier to the participation of transgender and non-binary young people, due to pressures surrounding gender expectations and performances.

However, while the data highlighted some evident challenges – around, for example, changing spaces, activity choice, teachers' understanding and peers' reactions – there were also some suggestions as to how PESS practice could be enhanced and made more inclusive of transgender and non-binary students. In this respect, participants highlighted the need for mixed gender classes, to alleviate the gendered focus of PE, as well as the deconstruction of the gendered curriculum. They also stressed the need for privacy and safe spaces, noting the need for 'gender neutral' areas or private cubicles. An examination of gender inclusive recreational sports contexts provides useful examples for the potential of mixed gender PESS in including transgender and non-binary young people and positively impacting their experience of PESS. The heteronormative context of PESS moulds the current possibilities to perform gender, reducing it to the ability or inability to reproduce hegemonic gender performances. However, by deconstructing the curriculum and shifting the organisation of PESS, a more gender inclusive PE can be shaped; one which does not focus on heteronormativity or gender expectations. Such a context would afford transgender and non-binary young people the freedom to express and perform their gender identities, with no strict set of 'rules' for gender enactment.

References

Ahmed, D. (2020). Physical education and transgender youth: Supporting all students. *Physical Education Matters*, 15(3), 23–25.

Alonso, B., & Zurbriggen, R. (2014). Transforming corporealities: Beyond the pedagogical normality. *Educar em Revista*, 1, 53–69.

Andrews, D., Nonnecke, B., & Preece, J. (2003). Electronic survey methodology: A case study in reaching hard-to-involve Internet users. *International Journal of Human-Computer Interaction*, 16(2), 185–210.

Azzarito, L. (2009). The panopticon of physical education: Pretty, active and ideally white. *Physical Education and Sport Pedagogy*, 14(1), 19–39.

Azzarito, L., & Hill, J. (2013). Girls looking for a 'second home': Bodies, difference and places of inclusion. *Physical Education and Sport Pedagogy*, 18(4), 351–375.

Azzarito, L., & Solomon, M.A. (2005). A reconceptualization of physical education: The intersection of gender/race/social class. *Sport, Education and Society*, 10(1), 25–47.

Barron, C., & Capous-Desyllas, M. (2017). Transgressing the gendered norms in childhood: Understanding transgender children and their families. *Journal of GLBT Family Studies*, 13(5), 407–438.

Bazeley, P. (2007). *Qualitative Data Analysis with NVivo*. Sage.

Beemyn, G., & Rankin, S. (2011). *The Lives of Transgender People*. New York: Columbia University Press.

Berkowitz, D., & Ryan, M. (2011). Bathrooms, baseball, and bra shopping: Lesbian and gay parents talk about engendering their children. *Sociological Perspectives*, 54(3), 329–350.
Billard, T.J. (2019). 'Passing' and the politics of deception: Transgender bodies, cisgender aesthetics, and the policing of inconspicuous marginal identities. In T. Docan-Morgan (Ed.) *The Palgrave Handbook of Deceptive Communication* (pp. 463–477). Palgrave Macmillan.
Broussard, K.A., & Warner, R.H. (2019). Gender nonconformity is perceived differently for cisgender and transgender targets. *Sex Roles*, 80(7), 409–428.
Butler, J. (1988). Acts and gender performative: An essay in phenomenology constitution and feminist theory. *Theatre Journal*, 40(4), 519–531.
Butler, J. (1996). *Bodies that Matter*. Routledge.
Butler, J. (1999). *Gender Trouble: Feminism and the Subversion of Identity*. Routledge.
Buzuvis, E. (2011). Caster Semenya and the myth of a level playing field. *The Modern American*, 6, 36–42.
Cahn, S.K. (1994). *Coming on Strong. Gender and Sexuality in Twentieth-century Women's Sport*. The Free Press.
Cameron, J. (1996). Throwing a dishcloth into the works: Troubling theories of domestic labour. *Rethinking Marxism*, 9(2), 24–44.
Campbell, H. (2000). The glass phallus: pub(lic) masculinity and drinking in rural New Zealand. *Rural Sociology*, 65(4), 562–581.
Caudwell, J. (2014). [Transgender] young men: Gendered subjectivities and the physically active body. *Sport, Education and Society*, 19(4), 398–414.
Devís-Devís, J., Pereira-García, S., López-Cañada, E., Pérez-Samaniego, V., & Fuentes-Miguel, J. (2018). Looking back into trans persons' experiences in heteronormative secondary physical education contexts. *Physical Education and Sport Pedagogy*, 23(1), 103–116.
Devís-Devís, J., Pereira-García, S., Valencia-Peris, A., Fuentes-Miguel, J., López-Cañada, E., & Pérez-Samaniego, V. (2017). Harassment patterns and risk profile in Spanish trans persons. *Journal of Homosexuality*, 64(2), 239–255.
Dismore, H. (2007). The attitudes of children and young people towards physical education and school sport, with particular reference to the transition from key stage 2 to key stage 3. Unpublished Doctoral Thesis, University of Kent.
Fagrell, B., Larsson, H., & Redelius, K. (2012). The game within the game: Girls' underperforming position in physical education. *Gender and ducation*, 24(1), 101–118.
Fisette, J.L. (2011). Exploring how girls navigate their embodied identities in physical education. *Physical Education and Sport Pedagogy*, 16(2), 179–196.
Foucault, M. (1977). *Discipline and Punish: The Birth of the Prison*. New York: Pantheon.
Frith, H. (2000). Focusing on sex: Using focus groups in sex research. *Sexualities*, 3(3), 275–297.
Garfinkel, H. (1967). *Studies in Ethnomethodology*. Englewood Cliffs: Prentice-Hall.
Gerdin, G. (2016). The disciplinary and pleasurable spaces of boys' PE: The art of distributions. *European Physical Education Review*, 22(3), 315–335.
GIDS (Gender Identity Development Service). (2021). Referrals to GiDS, financial years 2010–11 to 2020–21. https://gids.nhs.uk/number-referrals.
Grant, J.M., Mottet, L.A., Tanis, J., Harrison, J., Herman, J.L. & Keisling, M. (2011). *Injustice at Every Turn: A Report of the National Transgender Discrimination*

Survey. Washington, DC: National Center for Transgender Equality and National Gay and Lesbian Task Force.

Grossman, A.H., & D'Augelli, A.R. (2007). Transgender youth and life-threatening behaviors. *Suicide and life-threatening behavior*, 37(5), 527–537.

Hargie, O.D., Mitchell, D.H., & Somerville, I.J. (2017). 'People have a knack of making you feel excluded if they catch on to your difference': Transgender experiences of exclusion in sport. *International Review for the Sociology of Sport*, 52(2), 223–239.

Hargie, O., Somerville, I., & Mitchell, D. (2015). *Social Exclusion and Sport in Northern Ireland*. Retrieved from Social Exclusion and Sport in Northern Ireland | The Executive Office (executiveoffice-ni.gov.uk).

Hargreaves, J. (1994). *Sporting Females*. London: Routledge.

Hellen, M. (2009). Transgender children in schools. *Liminalis: Journal for Sex/Gender Emancipation and Resistance*, 81–99.

Hills, L. (2007). Friendship, physicality, and physical education: An exploration of the social and embodied dynamics of girls' physical education experiences. *Sport, Education and Society*, 12(3), 317–336.

Hills, L.A., & Croston, A. (2012). 'It should be better all together': Exploring strategies for 'undoing' gender in coeducational physical education. *Sport, Education and Society*, 17(5), 591–605.

(IQA) International Quidditch Association. (2013). *International Quidditch Association Rulebook*. Radford, VA: Impressed Books.

Johnson, C.W., Singh, A.A., & Gonzalez, M. (2014). It's complicated? Collective memories of transgender, queer, and questioning youth in High School. *Journal of Homosexuality*, 61(3), 419–434.

Jones, B.A., Arcelus, J., Bouman, W.P., & Haycraft, E. (2017). Barriers and facilitators of physical activity and sport participation among young transgender adults who are medically transitioning. *International Journal of Transgenderism*, 18(2), 227–238.

Kessler, S.J., & McKenna, W. (1978). *Gender: An Ethnomethodological Approach*. University of Chicago Press.

Kirk, D. (1999). Physical culture, physical education and relational analysis. *Sport, Education and Society*, 4(1), 63–73.

Lentillon-Kaestner, V., & Roure, C. (2019). Coeducational and single-sex physical education: students' situational interest in learning tasks centred on technical skills. *Physical Education and Sport Pedagogy*, 24(3), 287–300.

Lisahunter, Smith, W., & Emerald, E. (2014). *Pierre Bourdieu and Physical Culture*. London/New York: Routledge.

Lucas-Carr, C., & Krane, V. (2012). Troubling sport or troubled by sport. *Journal for the Study of Sport and Athletes in Education*, 6(1), 21–44.

Metcalfe, S. (2018). 'Trapped': Gender, identities and PE. Unpublished Doctoral Thesis, Durham University.

National Union of Students. (2012). *Out in Sport: LGBT Students' Experiences of Sport* [Research Report]. London.

O'Donovan, T., Sandford, R., & Kirk, D. (2014). Bourdieu in the changing room. In lisahunter, W.Smith & E. Emerald (Eds.) *Pierre Bourdieu and Physical Culture*. London: Routledge.

Paechter, C. (2006). Masculine femininities/feminine masculinities: Power, identities and gender. *Gender and Education*, 18(3), 253–263.

Pahlke, E., Bigler, R.S., & Patterson, M.M. (2014). Reasoning about single-sex schooling for girls among students, parents, and teachers. *Sex Roles*, 71(5–8), 261–271.

Parker, F.J. (1996). Teacher and student beliefs: a case study of a high school physical education class. Unpublished Doctoral Thesis, University of Massachusetts Amherst.

Pavlidis, A., & Connor, J. (2015). Men in a 'Women Only' sport? Contesting gender relations and sex integration in Roller Derby. *Sport in Society*, 19(8–9), 1349–1362.

Planella, J., & Pié, A. (2015). Pedagogías transfronterizas: cuerpo, cultura y teoría queer. In A. Pié & J. Planella (Coords.), *Políticas, prácticas y pedagogías trans*. Barcelona: UOC.

Plaza, M., Boiché, J., Brunel, L., & Ruchaud, F. (2017). Sport= male... But not all sports: Investigating the gender stereotypes of sport activities at the explicit and implicit levels. *Sex Roles*, 76(3–4), 202–217.

Plumridge, E., Fitzgerald, L., & Abel, G. (2002). Performing coolness: Smoking refusal and adolescent identities. *Health Education Research*, 17 (2), 167–179.

Puche, L., Moreno, E., & Pichardo, J.I. (2013). Adolescentes Transexuales en la Escuela. Aproximación Cualitativa y Propuestas de Intervención desde la Perspectiva Antropológica. In O. Moreno & L. Puche (Eds). *Transexualidad, Adolescentes y Educación: Miradas Multidisciplinares* (pp. 189–265). Madrid: Egales.

Sausa, L. (2005). Translating research into practice: Trans youth recommendations for improving school systems. *Journal of Gay & Lesbian Issues in Education*, 3(1), 15–28.

Schilt, K., & Westbrook, L. (2009). Doing gender, doing heteronormativity: 'Gender normals', transgender people, and the social maintenance of heterosexuality. *Gender & Society*, 23(4), 440–464.

Segrave, J.O. (2016). Challenging the gender binary: the fictive and real world of quidditch. *Sport in Society*, 19(8–9),1299–1315.

Semerjian, T.Z., & Cohen, J.H. (2006). 'FTM means female to me': transgender athletes performing gender. *Women in Sport & Physical Activity Journal*, 15(2), 28.

Serano, J. (2016). *Whipping Girl: A Transsexual Woman on Sexism and the Scapegoating of Femininity*. Hachette.

Stonewall. (2020). Glossary of terms. https://www.stonewall.org.uk/help-advice/glossary-terms#t.

Sutherland, S. (2015). *A Beginner's Guide to Discourse Analysis*. Macmillan International Higher Education.

Sykes, H.J. (2011). *Queer Bodies: Sexualities, Genders, and Fatness in Physical Education* (Vol. 36). Peter Lang.

Tagg, B. (2012). Transgenders netballers: Ethical issues and lived realities. *Sociology of Sport Journal*, 29(2), 151–167.

Tagg, B. (2014). Changing hegemonic masculinities in men's netball. *Sport in Society*, 17 (6), 689–705.

Taylor, S. (2013). *What Is Discourse Analysis?*. Bloomsbury.

Theberge, N. (2000). *Higher Goals: Women's Ice Hockey and the Politics of Gender*. Suny Press.

Tejada III, E. (2016). Transgressing gender normativity through gender identity development: Exploring transgender, non-conforming, and non-binary identities of college students. Thesis. University of Nebraska, Lincoln, retrieved from https://digitalcommons.unl.edu/cgi/viewcontent.cgi?article=1266&context=cehsedaddiss.

Travers, A. (2013). Thinking the unthinkable: Imagining an "un-American," girl-friendly, women-and trans- inclusive alternative for baseball. *Journal of Sport & Social Issues*, 13(1), 78–96.

Travers, A., & Deri, J. (2011). Transgender inclusion and the changing face of lesbian softball leagues. *International Review for the Sociology of Sport*, 46(4), 488–507.

Trujillo, G. (2015). Thinking from another place, thinking the unthinkable: Towards a queer pedagogy. *Educação e Pesquisa*, 41(SPE), 1527–1540.

Wallace, L., Buchan, D., & Sculthorpe, N. (2020). A comparison of activity levels of girls in single-gender and mixed-gender physical education. *European Physical Education Review*, 26(1), 231–240.

Walton-Fisette, J.L., Philpot, R., Phillips, S., Flory, S.B., Hill, J., Sutherland, S., & Flemons, M. (2018). Implicit and explicit pedagogical practices related to sociocultural issues and social justice in physical education teacher education programs. *Physical Education and Sport Pedagogy*, 23(5), 497–509.

West, C., & Zimmerman, D. (1991). Doing gender. In J. Lorber & S. Farrell (Eds.) *The Social Construction of Gender*. Sage.

Westbrook, L., & Schilt, K. (2014). Doing gender, determining gender: Transgender people, gender panics, and the maintenance of the sex/gender/sexuality system. *Gender & Society*, 28(1), 32–57.

Williamson, R., & Sandford, R.A. (2018). 'School is already difficult enough…': Examining transgender issues in physical education. *Physical Education Matters*, 13(3), 57–61.

Wright, J., & Laverty, J. (2010). Young people, physical activity and transitions. In J. Wright, & D. Macdonald (Eds.) *Young People, Physical Activity and the Everyday* (pp. 136–149). London: Routledge.

Chapter 7

Understanding How Voice Impacts on Trans Women's Participation in Sport

L. Stewart, J. Oates and P. O'Halloran

Importance of Voice in Sport Settings

The human voice is a powerful communication tool that allows individuals to sing, speak, yell and express emotion. A person's voice also provides clues as to their physical health, emotional state, gender identity and the meaning of their words (Colton et al., 2011; Oates, 2011). There are three main body systems that need to be coordinated for efficient voice production (Titze & Martin, 1998); the power supply (the respiratory system), the sound source (vibration of the vocal folds in the larynx), and the shaping or resonance of that sound source as it travels through the pharynx (throat), nasal and oral cavities and then out of the mouth and nose as sound waves that we hear as speech (Lowell et al., 2008).

One group of individuals who heavily rely on their voice is occupational voice users and this can include school teachers, telemarketers, auctioneers, barristers as well as sportspeople, sports coaches and umpires. Sport settings may not at first appear to be a communication setting where peoples' voices may be challenged but no game or training session can be successful without vocal communication. Many occupational voice users do not receive voice training and are unaware of how to protect, maintain, or enhance their voices.

Communication in sport is critical, especially in team sport when everyone is working towards the same goal. Clear and concise vocalisations between players, coaches, administrators and others involved with a team and the sport should not be underestimated. Sport is just like any other business and, without effective voice, the inability to communicate effectively could have a negative impact on the team and club's overall success (Eccles & Tenenbaum, 2004). For example, research has found that team communication is important for successful team coordination and that inexperienced teams often have difficulty with this skill due to miscommunication (Eccles & Tenenbaum, 2004). Additionally, research is required in this area to highlight the importance of communication in team sport.

In sport settings, high levels of noise can be generated from vocalisations. At any sporting event there is typically the familiar sound of spectators where their voices

DOI: 10.4324/9781003050568-7

serve as an emotional outlet and where shouts of joy and screams of anger convey meanings that are easily recognised worldwide. Then there are the umpires who need to project their voices to ensure that all players, staff and spectators know what decisions they have made during games. There is the sound of the coach instructing their team, whether that is from the bench, the side-lines, the club rooms or the coaches' box. It is not uncommon for coaches to yell at their players from the side-lines or to project their voice to the other side of the field to instruct their athletes on what to do next or how and when to change tactics. Finally, there are the players themselves. They are often talking or yelling to their teammates, coach and umpire, over the crowd and game noises being produced.

Sportspeople are often not educated on what is required to generate enough vocal power to get their message across distances, against those crowd noises, and the less than ideal acoustic environments (Verdolini & Ramig, 2001). One aspect that can impact on an individual's effective communication and use of voice is their vocal load. Vocal load is defined as the quantity, demand, type and contexts of voice use (Hunter et al., 2020). The production of voice relies on physiological efficiency and when an individual's vocal load is too heavy this can create vocal problems (e.g., vocal fatigue, effortful voicing or vocal strain) or potentially lead to a voice disorder (e.g., muscle tension dysphonia or phonotraumatic lesions such as vocal polyps or even haemorrhage of the vocal folds) (Hunter et al., 2020). It is important to remember that the human vocal folds are a layered structure comprising epithelium, connective tissue, ligament and muscle, with the upper most epithelium and connective tissue layers being most susceptible to damage with demanding voice use (Hunter et al., 2020). Almost all team sport settings would be categorised as challenging vocal environments that place heavy vocal demands on speakers. Individuals are required to speak in an array of environmental conditions depending on the sport setting. The need to project voice within these environments increases vocal load, compromises voice ergonomics, and imposes high stress on an individual's phonatory system (Hamdan et al., 2021). For instance, indoor arenas typically echo and have poor acoustics, meaning an individual has to project over crowd noise, music, potentially other games being played at the same time on different courts as well as speaking over other athletes and umpires. Outside sports require the speaker to project across distances, over crowd noises and natural or artificial elements such as wind, rain or traffic on the roads. Irrespective of where the game is played there are several factors that can impact on voice efficiency and vocal load.

Research conducted in soccer/football and Australia Football League settings has found that heavy vocal load and vocal demands required in sport have negatively impacted on individuals involved within this setting (Nerriere et al., 2009; Buckley et al., 2014; O'Neill & McMenamin, 2014; Fellman & Simber, 2017). Sports-related laryngeal trauma, although rare, has also been reported in the literature due to equipment or player contact to the neck and the laryngeal area not being protected (Hamdan et al., 2021). For example, Trinidade et al. (2015) found lacrosse players had sustained laryngeal injury from being hit by the lacrosse ball. Additionally, O'Neill and McMenamin (2014) detailed that sport is an emotionally driven environment and that the emotions experienced during games, and in particular periods of stress, can alter an individual's phonation pattern and result in an increase in vocal load. One of the most important factors whilst playing sport is strong respiratory muscles that allow players to engage in the game to the best of their ability. Similarly, the foundation for efficient voice production is the respiratory system (Stemple, 2018). If a player does not have efficient coordination between breathing and phonation, they will be challenged to engage in both the physicality of the game and communication required with their coach and their teammates (Kassing et al., 2004).

Trans people participating in sport will experience the same vocal demands as their fellow players who are cisgender. However, they may have the additional challenge of their gender identity being questioned by coaches, teammates and club officials in sport settings. This may occur for example if a trans woman has a more masculine voice that is not congruent with her female physical appearance. Further, it is well documented that trans people have difficulty being accepted by sporting communities due to their gender identity (Pitts et al., 2009; Hughto et al., 2015; Strauss et al., 2017).

Trans People and their Voice

An individual's voice is linked to their personal identity (Adler et al., 2019). Indeed, people are often recognised by others based on the auditory–perceptual qualities of their voice. Listeners often attribute gender of their communication partner based on the voice features that they can hear, particularly the pitch and resonance characteristics (Davies et al., 2015).

Misgendering someone, using a word, pronoun or other form of address that does not correctly reflect a person's gender is a daily occurrence for some trans individuals (Dolan et al., 2020). Misgendering can either be intentional, where a person purposefully refers to an individual using their incorrect pronoun, or unintentional (Dolan et al., 2020). It is well documented that misgendering can have a negative impact on trans people (Bradford et al., 2013; Testa et al., 2012). Trans individuals are one group who experience high levels of discrimination that may result in considerable anguish and social isolation (Testa et al., 2012). The permeating discrimination and stigma that some trans and gender-diverse individuals face can result in exclusion from society (Bith-Melander et al., 2010; Bradford et al., 2013; Grant et al., 2011). This may occur across workplaces, social environments and family life contexts (Pitts et al., 2009). Further, research has found trans people are at higher risk than the general population of engaging in substance abuse to cope with the felt discrimination and stigma (Bradford et al., 2013). They are also at higher risk of experiencing violence, self-harm, suicide, anxiety and depression (Bouman et al., 2017; Davy, 2011; Marshall et al., 2016; Testa et al., 2012).

The human voice is critical in building rapport, relationships, and communicating one's needs and wants (Neumann & Welzel, 2004). A trans person's ability to develop and maintain relationships is likely to be negatively influenced if their voice does not match their gender expression and identity. It is not uncommon for trans people to experience a break-down in relationships because their communication partner incorrectly attributes their gender (Hancock et al., 2011). Further, willingness to communicate is diminished when a person is misgendered due to their voice (Pasricha et al., 2008). This can occur via the telephone or in-person in various social and sport settings. Communication could potentially be reduced in sport settings if a trans person is misgendered by their peers, and this could impact directly and negatively on the individual and their teammates.

As a result of having a gender-incongruent voice, trans people may experience activity limitations in speaking, communicating and participating in society because their birth-assigned sex is exposed. Their voice could impact negatively on their participation and on acceptance of their peers in sport. The potential to experience voice difficulties when playing sport is high, given that trans people can feel the need to focus on producing and maintaining a voice that is perceived in line with their identified gender. Sport settings can also be vocally challenging environments (Davies et al., 2015). These challenges of maintaining their voice may lead to increased anxiety about being misgendered because of voice. Anxiety can lead to increased laryngeal and perilaryngeal muscle tension and constriction, and thus potentially exacerbate any vocal difficulties that these people experience. Such vocal misuse can potentially lead to vocal hyperfunction, vocal impairment and potential phonotrauma (damage to the vocal folds) (Hillman et al., 2016; Roy et al., 2016; Stepp et al., 2011).

Impact of Voice on Trans Women

Research examining trans women's voice has expanded over the past 30 years and includes both qualitative and quantitative research methods. Researchers have found that trans women often experience voice concerns (Young et al., 2020). Trans women are more likely than trans men to experience voice concerns because hormone therapy does not change the structure of their vocal folds (Ziegler et al., 2018). When trans men begin to take testosterone, their vocal folds thicken and their pitch is likely to lower into the cis male pitch range (Zimman, 2012). Due to there being no effect on vocal folds for trans women, they often participate in voice training and learn to modify their voice to develop characteristics that are more in line with the way they want to present their gender. One of the main explanations for a trans woman facing social exclusion is that her voice often divulges her birth-assigned sex (Neumann & Welzel, 2004; McNeill et al., 2008; Mount & Salmon, 2008; Pasricha et al., 2008; Hancock et al., 2011; Adler et al., 2019). Therefore, it is often important to trans women that they develop a voice perceived by listeners as 'female' to successfully live in their desired gender role in society (McNeil et al., 2008; Pasricha et al., 2008). A trans woman may have difficulty attaining a voice that is perceived by listeners as female because of their typically larger larynx and longer and thicker vocal folds, relative to cisgender women. Research has shown that acoustic voice features differ between cismale and cisfemale speakers; such as average fundamental frequency (pitch), fundamental frequency range and variability, average intensity (loudness), formant frequencies (resonance characteristics) and that these voice characteristics are critical to listener perceptions of gender (Gallena et al., 2018; Gelfer & Tice, 2013; Oates, 2018; Oates & Dacakis, 2015).

Trans women have identified that their voice can 'expose' their birth-assigned sex because they either do not have a feminine voice or have difficulty maintaining a feminine voice, which makes it challenging for some trans women to be identified by others as female (Neumann & Welzel, 2004; Pasricha et al., 2008). Research has found that trans people also experience high levels of body dissatisfaction (Witcomb et al., 2015). The parts of the body that were linked with the most dissatisfaction included: body hair, Adam's apple, chest area, stomach, waist, hips and bottom (Witcomb et al., 2015). Failure to be accepted as one's identified gender can lead to discrimination, harassment and potential embarrassment for these trans women (Dacakis et al., 2013). Research has indicated that trans women with gender-incongruent voices are likely to experience a range of psychosocial effects in their everyday lives (McNeil et al., 2008; Mount & Salmon, 2008; Hancock et al., 2011; Adler et al., 2019). Hardy et al. (2013) explain that, because some trans women believe they have a male sounding voice they reduce their participation and involvement in life activities, as they are unsure how people will treat them if their birth-assigned sex were to be identified. Many of the women in their study reported social participation restrictions because of their gender incongruent voice (Hardy et al., 2013). Some trans women reported that they avoided previously enjoyed leisure activities or going out and participating in activities because of their voice (Hardy et al., 2013). Voice directly impacts on self-confidence, stigma and is therefore likely to heighten feelings of social anxiety.

Trans Women's Experiences in Sport Settings

There is a relative paucity of research examining the experiences of trans women in sport. The majority of sport literature that has examined trans women's participation in sport has examined issues related to gender testing, hormone level testing and regulations regarding elite sport (Reeser, 2005; Symons & Hemphill, 2006; Buzuvis, 2011; Sullivan, 2011; Wahlert & Fiester, 2012; Knox et al., 2019). A study by the authors, Stewart at al. (2020) explored the role of voice for trans women's participation in sport. Twenty women participated in semi-structured in-depth interviews and completed the Trans Woman Voice Questionnaire (Dacakis et al., 2013). The questionnaire is a self-reported measure that provides data on how trans women perceive their voices and the impact of voice in their everyday lives. We reported that trans women identify having a voice that does not match their gender identity and feminine physical appearance as one of the major barriers to their sport engagement (Stewart et al., 2020). Sport is one of the most gendered social settings throughout the world and is one environment where dominance of binary conceptions of gender (i.e., female or male) persist. The trans women reflected that, because of the gendered environment, their voice is pivotal to ensuring that they are accepted as women in sport settings. In particular, a gender incongruent voice impacted on their performances in games and training, as well as on their ability to form connections and engage in their sporting clubs.

Communication in sport is multi-levelled and involves both interpersonal and organisational communication., i.e., communication is required between players, coaches, managers, club employees, and umpires/referees. Further, communication involves opposition players, spectators, fans and the media (Hambrick, 2017; McLaren & Spink, 2018; Yasuda, 2019). It is undeniable that communication between players, coaches and even umpires is key in team sport (Yasuda, 2019). We found that trans women in particular find communicating in sport settings challenging and that the women perceive a direct impact on their sport participation (Stewart et al., 2020). The women in the study revealed that they would purposefully not speak during games including to their teammates or coach because they were often misgendered and referred to as males. This disconnection and inability to speak during games directly impacted on the team's success. As a consequence, some of the trans women were not selected for the team in the following matches because of the effect this had on the overall team. When sharing their experiences, trans women explained that they stopped speaking because their voice sounded masculine and they would be subjected to stigma and discrimination by opposition and spectators with some being called 'freaks' and being questioned about their eligibility to play when they sounded like a man.

Trans women can purposefully limit their performance and interactions with teammates because they are self-conscious about their voices and are fearful of being misgendered. Our other previous research (Stewart, 2019) found that the physical environment of sport impacted directly on trans women's voice use. Sport is usually played in arenas/stadiums or at outdoor venues where sports people need to project their voices over several elements including loud music, across distances to teammates, and against natural elements and crowd noise. This demanding vocal load directly impacts on individuals being able to voice sufficiently (O'Neill & McMenamin, 2014). Without effective voicing and respiratory support these external conditions can make it challenging for transwomen to maintain a female voice. Because trans women need to increase their vocal loudness and effort when playing sport, a significant drop in pitch and increase in chest resonance can occur. These changes, in turn, can make their voices sound more masculine and lead to them being misgendered. The women that were interviewed explained that because of the changes in their voice they had to choose between communicating with reduced physical exertion or focus on the game and reduce their communication. The participants in the study explained this choice was based on being unsure of strategies to maintain a female voice in sport environments. Another barrier to these women maintaining their female voice was the experience of vocal fatigue. Vocal fatigue led them to resort to hand gestures because they could not vocalise. Participants perceived that they experienced fatigue because of poor vocal hygiene, inadequate hydration and inadequate breath support (Stewart et al., 2020). Ensuring sufficient hydration is important for efficient and effective voice production and vocal health. Hydration helps maintain the protective mucosal lining which coats the vocal folds and protects them from the natural friction that occurs during vocalisation (King et al., 2018). Conversely, with inadequate hydration the essential pliability of the mucous membranes is compromised and can lead to swelling of the folds. Swollen vocal folds do not vibrate as freely as healthy vocal folds do, thus hindering vocalisation (Fujiki et al., 2017; King et al., 2018). Swollen vocal folds, like any condition or injury to the body, are potentially vulnerable to further, more serious, and possibly permanent damage (Fujiki et al., 2017; King et al., 2018).

The physical environment is not the only aspect of sport engagement that may impact on voice, psychosocial factors can also equally impact on voice production and maintenance of female voice. Psychosocial factors for voice use can include: emotions, anxiety, stress or major life changes (Guzy, 2016; Kollbrunner & Seifert, 2017). Stewart et al. (2020) identified that the nature of the relationship between the trans woman and their communication partner was important. For instance, participants were more anxious speaking to the opposition and management because they did not have a relationship with those people and would place more emphasis on maintaining their female voice because they did not want to be misgendered or discriminated against. However, whilst speaking with teammates and their coaches with whom they have built rapport and friendships, the trans women did not place the same emphasis on maintaining their female voice. However, it is important to note that if the trans woman was not close with people on her team she would still focus more on her voice because it was perceived as less acceptable. It is important to note that for some trans women not being able to maintain their female voice impacted not only on their engagement in sporting games but also their participation in social events at their club because they were stressed about being in social situations and being misgendered. Similar research has also identified that the level of importance trans women place on maintaining their female voice differs depending on their communication partner (Pasricha et al., 2008). Another psychosocial factor that is perceived to impact on voice production is an individual's emotional state. Sport competitions are often emotionally driven and these emotions can change based on whether a team is winning or losing (Campo et al., 2019; Hopfensitz & Mantilla, 2019).

Trans women have explained it is the intensity of the experienced emotion rather than the type of emotion that affects their voice (Stewart et al., 2020). Experiencing intense emotions can result in reduced control over the voice, thus creating a barrier to these women being able to successfully communicate because their birth-assigned sex might be exposed (O'Neill & McMenamin, 2014).

Incongruent voice also impacts trans women currently transitioning to their identified gender. In Australia, some sporting policies do not allow transitioning women to engage in women-only competitions until they have fully transitioned. Therefore, many trans people engage in mixed competitions where women and men can compete together. Engaging in mixed level competitions provides its own unique challenges for trans women's participation. Stewart et al. (2020) detail how many women currently transitioning would often hide their trans status so that nobody knew they were transitioning. That is, they would purposefully avoid building connections with their teammates. which is in contrast to trans women who were fully transitioned. The women in the process of living as their true gender identity explained that they believed that people would not understand what they were going through (Stewart, 2019). Trans women currently transitioning are commonly misgendered and referred to as male based on their voice (Stewart et al., 2020). The women explained that constantly being misgendered decreased their self-confidence, self-worth, and made them feel inadequate. Trans women believed that they might be shamed about their gender expression, often refusing to go to club functions and only talking when necessary. Limiting their participation in their sporting club impacted negatively on their sense of belonging in the club culture and prevented them from expanding their social networks (Stewart, 2019). Trans women perceived that there is a clear link between their gender incongruent voice and feeling unwelcome, the trans women felt unaccepted, often experiencing the stigma and discrimination in sport environments.

Outweighing the Negative: Positive Factors of Engaging in Sport

Despite experiencing difficulties and barriers to sport participation due to their gender-incongruent voice, trans women have reported positive aspects of participating in sport. One concern for trans women is the impact that hormone therapy has on their bodies. To counteract those negative effects (such as weight gain or change in mental state), the women explained that a positive aspect of engaging in sport is maintaining their physical health and that this is a key reason for their continued participation (Stewart, 2019). Sport can make a substantial contribution to the wellbeing of people. Some of the physical health benefits of sport participation include reduced risk of obesity and diabetes, increased cardiovascular fitness, improved coordination and balance, a greater ability to physically relax, and improved sleep (Collins, 2014; Eime et al., 2013;

Fujiwara et al., 2014; Gilchrist & Wheaton, 2017; Hoye et al., 2015; Moon & Heo, 2011; Sherry et al., 2015).

Sport also has the ability to increase individuals' social participation, connectedness and engagement within their community, enhancing their mental wellbeing (Coalter, 2007; Gilchrist & Wheaton, 2017; Sherry et al., 2015). Indeed, trans women have explained that engaging in sport encouraged them to get out of their homes, not feel isolated, and improved their physical vitality. The women detailed how being a trans person can be very lonely and isolating but knowing that they have training and games to attend encourages them to leave the house (Stewart et al., 2020). Indeed, researchers have found that there is a link between physical activity and mental wellbeing (Al-Qahtani et al., 2018; Craft & Perna, 2004). Dale and colleagues (2019) conducted a narrative review of the literature examining the impact of physical activity on reducing depression as a mental health treatment option and found that consistent exercise has a positive effect on mental wellbeing. Another positive aspect of participating and engaging in sport, despite the negative barriers, was simply enjoying sport and finding the game entertaining. Trans women are able to meet people with similar interests and work together towards a shared goal within team sport with likeminded people (Stewart et al., 2019).

The Role of Sport Organisations in Supporting Trans Sports People

There is evidence that participation in sport can be a potential facilitator for marginalised groups worldwide (Bloom et al., 2005; Coalter, 2007; Dagkas & Armour, 2012; Jeanes et al., 2018). However, for marginalised groups to successfully integrate and engage in sport, policies need to be put into place to allow these individuals to thrive and enjoy the positive health and wellbeing benefits that sport is known to create. Currently, in Australia there is a lack of policies and procedures in place to protect trans women engaging in sport (Stewart, 2019). National Sporting Organisations have detailed that they rely on membership protection policies to meet current needs (Stewart, 2019). However, these do not adequately meet the needs of their athletes. Therefore, the creation of policies that relate specifically to trans populations are needed. Specific policies may reduce barriers and enhance facilitators to assist trans women's engagement in sport. Research has found that policies and procedures that are enacted by sporting institutions directly affect the capacity of minority groups to engage in sport (Sawrikar & Muir, 2010; Kelly et al., 2014; Fahlén, 2017). Whilst sporting organisations cannot help trans women develop a gender congruent voice, they can protect these women from experiencing prejudice, stigma and being discriminated against based on their gender. Policies referring to trans women often determine their eligibility to participate and the fairness of the competition if they play against cisgender women. Very few policies have been created and implemented to protect these women and their specific needs.

Since 2018 in Melbourne, Australia, local councils have created 'trans and gender diverse nights' where swim nights have been created to allow trans and gender-diverse people to safely access pools and welcome them to exercise. Recently these facilities have grown to include gym facilities and group fitness classes. Trans-only physical activity sessions have also begun to take place across the United Kingdom where trans people have welcomed the opportunity to not be surveyed or receive backlash from the public (Caudwell, 2020). Whilst this is a welcoming and open opportunity for trans people to meet others from similar backgrounds and exercise, it is important that sporting organisations and Governments continue to work together to ensure trans and gender-diverse individuals are accepted into mainstream sessions and are safe to complete in sporting activities without the worry of public backlash.

One potential way to mitigate the voice problems experienced by trans women and reduce voice barriers is by utilising voice training implemented by speech language pathologists (SLP). An SLP is a specialist who diagnoses and treats a range of conditions and who works with people who experience communication and swallowing disorders (Speech Pathology Australia, 2020). An SLP is trained to provide voice training and voice feminisation for trans women (Dacakis, 2002; Dacakis, 2018). Voice feminisation training conducted by an SLP may address the vocal fatigue, vocal hyperfunction and vocal misuse behaviours reported by trans women. Voice feminisation is voice training that assists trans women to increase the alignment between their voice and gender, and is considered critical to some women's gender transition (Kim, 2017). SLPs could be effective in assisting trans women to reduce potential barriers to their voice by assisting them to understand how they use their voice throughout the day and in sport settings. Research has identified that voice training provided by SLPs can be effective in assisting trans women to achieve a gender congruent voice (Neumann & Welzel, 2004; Mount & Salmon, 2008; Oates, 2012; Davies et al., 2015). It is important that the SLP provides evidence-based practice when setting goals with their trans women clients (Leung et al., 2018). Current evidence suggests that targeting increased speaking pitch, feminising resonance, and increasing vocal flexibility can assist trans women to develop a more gender congruent voice (Davies et al., 2015; Leung et al., 2018; Nygren, Nordenskjöld, Arver, & Södersten, 2016). For sport settings in particular, it is important that the SLP educate trans women about voice care and techniques for safe vocal projection to minimise vocal misuse and potential phonotrauma, whilst improving vocal health (Colton et al., 2011, p. 75). Trans women in particular have identified they want to be trained in knowing how to speak in arenas and wide-open spaces, projecting their voice, maintaining adequate breath support and using female paralinguistic behaviours (Stewart, 2019). For voice training to be effective, it is also important that the SLP introduces the concept of generalisation early in training because it focuses on maintaining voice changes in everyday situations (Davies et al., 2015). Finally, because the characteristics of a person's voice do not guarantee that listeners will perceive their gender in line with their wishes and gender identity (Azul et al., 2020), it is also important that speech pathologists discuss this caveat with their clients and assist them to develop strategies to cope with the possibility that they will be misgendered, misunderstood or even excluded, regardless of their voice characteristics.

Conclusion

The evidence within the literature on voice and sport is almost non-existent, with most occupational voice literature focusing on teachers, singers and actors. However, it is clear from the available research that voice is a critical factor to those involved in sport, and further research exploring this relationship is warranted. This information will enhance team communication and activity, as well as potentially reduce vocal fatigue and encourage vocal unloading. There is beginning to be some understanding of how voice is one, if not the greatest, barrier to trans women's acceptance by peers in sport settings. Gender incongruent voice can result in stigma, discrimination and negative experiences. The heavy vocal load experienced in sport environments must also be addressed and considered in future research. This is because there is a link between the physical environment of sport and negative effect on voice production, due to poor acoustics, natural elements, long distances required for vocal projection and crowd noises, as well as risk of laryngeal injuries and development of hyperfunctional voice. Perhaps one of the most difficult aspects of trans women's participation in sport is that they must choose between their athletic performance and being correctly identified as their true gender because of several forces impacting on vocal function.

Whilst experiencing voice problems and developing potential voice disorders may be common for all athletes, coaches and staff, being misgendered has not been a concern to the engagement in sport for most people. However, trans women are having to compete with both the psychosocial and physical barriers to the voice production. They cannot communicate with their team and coach; therefore, they withdraw from club activities based on having a gender incongruent voice. No studies have yet demonstrated the relative effectiveness of specific intervention methods or the relative effectiveness of targeting particular voice features for trans feminisation to assist with these women's participation and acceptance in sport. Future research and voice training should address the needs of these women. Additionally, development of policies specific to trans women's participation in sport are sorely needed so that these women are able to participate without experiencing barriers such as stigma and discrimination. It is important to note that voice is personal and unique and even if trans and gender diverse people are happy with their voice and vocal function, their communication partner may attribute them the incorrect gender, which is why inclusive policies, supportive facilities, and positive attitudes are critical in the support of trans women engaging in sport.

References

Adler, R., Hirsch, S., & Pickering, J. (Eds.) (2019). *Voice and Communication Therapy for the Transgender/Gender-Diverse Client: A Comprehensive Clinical Guide* (3rd ed.). San Diego: Plural.

Al-Qahtani, A.M., Shaikh, M.A.K., & Shaikh, I.A. (2018). Exercise as a treatment modality for depression: A narrative review. *Alexandria Journal of Medicine*, 54(4), 429–435. https://doi.org/10.1016/j.ajme.2018.05.004.

Azul, D., Hancock, A., & Nygren, U. (2020). Forces affecting voice function in gender diverse people assigned female at birth. *Journal of Voice*. https://doi.org/10.1016/j.jvoice.2020.01.001.

Bith-Melander, P., Sheoran, B., Sheth, L., Bermudez, X., Drone, L., Wood, W., & Schroeder, K. (2010). Understanding sociocultural and psychological factors affecting transgender people of color in San Francisco. *Journal of the Association of Nurses in AIDS Care*, 21(3), 207–220.

Bloom, M., Grant, M., & Watt, D. (2005). *Strengthening Canada: The Socio-economic Benefits*. Ottawa, Canada: The Conference Board of Canada.

Bouman, W., Claes, L., Brewin, N., Crawford, J., Millet, N., Fernandez-Aranda, F., & Arcelus, J. (2017). Transgender and anxiety: A comparative study between transgender people and the general population. *International Journal of Transgenderism*, 18 (1), 16–26. https://doi.org/10.1080/15532739.2016.1258352.

Bradford, J., Reisner, S., Honnold, J., & Xavier, J. (2013). Experiences of transgender-related discrimination and implications for health: Results from the Virginia transgender health initiative study. *The American Journal of Public Health*, 103(10), 1820–1829.

Buckley, K., O'Halloran, P., & Oates, J. (2014). Occupational vocal health of elite sports coaches: An exploratory pilot study of football coaches. *Journal of Voice*, 29(4), 476–483. doi:10.1016/j.jvoice.2014.09.017.

Buzuvis, E. (2011). Transgender student-athletes and sex-segregated sport: Developing policies of inclusion for intercollegiate and interscholastic athletics. *Journal of Sports and Entertainment Law*, 21(1), 1–60.

Campo, M., Mackie, D., Champely, S., Lacassagne, M.F., Pellet, J., & Louvet, B. (2019). Athletes' social identities: Their influence on precompetitive group-based emotions. *Journal of Sport and Exercise Psychology*, 1(3), 1–6. doi:10.1123/jsep.2018-0282.

Caudwell, J. (2020). Transgender and Non-binary Swimming in the UK: Indoor Public Pool Spaces and Un/Safety. *Frontiers in Sociology*, 5, 64–64. https://doi.org/10.3389/fsoc.2020.00064.

Coalter, F. (2007). *A Wider Social Role for Sport: Who's Keeping the Score?* Abingdon, UK: Routledge.

Collins, M. (2014). *Sport and Social Exclusion*. Routledge.

Colton, R.H., Casper, J.K., & Leonard, R. (2011). *Understanding Voice Problems: A Physiological Perspective for Diagnosis and Treatment*. Lippincott Williams & Wilkins.

Craft, L.L., & Perna, F.M. (2004). The Benefits of Exercise for the Clinically Depressed. *Primary Care Companion to the Journal of Clinical Psychiatry*, 6(3), 104–111. https://doi.org/10.4088/PCC.v06n0301.

Dacakis, G. (2018). Consideration for Intake and Assessment. In R. Adler, S. Hirsch, & J. Pickering (Eds.) *Voice and Communication Therapy for the Transgender/Gender-Diverse Client* (3rd ed., pp. 45–68). San Diego: Plural Publication.

Dacakis, G. (2002). The role of voice therapy in male-to-female transsexuals. *Current Opinion in Otolaryngology & Head and Neck Surgery*, 10(3) 173–177.

Dacakis, G., Davies, S., Oates, J., Douglas, J., & Johnston, J. (2013). Development and preliminary evaluation of the transsexual voice questionnaire for male-to-female transsexuals. *Journal of Voice*, 27(3), 312–320. doi:10.1016/j.jvoice.2012.11.005.

Dagkas, S., & Armour, K. (2012). *Inclusion and Exclusion through Youth Sport*. London, UK: Routledge.

Dale, L.P., Vanderloo, L., Moore, S., & Faulkner, G. (2019). Physical activity and depression, anxiety, and self-esteem in children and youth: An umbrella systematic review. *Mental Health and Physical Activity*, 16, 66–79.

Davies, S., Papp, V., & Antoni, C. (2015). Voice and Communication Change for Gender Nonconforming Individuals: Giving Voice to the Person Inside. *International Journal of Transgenderism*, 16(3), 117–159. doi:10.1080/15532739.2015.1075931.

Davy, Z. (2011). *Recognizing Transsexuals: Personal, Political and Medicolegal Embodiment*. London, UK: Routledge.

Dolan, I.J., Strauss, P., Winter, S., & Lin, A. (2020). Misgendering and experiences of stigma in health care settings for transgender people. *The Medical Journal of Australia*, 212(4), 150–151.

Eccles, D.W., & Tenenbaum, G. (2004). Why an expert team is more than a team of experts: A social-cognitive conceptualization of team coordination and communication in sport. *Journal of Sport and Exercise Psychology*, 26(4), 542–560.

Eime, R., Young, J., Harvey, J., Charity, M., & Payne, W. (2013). A systematic review of the psychological and social benefits of participation in sport for adults: Informing development of a conceptual model of health through sport. *International Journal of Behavioral Nutrition and Physical Activity*, 10(1), 135.

Fahlén, J. (2017). The corporal dimension of sports-based interventions: Understanding the role of embedded expectations and embodied knowledge in sport policy implementation. *International Review for the Sociology of Sport*, 52(4), 497–517. doi:10.1177/1012690215607083.

Fellman, D., & Simberg, S. (2017). Prevalence and risk factors for voice problems among soccer coaches. *Journal of Voice*, 31(1), 121.e9–121.e15. doi:10.1016/j.jvoice.2016.02.003.

Fujiki, R.B., Chapleau, A., Sundarrajan, A., McKenna, V., & Sivasankar, M.P. (2017). The interaction of surface hydration and vocal loading on voice measures. *Journal of Voice*, 31(2), 211–217. doi:10.1016/j.jvoice.2016.07.005.

Fujiwara, D., Kudrna, L., & Dolan, P. (2014). *Quantifying the Social Impacts of Culture and Sport*. London, UK: Department of Culture, Media and Sport.

Gallena, S.J., Stickels, B., & Stickels, E. (2018). Gender perception after raising vowel fundamental and formant frequencies: Considerations for oral resonance research. *Journal of Voice*, 32(5), 592–601. doi:10.1016/j.jvoice.2017.06.023.

Gelfer, M., & Tice, R. (2013). Perceptual and acoustic outcomes of voice therapy for male-to-female transgender individuals immediately after therapy and 15 months later. *Journal of Voice*, 27(3), 335–347. doi:10.1016/j.jvoice.2012.07.009.

Gilchrist, P., & Wheaton, B. (2017). The social benefits of informal and lifestyle sports: A research agenda. *International Journal of Sport Policy and Politics*, 9(1), 1–10.

Grant, J.M., Mottet, L., Tanis, J., Min, D., Herman, J.L., Harrison, J., & Keisling, M. (2010). *National Transgender Discrimination Survey Report on Health and Health Care: Findings of a Study by the National Center for Transgender Equality and the National Gay and Lesbian Task Force*. Retrieved from http://transequality.orgissues/resources/national-transgender-discrimination-survey-full-report.

Guzy, A. (2016). Psychosocial factors and problems with voice production. *European Health Psychologist*, 18(S), 990. doi:10.1080/14015430119969.

Hambrick, M.E. (2017). Sport communication research: A social network analysis. *Sport Management Review*, 20(2), 170–183. doi:10.1016/j.smr.2016.08.002.

Hamdan, A., Sataloff, R., & Hawkshaw, M. (2021). *Voice Disorders in Athletes, Coaches and Other Sports Professionals*. Springer.

Hancock, A., Krissinger, J. & Owen, K. (2011). Voice perceptions and quality of life of transgender people. *Journal of Voice*, 25(5), 5553–5558. doi:1-.1016/j.jvoice.2010.07.013.

Hardy, T., Boliek, C., Wells, K., & Rieger, J. (2013). The ICF and male-to-female transsexual communication. *International Journal of Transgenderism*, 14(4), 196–208. doi:10.1080/15532739.2014.890561.

Hillman, R., Mehta, D., Stepp, C., Van Stan, J., & Zanartu, M. (2016). Objective assessment of vocal hyperfunction. *The Journal of the Acoustical Society of America*, 139(4), 2193–2194.

Hopfensitz, A., & Mantilla, C. (2019). Emotional expressions by sports teams: An analysis of world cup soccer player portraits. *Journal of Economic Psychology*, 75, 102071. doi:10.1016/j.joep.2018.04.008.

Hoye, R., Nicholson, M., & Brown, K. (2015). Involvement in sport and social connectedness. *International Review for the Sociology of Sport*, 50(1), 3–21.

Hughto, W., Reisner, S., & Pachankis, J. (2015). Transgender stigma and health: A critical review of stigma determinants, mechanisms, and interventions. *Social Science & Medicine*, 147, 222–231.

Hunter, E.J., Cantor-Cutiva, L.C., Van Leer, E., Van Mersbergen, M., Nanjundeswaran, C. D., Bottalico, P., … & Whitling, S. (2020). Toward a consensus description of vocal effort, vocal load, vocal loading, and vocal fatigue. *Journal of Speech, Language, and Hearing Research*, 63(2), 509–532. doi:10.1044/2019_JSLHR-19-00057.

Jeanes, R., Spaaij, R., Magee, J., Farquharson, K., Gorman, S., & Lusher, D. (2018). 'Yes we are inclusive': Examining provision for young people with disabilities in community sport clubs. *Sport Management Review*, 21(1), 38–50.

Kassing, J.W., Billings, A.C., Brown, R.S., Halone, K.K., Harrison, K., Krizek, B., … & Turman, P.D. (2004). Communication in the community of sport: The process of enacting, (re) producing, consuming, and organizing sport. *Annals of the International Communication Association*, 28(1), 373–409.

Kelly, B., King, L., Bauman, A.E., Baur, L.A., Macniven, R., Chapman, K., & Smith, B. J. (2014). Identifying important and feasible policies and actions for health at community sports clubs: A consensus-generating approach. *Journal of Science and Medicine in Sport*, 17(1), 61–66. doi:10.1016/j.jsams.2013.02.011.

Kim, H.T. (2017). A new conceptual approach for voice feminization: 12 years of experience. *The Laryngoscope*, 127(5), 1102–1108. doi:10.1002/lary.26127.

King, R.E., Steed, K., Rivera, A.E., Wisco, J.J., & Thibeault, S.L. (2018). Magnetic resonance imaging quantification of dehydration and rehydration in vocal fold tissue layers. *PloS one*, 13(12). doi:10.1371/journal.pone.0208763.

Knox, T., Anderson, L., & Heather, A. (2019). Transwomen in elite sport: Scientific and ethical considerations. *Journal of Medical Ethics*, 45(6), 395–403.

Kollbrunner, J., & Seifert, E. (2017). Encouragement to increase the use of psychosocial skills in the diagnosis and therapy of patients with functional dysphonia. *Journal of Voice*, 31(1), 132. doi:10.1016/j.jvoice.2015.11.021.

Leung, Y., Oates, J., & Chan, S.P. (2018). Voice, articulation, and prosody contribute to listener perceptions of speaker gender: A systematic review and meta-analysis. *Journal of Speech, Language and Hearing Research*, 61(2), 266–297. doi:10.1p44/2017_JSLHR-S-17-0067.

Lowell, S. Y., Barkmeier-Kraemer, J. M., Hoit, J. D., & Story, B. H. (2008). Respiratory and laryngeal function during spontaneous speaking in teachers with voice disorders. *Journal of Speech, Language, and Hearing Research*. doi:10.1044/10924388(2008/025).

Marshall, E., Claes, L., Bouman, W., Witcomb, G., & Arcelus, J. (2016). Non-suicidal selfinjury and suicidality in trans people: A systematic review of the literature. *International Review of Psychiatry*, 28(1), 58–69.

McLaren, C.D., & Spink, K.S. (2018). Examining communication as information exchange as a predictor of task cohesion in sport teams. *International Journal of Sport Communication*, 11(2), 149–162. doi:10.1123/ijsc.2018-0004.

McNeill, E., Wilson, J., Clark, S., & Deakin, J. (2008). Perception of voice in the transgender client. *Journal of Voice*, 22(6), 727–733. doi:10.1016/j.jvoice.2006.12.010.

Moon, T.Y., & Heo, C.U. (2011). Impact of participation in sport for all on leisure satisfaction, psychological wellbeing and subjective wellbeing. *Journal of the Korea Academia-Industrial Cooperation Society*, 12(9), 3984–3993.

Mount, K. & Salmon, S. (2008). Changing the vocal characteristics of a postoperative transsexual patient: A longitudinal study. *Journal of Communication Disorders, 21 (3)* 229–238. doi:10.1016/0021-9924(88)90031-90037.

Nerriere, E., Vercambre, M., Gilbert, F., & Kovess-Masfety, V. (2009). Voice disorders and mental health in teachers: A cross-sectional nationwide study. *BMC Public Health*, 9, 370. doi:10.1186/1471-2458-9-370.

Neumann, K., & Welzel, C. (2004). The importance of voice in male-to-female transsexualism. *Journal of Voice, 18*(1), 153–167. doi:10.1016/S0892-1997(03)00084-00085.

Nygren, U., Nordenskjöld, A., Arver, S., & Södersten, M. (2016). Effects on voice fundamental frequency and satisfaction with voice in trans men during testosterone treatment—a longitudinal study. *Journal of Voice*, 30(6), 766–e23. doi:10.1016/j.jvoice.2015.10.016.

Oates, J. (2011), Voice Impairment. In K. Hilari & N. Botting (Eds.) *Impact of Communication Disability across the Lifespan*. (pp. 243–262). Guilford: J & R Press.

Oates, J. (2012). Evidence-based practice in voice therapy for transgender/transsexual individuals. In R. Adler, S. Hirsch, & M. Morduant (Eds.,) *Voice and Communication Therapy for the Transgender/Transsexual Client* (2nd ed., pp. 45–68). San Diego: Plural Publication.

Oates, J. (2018). Evidence-based practice in voice therapy for transgender/transsexual individuals. In R. Adler, S. Hirsch, & J. Pickering, *Voice and Communication Therapy for the Transgender/Gender-Diverse Client* (3rd edn, pp. 45–68). San Diego: Plural Publication.

Oates, J., & Dacakis, G. (2015). Transgender voice and communication: Research evidence underpinning voice intervention for male-to-female transsexual women. *Perspectives on Voice and Voice Disorders*, 25(2), 48.

O'Neill, J., & McMenamin, R. (2014). Voice use in professional soccer management. *Logopedics Phoniatrics Vocology*, 39(4), 169–178. doi:10.3109/14015439.2013.825008.

Pasricha, N., Dacakis, G., & Oates, J. (2008). Communication satisfaction of male-to-female transsexuals. *Logopedics Phoniatrics Vocology*, 33(1), 25–34. doi:10.1080/14015430701514500.

Pitts, M., Couch, M., Mulcare, H., Croy, S., & Mitchell, A. (2009). Transgender people in Australia and New Zealand; Health, wellbeing and access to health services. *Feminism & Psychology*, 19(4), 475–495.

Reeser, J. (2005). Gender identity and sport: Is the playing field level? *British Journal of Sports Medicine* 39(10), 695–699.

Roy, N., Fetrow, R., Merrill, R., & Dromey, C. (2016). Exploring the clinical utility of relative fundamental frequency as an objective measure of vocal hyperfunction. *Journal of Speech, Language, and Hearing Research: JSLHR*, 59(5), 1002–1017.

Sawrikar, P., & Muir, K. (2010). The myth of a 'fair go': Barriers to sport and recreational participation among Indian and other ethnic minority women in Australia. *Sport Management Review*, 13(4), 355–367. doi:0.1016.j.smr.2010.01.005.

Sherry, E., Schulenkorf, N., & Chalip, L. (2015). Managing sport for social change: The state of play. The state of play. *Sport Management Review*, 18(1), 1–5.

Speech Pathology Australia. (2020). What is a Speech Pathologist? Retrieved from https://speechpathologyaustralia.org.au/SPAweb/Resources_for_the_Public/What_is_a_Speech_Pathologist/SPAweb/Resources_for_the_Public/What_is_a_Speech_Pathologist/What_is_a_Speech_Pathologist.aspx?hkey=7e5fb9f8-c226-4db6-934c-0c3987214d7a.

Stepp, C.E., Merchant, G.R., Heaton, J.T., & Hillman, R.E. (2011). Effects of voice therapy on relative fundamental frequency during voicing offset and onset in patients with vocal hyperfunction. *Journal of Speech Language and Hearing Research*, 54(5), 1260–1266.

Stemple, C (2018). Anatomy and physiology. In J.C. Stemple, N. Roy, & B.K. Klaben (2018). *Clinical Voice Pathology: Theory and Management*. Plural Publishing.

Stewart, L., Oates, J., & O'Halloran, P. (2020). 'My voice is my identity': The role of voice for trans women's participation in sport. *Journal of Voice*, 34(1), 78–87. doi:10.1016/j.jvoice.2018.05.015.

Stewart, L. (2019). Participation of trans women in sport. Unpublished Doctoral Thesis, La Trobe University.

Strauss, P., Cook, A., Winter, S., Watson, V., Wright Toussaint, D., & Lin, A. (2017). *Trans Pathways: The Mental Health Experiences and CARE PATHWays of Trans Young People. Summary of Results*. Perth, Australia: Telethon Kids Institute.

Sullivan, C.F. (2011). Gender verification and gender policies in elite sport: Eligibility and 'fair play'. *Journal of Sport and Social Issues*, 35(4), 400–419.

Symons, C., & Hemphill, D. (2006). Transgendering sex and sport in the Gay Games. In J. Caudwell (Ed.) *Sport, Sexualities and Queer/Theory*. (pp. 109–128) Routledge.

Testa, R.J., Sciacca, L.M., Wang, F., Hendricks, M.L., Goldblum, P., Bradford, J., & Bongar, B. (2012). Effects of violence on transgender people. *Professional Psychology: Research and Practice*, 43(5), 452.

Titze, I.R., & Martin, D.W. (1998). Principles of voice production. *The Journal of the Acoustical Society of America*, 104. doi:10.1121/1.424266.

Trinidade, A., Shakeel, M., Stickle, B., & Ah-See, K.W. (2015). Laryngeal fracture caused by a Lacrosse ball. *Journal of the College of Physicians and Surgeons*, 25(11), 843–844.

Verdolini, K., & Ramig, L. (2001). Review: Occupational risks for voice problems. *Logopedics Phoniatrics Vocology*, 26(1), 37–46. doi:10.1080/14015430119969.

Wahlert, L., & Fiester, A. (2012). Gender transports: Privileging the 'natural' in gender testing debates for intersex and transgender athletes. *The American Journal of Bioethics* 12(7), 19–21.

Witcomb, G.L., Bouman, W.P., Brewin, N., Richards, C., Fernandez-Aranda, F., & Arcelus, J. (2015). Body image dissatisfaction and eating-related psychopathology in trans individuals: A matched control study. *European Eating Disorders Review*, 23(4), 287–293. https://doi.org/10.1002/erv.2362.

Yasuda, Y. (2019). The relationship between cohesion, collective efficacy, communication and performance outcomes in youth team sports. Master's thesis, Kinesiology.

Young, V.N., Yousef, A., Zhao, N.W., & Schneider, S.L. (2020). Voice and stroboscopic characteristics in transgender patients seeking gender-affirming voice care. *The Laryngoscope*.

Ziegler, A., Henke, T., Wiedrick, J., & Helou, L. B. (2018). Effectiveness of testosterone therapy for masculinizing voice in transgender patients: A meta-analytic review. *International Journal of Transgenderism*, 19(1), 25–45.

Zimman, L. (2012). Voices in transition: Testosterone, transmasculinity, and the gendered voice among female-to-male transgender people. Boulder, CO: University of Colorado at Boulder. PhD Dissertation.

Chapter 8

Representing Diverse Genders in Sports Media

The Discursive Production of Cisgenderism in the UK Press

G. Knott-Fayle, E. Peel and G.L. Witcomb

Introduction

Conventional sex and gender ideals dominate sporting discourse and organisation (Lenskyj, 2013; Magrath, 2018). This chapter examines the discursive and rhetorical construction of trans, intersex[1] and non-binary athletes in the context of the UK national press. In particular, we examine how cisgender identities are naturalised in sports media through the discursive exclusion of trans, intersex and non-binary athletes. In this chapter we consider how the relationship between sport and media, and the resulting sports media discourse contributes to this limiting, cisgenderist understanding of identities. We do this through a discursive reflexive thematic analysis (RTA) of UK national newspapers' representations of trans, intersex and non-binary athletes. Our analysis produces three interlocking themes, namely: un/natural athletic bodies; contested rights; and deviation signals deviancy. Taken together, these themes demonstrate how scientific, political and ethical discourses are deployed in the UK press in ways that naturalise cisgender identities and destabilise trans, intersex and non-binary ones.

Whilst it is important not to collapse trans, intersex and non-binary identities into each other, this chapter considers how the media representations of non-normative sex and gender identities contribute to the production of cisgenderism in sports media. That is not to say that the manifestations of cisgenderism are homogenous, but rather that trans, intersex and non-binary identities are all marginalised by cisgenderism.

Sport and the media have a well-established, economically driven relationship. Media technologies have allowed sports to be broadcast further and more accessibly around the globe. This is visible in the growth of sporting mega-events and viewing figures of those events. For example, 3.6 billion people watched some of the 2016 Summer Olympic Games (Statista, 2016). Over 1 billion viewers watched the 2018 Men's World Cup Final match (FIFA, 2018). These unprecedented figures demonstrate the importance of media to sports popularity. Similarly, these viewing figures also present the media with important economic opportunities. The commercial potential for media is evident in

DOI: 10.4324/9781003050568-8

the size of the bids for the broadcast rights to sporting events. For example, the English Premier League, founded in 1992, sold the rights to its first season for £305 million – a TV deal which has grown to exceed £8 billion (Magrath, 2018). This is not an anomalous case, but rather is illustrative of sports media relationships around the world. Consequently, sporting events have often driven media revenue and advancements in media technology – advancements which have facilitated an unprecedented growth in the reach of sporting events.[2]

Whilst this mutually beneficial relationship can be characterised by an ever-increasing ability to transmit events across space, equally significant is the representation of societal identities and values. This aspect of communication is described in the 'ritual view' of communication. As Carey (1989) has outlined '[a] ritual view of communication is directed not towards the extension of messages in space but towards the maintenance of society in time; not the act of imparting information but the representation of shared beliefs' (p. 18). This is clear when one considers, for example, media coverage of the Olympic Games. In one sense, this coverage simply disseminates images of athletes running, jumping, throwing and so on, across the globe. However, these images are enmeshed with messages about nationality, with athletes' bodies adorned with national symbolism (Hogan, 2003; Shin, 2014), neoliberal messages exalting the power of economic growth for the host country (Silk, 2014) and big sponsors using the events as prime advertising opportunities (Silk & Andrews, 2001).

Consequently, the coverage of sporting events, actors and debates should not be taken at face value. Instead, critical researchers need to examine what stories, and what shared beliefs, are represented in, and through, sports media. Moreover, it is necessary to consider what forms of society are maintained by such representations. Representations are particularly significant in the case of sports coverage, which has garnered such a preeminent cultural position. In light of this, this chapter offers a discursive reflexive thematic analysis (RTA; Braun & Clarke, 2019) of UK newspapers' representations of trans, intersex and non-binary athletes. We focus now on representations of sex, gender and sexuality in sports media before turning our attention to discussion of cisgenderism specifically in sports coverage.

Sex, Gender and Sexuality in Sports Media

Sports media has long been steeped in sex, gender and sexuality conventions. Indeed, '[t]hroughout the 20th and 21st century, a salient media message has been the usefulness of sport as a social control mechanism, with two important complementary functions: to shape young people's behaviour in socially acceptable ways and to define and entrench hegemonic femininity and masculinity' (Lenskyj, 2012, p. 146). Hegemonic masculinity and femininity represent paradigmatic nodes which have structured social control in sporting contexts. Hegemonic masculinity has been described as 'the currently most honored way of being a man, it required all other men to position themselves in relation to it, and it ideologically legitimated the global subordination of women to men' (Connell & Messerschmidt, 2005, p. 832). Thus, hegemonic masculinity and femininity are interlinked as hierarchical binary nodal points in the gender identity system. In the sports media context, athletes are persuaded to strive for these hegemonic ideals, with adherence to hegemonic values a prerequisite for positive media coverage – a necessity for the acquisition of sponsorship deals (Blinde & Taub, 1992; Spencer, 2003).

Men's sports are largely presented as hegemonically masculine sites, which are defined by explicit homophobia and misogyny (Messner, 1992; Anderson, 2002; Magrath, 2018). As Messner wrote '[t]he extent of homophobia in the sports world is staggering. Boys (in sports) learn early that to be gay, to be suspected of being gay, or even to be unable to prove one's heterosexual status is not acceptable' (Messner, 1992, p. 34). This formulation of hegemonic masculinity manifests in sports media through the glorification of pain, powerful muscles, and aggression – a discursive practice described by Messner et al. (2000, p. 380) as 'the televised sports manhood formula'. There is evidence that the open hostility towards gay athletes has lessened over the last two decades with sporting discourse, authorities and teams espousing a more inclusive tone (Cleland & Magrath, 2020). However, the lacuna of openly gay athletes attests to a perpetuation of heteronormative constraints. Hegemonic masculinity is thus produced in sports media by an alienation of marginalised masculinities, defined by associations with homosexuality and femininity.

What may be termed hegemonic femininity is defined in a subordinate relationship to hegemonic masculinity (Connell & Messerschmidt, 2005). Female athletes need to navigate complex notions of hegemonic femininity because the sporting sphere is inherently androcentric. The founder of the modern Olympics, Pierre de Coubertin, described the Olympics as an 'exaltation of male athleticism' (quoted in Lenskyj, 2013, p. 23). Women were thus excluded from participation and were 'reduced to spectator and mothers, bearing and raising athletic sons' (Lenskyj, 2013, p. 23). The continuing impact of this conception of sport is apparent as female athletes are commonly perceived as masculine (Messner et al., 2003). This perceived masculine expression is stabilised in conventional sex, gender and sexuality notions by reading it as proof of non-heterosexuality.

As a departure from hegemonic femininity, assumptions of lesbianism have led to loss of sponsorship, for example tennis player Billie-Jean King lost sponsorship following public knowledge of her sexuality, and later Martina Navratilova was unable to secure the same level of sponsorship deals as many of her peers (Blinde & Taub, 1992; Spencer, 2003). More recently the revocation of sponsorship is perhaps less explicit, but female athletes still have to navigate competing expectations about being a woman and being an athlete – failure to do so often resulting in either negative coverage or simply a lack of media presence (Tredway, 2014; Schultz, 2014). Lenskyj (1994) discussed the particular heteronormative constraint foisted on '[s]portswomen, already seen as nonconforming, [that they] should at least present themselves as unequivocally heterosexual, and this hyperfeminine image is seen as an effective marketing strategy for female sport' (Lenskyj, 1994, p. 359). The continued prevalence of this enforced heterosexual, feminine expression has led some to describe how, in the sporting context, the female apologetic 'translates into a lesbian apologetic' (Schultz, 2014, p. 4). Thus, sports media contributes to gender hegemony by policing subordinated masculinities and femininities through narratives of deviant behaviour and related loss of necessary sporting capital. Subordinated gender expressions are thus persuaded to strive to adhere to these hegemonic paradigms. Consequently, binary masculine and feminine expressions structure discourse in sport and sports media. In this policing of the available sex, gender and sexuality expressions, gender hegemony, as we now go on to discuss, contributes to a cisgender system by enforcing a rigid binary conception of sex and gender.

Fairness in Cisgenderist Sports Media

Polarised gender ideals have a fundamental structuring impact which excludes trans, intersex and non-binary athletes. As conventional masculinity and femininity bolsters a two sex/gender system, athletes who fall outside of that binary are further subordinated. This structuring effect of hegemonic masculinity and femininity underpins cisgenderism in sports media. The regulations and practice around South African runner Caster Semenya provide a prototypical instance of how cisgenderism operates in sports media. Semenya became the focal point of public and academic debate around intersex identities in sport that generated contestation over the definition of the female sporting category more broadly. In 2009, when Semenya won the gold medal at the women's 800 metre race in the World Championships in Germany, public discourse quickly turned to scrutinise Semenya's body. Suspicions over her sex arose and were justified in sports media, particularly in western contexts, due to Semenya's supposedly masculine, muscular physiology (Cooky et al., 2013). What ensued was severe scrutiny of Semenya's body and speculation over her physiology and genital configuration.

News reports (cf. Williams, 2011) related to the International Association of Athletics Federations' (IAAF; now known as World Athletics) regulations on the female sporting category followed. These regulations stipulated that athletes in the female sporting category must have testosterone levels below 10nmol/L (IAAF, 2018). These regulations were successfully challenged by Indian sprinter Dutee Chand in 2015 – a ruling which required the IAAF to either change the regulations or prove their credibility with further evidence. The IAAF returned with data suggesting that intersex athletes had an unfair advantage (Bermon & Garnier, 2017; Eklund et al., 2017) – although the validity of these studies has been challenged (Sonksen et al., 2018). Following this, the regulations were changed to stipulate that athletes in the female category, competing in races between 400m and one mile, had to have testosterone levels below 5nmol/L

(IAAF, 2018). These new regulations were also challenged, this time by Semenya and Athletics South Africa. However, the Court for the Arbitration of Sport ruled against Semenya. The ruling stated that, because the regulations 'establish restrictions that are targeted at a subset of the female/intersex athlete population, and do not impose any equivalent restrictions on male athletes, it follows that the Regulations are prima facie discriminatory on the grounds of legal sex' (CAS, 2019, p. 2). However, it further concluded that the regulations are 'reasonable and proportionate' (CAS, 2019, p. 5) in order to protect fairness in female sports. Consequently, discrimination predicated on sex was enshrined as a necessary practice in the construction of fairness as it was conceived by sporting authorities.

Fairness coheres, in sporting discourse, around the concept of the 'level playing field'. Cooky and Dworkin (2013) unpack this sacrosanct sporting principle by highlighting that sport is not a level playing field but rather, 'it is a site wherein broader forms of inequality are accepted, tolerated, and ignored' (p. 107). Furthermore, it is an inherently cisgendered concept that is predicated upon the assumption that there are only two binary sexes that can be empirically, and irrefutably, tested for (cf. Fausto-Sterling 2000; 2018). However, 'reaffirming the sex binary is central to sex testing procedures' (Cooky & Dworkin, 2013, p. 106) and so the concept of the 'level playing field' is fundamentally conceptualised in, and itself reproduces, a cisgender sports system.

The coverage of the regulations of the female sporting category highlighted a conflation between trans and intersex identities (Lucas & Newhall, 2018). For example, Nicholas Hellen writes in *The Sunday Times* 'transgender athletes are to face tougher restrictions on competing in the Olympic Games and international athletics with a halving in the maximum testosterone permitted for women's events' (Hellen, 2018). As Lucas and Newhall (2018) point out, this constitutes an amalgamation of trans and intersex athletes because, '[n] either Caster Semenya nor Dutee Chand, the two women who have faced sanctioning from the IAAF and IOC because of testosterone levels, identify as transgender' (p. 100). Cisgenderist sports media thus works negatively for trans and intersex athletes through a conflation of all potentially non-cisgender[3] identities.

When we examine cisgenderism in sports media then, it requires the examination of a number of non-normative sex and gender identities in tandem. That is not to say that the manifestation of cisgenderism is homogenous, but rather that trans, intersex and non-binary identities are both alienated, subjugated and excluded at the hands of cisgenderist ideology. Indeed, transgender athletes have tended to be conceptualised in very narrow terms in sports media 'ignoring the different contexts within which trans people exist' (Lucas & Newhall, 2018, p. 101). This narrow definition of trans athletes is rooted in medicolegal notions of categorisable bodies (Currah, 2006; Valentine, 2007). In other words, trans athletes are narrowly constructed through medicalised language which requires bodies to adhere to cisgender notions of sex, gender and sexuality. These medicalised notions of trans athletes in sporting discourse attach to the concept of fairness based on bodily categorisations. This discourse 'operates to define transgender as always about the body and trans athletes as fakes/cheats' (Lucas & Newhall 2018, p. 109). Trans athletes are, thus, defined first and foremost by their biology, which is held up as proof of their wrong categorisation and thus as breaching sporting fair play.

The cisgenderist reimagining of trans athletes through medicolegal discourse presents them as abnormal or deviant and in need of '"corrective" treatment and "normalizing" procedures that eliminate alleged physiological advantages in order to "fairly" compete with cisgender athletes' (Fischer & McClearen, 2020, p. 152). In other words, trans athletes who are presented as not adhering to an expected practice of realigning their identities in cisgender terms are doubly excluded – first from the cisgender system, then from the cisgenderist prescription of trans acceptability. Trans athletes therefore have a route to recognition, but it is contingent upon subscribing to cisgenderist notions of binary identity realignment. This narrow trans narrative in sports media, which sustains cisgenderist conventions, further compounds 'the non-existence of non-binary, genderfluid, or genderqueer athletes' (Lucas & Newhall, 2018, p. 120). Sporting participants who reject adherence to cisgender norms are not just alienated but rendered invisible in sports media discourse. This exclusionary practice in the narrow binary trans narrative hints that it 'is more about maintaining the sex/gender system than it is about providing access to sport and physical activity' (Lucas & Newhall, 2018, p. 120). Insofar as this is the case, the contestation over non-cisgender athletes' identities represents an exclusionary process which simultaneously secures cisgender identities as subjects and non-cisgender people as the 'abject outside' (Butler 1993). That is, the 'constitutive outside to the domain of the subject' (Butler, 1993, p. 3). In other words, the cisgender sports media system makes trans, intersex and non-binary identities 'unliveable', when they do not live up to cisgenderist expectations, and constitutes the defining limitation of the cisgender system itself. This representation of non-cisgender people as incoherent or unstable when they do not adhere to cisgender expectations demonstrates the discursive process by which cisgenderism is stabilised as the norm. This process of stabilisation concurrently hints at its inherent instability. Thus, the contestation over non-cisgender athletes' identities is indicative of the preservation and vulnerability of the cisgender system.

Sports media narratives, influenced by the hegemonic masculine and feminine ideals, are organised around assumptions of deviancy and exclude athletes who identify within the umbrella of trans, intersex and/or non-binary. In so doing, cisgender male and cisgender female identities are naturalised as sporting subjects. We consider in this chapter *how* this naturalisation of cisgender subjects through exclusion and destabilisation of trans, intersex and non-binary athletes occurs in the context of the UK national press.

Methodology

The analysis in this chapter focuses on UK national newspapers print and online editions. Despite the increasing hybridity of the media system (Chadwick, 2013) newspapers, particularly online editions, remain important parts of public media discourse, with 38% of British adults citing newspapers as a source of their news (Ofcom, 2019). Furthermore, on the grounds of quality, trustworthiness and impartiality, 58% of users rated newspapers positively compared to, for example, the 37% of social media users (Ofcom, 2019). Despite its refraction through 'the prism of the hybrid media system' the venerable position and resources available to traditional newspaper actors, as well as the shift to online platforms, attests to 'the enduring power of the traditional newspaper' (Chadwick, 2013, p. 54).

All articles were obtained through the NexisUK database with the search terms 'Transgender'+'Sport', 'Intersex' and 'Non-binary'. The trans search required the further search term 'Sport' because 'Transgender' on its own retrieved too large a dataset to analyse, with a large number of non-sport related articles. The 'Intersex' and 'Non-binary' searches generated more manageable datasets that were filtered for articles that were sports related. The total newspaper article data-set was 183, combining 'Transgender'+'Sport' (n=131), 'Intersex' (n=45) and 'Non-binary' (n=7). The searches had no time limit set but the first mentions of the search terms occurred in an article from 10 July 1996 and the search was conducted on 20 March 2019 making this the *de facto* time span.[4]

All articles were from national UK newspapers and the search terms had to appear in the headline or lead paragraphs. The articles were analysed using a combined discursive psychology and reflexive thematic analysis approach. Discursive psychology is concerned with the ways that ideological thinking is expressed in everyday communication such as in newspaper texts. In particular discursive psychology is concerned with how the self, others and the world are constructed through communicative events (Wetherell & Potter, 1992; Potter & Wetherell, 1987). Reflexive thematic analysis involves 'identifying, analysis and reporting patterns (themes) within data' (Braun & Clarke, 2006, p. 79). Themes are not simply unified ideas which occur in multiple articles but rather 'patterns of shared meaning underpinned or united by a core concept' (Braun & Clarke, 2019, p. 593). In other words, themes may not necessarily be conceptually monolithic or homogenous – in fact, the richness of an analysis can be hampered by such internal uniformity. Discursive psychology is beneficial to the reflexive thematic analysis in this chapter because of the aim to understand how sports media is constituted as cisgender through the construction of a non-cisgender 'Other'. The discursive psychological concept of the interpretative repertoire is particularly useful in furthering this analytic aim. Interpretative repertoires are 'broadly discernible clusters of terms, descriptions and figures of speech often assembled around metaphors or vivid images' (Wetherell & Potter,

1992, p. 90). The interpretative repertoire concept usefully captures the way that actors draw on ideological concepts to construct subject positions in communicative events.

The newspaper articles were coded for discursive themes in order to examine how ideological themes were employed to achieve different actions. Consequently, particular attention was paid to the latent ideas in the articles. Drawing on discursive psychology's methodological procedures (Wiggins, 2017), these latent ideas were accessed through fine-grained, micro level analyses at the textual level which are understood as connected to macrolevel, ideological discourses.

Analysis

The analytical process generated three main themes: un/natural athletic identities; contested rights; deviation signals deviancy. These three themes broadly map onto scientific, political and ethical discourses. The analysis considers how conventional, cisgender ideals are expressed and constituted in these three discursive sites particularly through the exclusion (and justifications for such exclusion) of trans, intersex and non-binary athletes.[5]

Un/natural Athletic Bodies

Trans and intersex athletes are often represented through scientific, biological language. Expressed in the everyday context of the press, a medical repertoire is produced which demarcates a conception of un/natural which cuts across trans and intersex athletes in complex ways. In other words, a medical repertoire is used to represent trans and intersex athletes as natural, or unnatural, in different ways at different moments. The use of this medical repertoire represents a situated use of parts of the medicolegal discourse of categorisable bodies (Currah, 2006; Valentine, 2007).

The medical repertoire presents an ostensible truth about the bodies of trans athletes through empiricist discourse in which 'the description is of a thing… and that thing exists, as described, without the describer having any influence on it' (Potter, 1996, p.150). Whilst it has been noted that medicalised sporting categorisation 'operates to define transgender as always about the body' (Lucas & Newhall, 2018, p.209), this process can also be read in terms of the severing of trans athletes' physiology and identity, with the former discursively reified as empirically evident. The medical repertoire purports to peel back the social skin of trans athletes and get at the truthful core underneath.

In an article in *The Sunday Times*, for example, Martina Navratilova writes:

> Simply reducing hormone levels – the prescription most sports have adopted – does not solve the problem. A man builds up muscle and bone density, as well as a greater number of oxygen-carrying red blood cells, from

> childhood. Training increases the discrepancy. Indeed, if a male were to change gender in such a way as to eliminate any accumulated advantage, he would have to begin hormone treatment before puberty. For me, that is unthinkable.
>
> (Navratilova, 2019)

This extract uses physiological processes, described through the medical repertoire 'oxygen-carrying red blood cells' and 'muscle and bone density' to categorise the body of trans athletes in the female category as male. Despite the physiological changes that hormone therapy enacts upon the body, this is presented as not enough to alter a physiological, male core. This biological construction is presented as proof that trans athletes are, deep-down, 'really' male. This un/natural dichotomy dissects the bodies and identities of trans athletes – the former sex/biology positioned as natural and real, the latter identity as a social decision which is draped over that biological frame.

Intersex athletes are not expressed in the same contested terms. However, they are still caught up in a medicalised conception of un/natural in which they are presented in purely biological terms and the cultural and social facets of their identities are withheld. In the case of intersex athletes, the medical repertoire is so dominant that the social aspects of their identity present less of a contest to their biologically determined portrayal. *The Times*, for example, states of intersex identities, 'This isn't about feeling you are one gender when you were born another, or your sexual preferences; it's basic biology' (Gill, 2015). This passage implicitly presents trans identities as a 'feeling' and contrasts that with the 'basic biology' of intersex. A clear distinction is made between sociological, cultural expressions and fundamental biological facticity. Intersex identities are pinned to the latter, as a matter of 'basic biology' and, because they are not about feelings, they are denied socio-cultural significance. The division between natural and unnatural is reasserted through the strict confinement of intersex to discursive representations of natural science.

Bound as they are to biology in the medical repertoire, intersex athletes' physiology is defined as a biological anomaly. An article in *The Telegraph* writes of Caster Semenya:

> The 25-year-old who has internal testes but no womb or ovaries due to an abnormality, has been dominating middle-distance running since a ruling which previously forced her to take drugs to cut her testosterone was overturned.
>
> (Morgan, 2016)

Here, divergence from typical female anatomy ('internal testes but no womb or ovaries') is presented as an 'abnormality'. The conventional female body is the benchmark against which this divergence is measured as abnormal or anomalous. Thus, the confinement of intersex athletes to scientific discourse does not render the intersex athlete natural in any simple sense. Instead, intersex athletes are at the mercy of medicalised notions of abnormality based upon biological assumptions of physiological averages.

The Guardian deploys a similar use of the medical repertoire in an earlier article when Semenya first rose to prominence. This article quotes a consultant gynaecologist in its description of Semenya, stating, 'The male hormone is what gives bulk to muscles and bones so they are at an advantage. I have seen pictures of this girl and she has no waist and very masculine musculature' (Bowcott, 2009). As with the previous extract, this article uses a perceived lack of adherence to conventional feminine norms ('she has no waist') as evidence of the existence of male physiology in the form of 'the male hormone' – presumably referencing testosterone. This quote produces multiple actions by quoting a medical professional. The authority that the audience is expected to ascribe to a medical professional makes the relatively ambiguous descriptions 'male hormone', 'she has no waist' and 'masculine musculature' appear more valid than they might otherwise have done. Furthermore, the experiential authority of the medical professional who has 'seen pictures of this girl' is combined with the authority of their professional status to render both the description and the conclusion objectively sound. That a gynaecologist is used is pertinent to the construction of intersex athletes as simply a biological phenomenon. That is to say, whilst the gynaecologist articulated those words, the journalist choreographs the article using actors and quotes to achieve certain things. As Attenborough (2016) describes it, 'only that which a journalist decides is relevant to understanding someone's talk/text will appear in the report' (p.259). In this case, Semenya is articulated as medically abnormal for diverging from female norms.

The positioning of intersex athletes as biological anomalies is stretched further in an article in *The Times* which reads:

> An insecticide used to kill malaria carrying mosquitoes in the northern Limpopo province of South Africa, the area where the Olympic runner Caster Semenya grew up, is responsible for the high number of 'genital ambiguity' cases in the area, scientists believe.
>
> (Graham, 2016)

Rather than a naturally occurring 'abnormality', this extract represents intersex characteristics as an externally enforced accident or mutation. In other words, there is a further use of the medical repertoire to portray the bodies of intersex athletes as being the result of unnatural interference, from toxicity in the environment, in the natural workings of biology.

The reproduction of an un/natural dichotomy in the medical repertoire has implications for the attribution of agency. Intersex athletes are reified as part of the empirical discourse of the medical world. However, this reification comes at the expense of their subjectivity because they are positioned as passive objects upon which biology occurs. As a result, intersex athletes' bodies become objects of scrutiny in sports media as described by Cooky et al. (2013). Trans athletes on the other hand are ironised as socially produced identities which do not adhere to their 'real' biology. This discursive practice enforces ill-fitting cisgenderist categories upon trans athletes. But it also has the effect of constructing trans athletes as agentic subjects. In so doing, the un/natural dichotomy produced and enforced problematically on trans and intersex athletes has sociopolitical implications, which we now explore under the 'contested rights' theme.

Contested Rights

The way that the medical repertoire mediates trans and intersex athletes' bodies contributes to debates around recognition and rights. Put simply, trans athletes' rights are positioned antithetically to women's rights; that is, as active subjects damaging women's rights and sporting spaces through their own rights claims. Alternatively, whilst intersex athletes are often represented as disruptive to the women's category, their divergence from expected female biology is also seen as a surmountable barrier to inclusion in the discourse of women's rights. Fundamentally, however, both of these position rights recognition and sporting inclusion conditional on adherence to cisgender narratives.

The rights of trans athletes and those of female athletes are frequently positioned oppositionally, with trans rights encroaching on women's rights. For example, an article in *The Sunday Times* headlined 'Sex changes spark new dilemmas: Sport, prisons and schools are struggling to deal with the rise of transgender rights' states:

> In Michigan, a woman had her gym membership revoked after she complained about a transgender person in the women's locker room. One of the most controversial issues has been participation in female sports events. In Connecticut, Andraya Yearwood, a 15-year-old transgender student with male anatomy and noticeable stubble who identifies as a girl, has become a star of the female sprint team. In 2014, a mixed martial arts competitor called Fallon Fox gave a female opponent, Tamikka Brents, concussion and broken eye socket… Eight years earlier Fox had undergone a sex-change operation from man to woman.
>
> (Shipman, 2017)

This passage positions trans rights and women's rights in the sporting context as antithetical. This is done by, firstly, discursively denying the femaleness of trans athletes in the female sporting category. This is achieved in part through 'the forced imperative to always be out' (Lucas & Newhall, 2018, p.120). Andraya Yearwood, for example, is nominalised as 'a 15-year-old transgender student'. This description places transgender at the forefront of her identity, regardless of how this sits with her experience. It works to withhold female identification from her. Furthermore, the explicit mention of her 'male anatomy and noticeable stubble' works to establish her as biologically male. A similar practice takes place in the descriptions of Fallon Fox and Tamikka Brents. Fox is described as 'a mixed martial arts competitor' while Brents is 'a female opponent'. Thus, Fox is denied female recognition, and tied to the male identity in the focus on her 'sex-change operation from man to woman'. Consequently, Fox is presented as a male fighter, while her opponent is explicitly marked as female.

Secondly, the rights of these separately marked actors are depicted competitively. Fox's and Brents' bout symbolises this oppositional positioning. However, the legitimisation that sporting participants receive as willing actors in a regulated contest is removed with Fox's description as a male fighter and Brents' as a female opponent. Consequently, the 'concussion and broken eye socket' are presented as evidence of the attacks that women face at the hands of trans rights. The opening line of the passage above describes how 'a woman had her gym membership revoked after she complained about a transgender person in the women's locker room'. In this formulation, a (presumably) cisgender woman is presented as a victim of punishment for her attempts to protect women's only spaces from an actor marked as non-female. This works to further construct a world in which women's rights are not just oppositional to trans rights, but policy is stacked in the favour of the latter – leaving them as unprotected to attack as Fox's opponent.

In contrast to trans athletes, intersex athletes are presented as biologically anomalous women who may be granted women's rights as long as they realign their biology with female averages – despite elite female athletes being, by definition, not average. For example, the article from *The Sunday Times* also states:

> 'Intersex' athletes with both sex organs and high levels of testosterone will be able to compete in female races at the World Athletics Championships in London next month. Athletics' world governing body is preparing to return to the Court of Arbitration for Sport (CAS) to argue that female competitors should undergo corrective treatment to lower any high levels of testosterone so that they can compete on a 'level playing field' with other women.
>
> (Shipman, 2017)

In this passage, intersex athletes are presented as biologically anomalous relative to expected female biology in their description as having 'both sex organs and high levels of testosterone'. However, they are simultaneously described as 'female competitors' and positioned as female relative to 'other women'. The extract hints at the potential for women's rights discourses to include intersex athletes. For this to happen, however, intersex athletes must adhere to conventional female norms through 'corrective treatment'. In other words, rights recognition is dependent upon cisgender aesthetics and norms around testosterone levels.

In contrast to making physical alignment with cisgender norms prerequisite for support, some articles reject this somatic stipulation but, instead, produce cisgender alignment discursively. Therefore, adherence to cisgender norms remains imperative for support of intersex athletes. For example, Navratilova's article in *The Sunday Times*, states:

> That brings me to the most controversial current case, involving Caster Semenya, the Olympic 800m champion. She was designated female at birth and has been raised as a female throughout her life. Suspicions were aroused because she was such a dominant runner and her body shape looked male. It turned out that Semenya has a condition called hyperandrogenism, which produces naturally occurring, but elevated, levels of testosterone. She has never taken medication or sought an advantage. She has just trained and run.
>
> (Navratilova, 2019)

In this extract support is given to Semenya. However, it is predicated upon a deliberate construction of her female credentials – that is that she 'was designated female at birth and has been raised as female'. Thus, whilst the previous article described a need for physical changes in the form of 'corrective treatment' to align intersex athletes with cisgender female norms, Navratilova's article discursively produces this alignment. Consequently, rights recognition for intersex athletes is rendered dependent on physical or discursive construction in the image of cisgender femaleness.

In the same article, a similar process of establishing cisgender female credentials as a precursor to arguments of rights recognition is visible in relation to trans athletes. Navratilova wrote, 'Let me make a critical distinction between transgender and transsexual athletes. Transsexuals have decided to change their gender and have had the deed done, surgically. They have made the full commitment' (Navratilova, 2019). In this passage Navratilova distinguishes between trans athletes who have surgically altered their physiology and those who have not. This distinction is described with the former having made a 'full commitment', the latter therefore portrayed as non-committal. This argument reproduces cisgenderist narratives in which the authenticity of trans identities is called into question (Knott-Fayle, Peel & Witcomb, 2021). This supposed fully committed change rectifies the perceived discrepancy between identity and physiology. This surgical alteration leads Navratilova to describe how she 'had no objection' when Renee Richards 'changed his sex through surgery… and began to compete as a woman' (Navratilova, 2019).

On the one hand, this distinction highlights that the category of woman is not immutable or necessarily out of reach for all trans athletes. On the other hand, it is only accessible if one aligns the body and social identity with cisgender expectations. In other words, indicative of the narrow binary trans narratives described by Lucas and Newhall (2018), Navratilova predicates her support for trans athletes upon the removal of non-binary identity facets. This exemplifies the coverage of non-binary athletes more broadly which is characterised by a non-existence. Not only is there a paucity of articles related to non-binary sporting participation – a mere seven – but the content of those articles differs from the contested representations of trans and intersex athletes. Non-binary participation is discussed in relation to amateur, social or peripheral sporting events.

One article in *The Sun,* for example, reports that, 'Girton College launched one-hour weekly slots for females and those identifying as non-binary, who feel their gender is neither male nor female' (Pattinson, 2019). *The Times* also reports on these events, writing, 'Cambridge University students are embroiled in a gender identity row over a poster that asked men to keep out of the gym and swimming pool once a week, reserving it for women and non-binary people' (Bennett, 2019). Where non-binary identities are discussed in relation to sport there is a tendency for this to be confined to amateur-level matters such as the organisation of a student gym. These articles evidence an exclusion of non-binary athletes from discussions of elite level or competitive sport.

The only article that discusses non-binary participation in competitive sports, does so in relation to the Highland Games. This article in *The Telegraph* reads, 'The organisers of the Highland Games are considering how to include competitors with a "non-binary" gender following demands that traditional men-only events should not receive public funding' (Johnson, 2019). Whilst the Highland Games are competitive, they have limited cultural impact compared to the international sporting events which trans and intersex athletes are discussed in relation to. Thus, trans and intersex athletes represent contested terrain in the sports media landscape, whereas non-binary athletes are invisible – particularly in discourse related to competitive sports. In the final theme, we move from the representation of contested rights and partial inclusion to the emphasis on negativity associated with non-cisgender athletes in sports-media.

Deviation Signals Deviancy

The previous two themes have highlighted how trans, intersex and non-binary athletes are portrayed as deviating from cisgender conventions laid out in scientific and political discourse. These portrayals are, however, not ethically neutral. Akin to discourses of deviancy in representations of subordinate femininities (Blinde & Taub, 1992; Tredway, 2014), cisgender deviation underpins narratives about trans and intersex athletes as cheats and even criminals.

For intersex athletes the ascription of deviancy is fuelled largely by the World Athletics' official argument that intersex athletes need to 'lower any high levels of testosterone so that they can compete on a "level playing field" with other women' (Shipman, 2017). Invocation of the 'level playing field', already established through Cooky and Dworkin's (2013) work as a fundamentally cisgenderist concept, discursively intertwines intersex athlete's non-binary physiology to the upsetting of an ostensible equilibrium in sport. It is no surprise then that intersex athletes are articulated through the allegorical figure of the doping athlete – the paradigmatic sporting cheat. For intersex athletes this construction manifests in the descriptions of their testosterone levels.

The Guardian, for example, in an article about the debate around intersex athletes, reads 'Testosterone has several potential performance enhancing effects on the body, including boosting the oxygen-carrying capacity of the blood, building lean muscle mass and increasing mental drive and aggressiveness' (Kelner & Rudd, 2017). This extract demonstrates an interdiscursivity between doping and intersex athletes in which natural testosterone levels are described in terms of their 'performance enhancing effect', akin to the language of performance enhancing drugs.

Trans athletes are similarly represented through a doping discourse. However, for trans athletes this figure is invoked in a way that establishes intentionality more explicitly than it does with intersex athletes. In legalese, this differentiation is manifest in the difference between *actus reus*, the illegal action, and *mens rea*, the criminal intent. Edwards (2008) describes how the latter becomes a discursive topic when trying to discern culpability for an action. In contrast to intersex athletes, trans athletes are represented as fulfilling the criteria for culpability in a legal sense – that is, as both gaining advantage *and* doing so deliberately. This is an important ethical distinction, one which is articulated clearly in Navratilova's article in *The Sunday Times*, where she writes:

> It turned out that Semenya has a condition called hyperandrogenism which produces naturally occurring, but elevated, levels of testosterone. She has never taken medication or sought an advantage. She has just trained and run.
>
> (Navratilova, 2019)

In this excerpt, Navratilova contrasts intersex athletes and trans athletes through the ascription of the former's 'naturally occurring' testosterone levels, implicitly positioning trans testosterone as unnatural. This comparison is interesting because any testosterone that trans athletes in the female category have is also naturally occurring – the only synthetic change will have been to reduce it. That this is the case highlights that what counts as natural is, itself, anything but natural. Rather it is a rhetorical device used to demonstrate intentionality on the part of trans athletes. This is a repertoire in which '[t]o be seen to have transgressed… is one thing; to be seen to have done so *deliberately* is something else entirely' (Attenborough, 2016, p.234). Therefore, trans athletes are articulated through a repertoire of deviancy and criminality which works to establish guilt, that is both *actus reus* and *mens rea*, in the sporting context.

An article in *The Times* exemplifies the explicit nature of this recriminatory discourse:

> If someone has grown up and developed a male body and then transitioned to being a woman, then they will still have a male body, with the muscle development and muscle memory. It is the same effect as if a woman had been doping for years.
>
> (Ziegler, 2019)

Describing male puberty in this context as the same as 'doping for years' solidifies the doped athlete – the paragon of deliberate sporting deviancy – as the underpinning allegory of the trans athlete. The entrenchment of this allegory fortifies the trans athlete as a guilty party.

This distinction between trans and intersex athletes along the lines of intentionality is rooted in an entrenched conception of gender fraud and deception in the case of trans people. This conception has manifested in legal cases (Sharpe, 2017), as well as in media discourse (Halberstam, 2005; Billard, 2018). This narrative of deception and fraud is rooted in an assumption that trans people who do not disclose their gender assigned at birth before engaging in sexual intercourse are rapists. As a result of this assumption, 'transgender individuals living out their authentic gender identities could become criminal deception when cisgender… individuals are not aware of the genders transgender people were assigned at birth' (Billard, 2018, p.463). This recalls Lucas and Newhall's assertion that 'trans women are always already liars and cheats trying to "trick" people' (Lucas & Newhall, 2018, p.119). In a sporting context this idea of gender fraud and deception manifests in a perception of trans athletes as seeking an unfair advantage.

The establishment of sporting deviancy is, however, seen to symbolise a more fundamental criminality in trans athletes. For example, to revisit the article in *The Sunday Times* which described Fallon Fox's MMA bout:

> In 2014, a mixed martial arts competitor called Fallon Fox gave a female opponent, Tamikka Brents, concussion and a broken eye socket. Brents said: "I've never felt so overpowered ever in my life". Eight years earlier, Fox had undergone sex-change operation from a man to a woman.
>
> (Shipman, 2017)

By calling into question the legitimacy of the contest itself, as discussed in the previous section, the passage reads like a description of a brawl or of domestic abuse rather than a sporting contest. Brents' statement that she had 'never felt so overpowered' reaffirms this description of a woman being beaten by Fox who is marked as having 'undergone a sex-change operation from a man to a woman'. Thus, the description of the bout subordinates sporting discourse and is reframed by a repertoire of social deviancy, specifically of violent criminal behaviour.

The article also discusses how, 'A double rapist... who had a £10,000 sex change on the NHS and changed his name to Jessica Winfield was moved to a women's prison.' Trans identities here are tied to criminal behaviour. In particular, male anatomy and physiology are presented as weapons in sexual assault. This crystallises a conception of trans people as deviant. This interdiscursivity manifests in the description of Fox's bout, as well as in the statement:

> A ruling in May 2016 by the Obama administration that state schools must allow transgender students to use toilets and changing rooms of the gender with which they identify led to a spate of cases where teenagers with male anatomy began using female lavatories.
>
> (Shipman, 2017)

This passage focuses specifically on the male anatomy of teenagers in the changing room recalling the previous excerpt from the same article which used male anatomy as a signifier of sexual assault. The same interdiscursive move is apparent in an article in *The Telegraph:* 'Trans activists want the right to self-identify, but opponents argue that reform of the act will mean there are no longer any "women-only" safe spaces, such as changing rooms and prisons' (Singh, 2018). Repertoires of criminality are deployed to construct trans athletes as not just deviant in a sporting context, but in a broader social one as well.

This position was reasserted in the number of articles dedicated to the attempted murder of a UK Athletes employee, Ralph Knibbs (Sheridan, 2016; Smith, 2017; Perraudin, 2017; Pidd, 2017). These articles tended to focus on the transgender identity of the athlete who attacked Knibbs. For example, *The Mirror* reads, 'Transgender athlete gets 18 years for murder bid: Knifing was frenzied, says judge' (Smith, 2017). The article reports, 'Born Michael Jameson, Jeska had a gender reassignment in 2000. She admitted attempted murder and actual bodily harm.' The transgender identity is placed at the forefront of the criminal attack. The same article states that, 'Birmingham crown court was told that she feared being exposed as transgender'. Thus, the gender status of the athlete is positioned as germane to the events. However, because of the mental and emotional stress that trans athletes feel at the risk of 'failing' sex tests and being removed from the sporting category that matches their identity, the sex-testing regulations and procedures themselves are also pertinent to the events. This facet of the events is mostly obscured, the only hint stemming from a quote from her parents, 'Stress had triggered a mental health crisis.' The lack of attention paid to these procedures and their impact highlights the entrenchment of narratives in which trans athletes are pathologised as unstable, violent and deviant, specifically as a result of their trans identity.

Conclusion

In this chapter we explored how sports media, in the context of the UK national press, constructs appropriate and recognisable athletic bodies in cisgender terms. With hegemonic masculinity and femininity so embedded in sporting discourses, we examined how this gender hegemony feeds into a fundamentally cisgender system. In particular, we considered how the bodies and identities of trans and intersex athletes are caught up in the boundary of legitimacy and intelligibility. This discursive process is enacted on medicolegal, political and ethical grounds. Trans and intersex athletes have marginal access to the sports media system. However, this access is dependent on the excision of all things non-binary from their identities. When non-binary aspects of gendered identities seep into sports media discourse, this is held up as proof of deviant behaviour and therefore justification for exclusion from participation (cf. Chapter 9, this volume).

Different rhetorical concepts are used to construct trans, intersex and non-binary athletes in different ways, and position them relative to each other and to cisgender women. The concept of what counts as natural, for example, is utilised in different ways at different times. Trans athletes in the female category are presented as being naturally male. However, their imagined testosterone levels are portrayed as unnatural, akin to doping or taking performance enhancing drugs. Relatedly, the concept of deviancy is rhetorically repositioned so trans athletes are portrayed as cheating for trying to procure an athletic advantage. In contrast to this deontological prescription of morality, trans athletes are then represented as deviant in teleological terms, when male puberty is described as having the same effect as doping for years. This highlights how sports media uses rhetorical concepts in fluid ways so as to constantly construct trans and intersex athletes as on the margins of intelligibility.

This rhetorical process shows a more fundamental disdain for non-binary identities in sports media. Trans and intersex athletes take up different peripheral positions in relation to the cisgender system. However, the discursive and practical contest that is enacted in relation to their positioning hints at a further excluded outsider to the cisgender sports media system – non-binary athletes. With this being the case, the non-binary experience is produced as the 'abject outside' (Butler, 1993) to the cisgender system with trans and intersex athletes recognisable in truncated ways whilst non-binary athletes remain excluded and inarticulable. Consequently, in UK sports press representations, trans, intersex and non-binary are constructed and function as 'a constitute outside to the subject' (Butler, 1993, p. 3). In other words, the cisgender subject is produced and secured through the abjection of the non-cisgender athlete's identity. This is evidenced in the mere seven articles related to non-binary sporting participation in the UK national press. The content of these articles also differs from trans and intersex athlete representations focusing on community and amateur sports rather than competitive ones. It is important not to collapse trans, intersex and non-binary athlete identities into each other and recognise that they take up different discursive positions in the UK press sports media. However, it is also germane that these different positions constitute the paradigmatic cisgender athlete as natural, normal and desirable. That is, trans, intersex and non-binary representations are used to constitute a cisgender sports media system. It is important to note, however, that the need to perpetually secure the cisgender system and binary male and female actors as its subjects, hints at its inherent instability. Thus, the contestation that trans and intersex athletes draw out of the cisgender sports media system represents the simultaneous stabilisation and destabilisation of that cisgender structure.

Notes

1 There has been a shift towards using the term 'differences of sexual development' (DSD) in the media and in some academic fields in recent years. However, we have chosen to use 'intersex' out of concern for the medicalised root of the DSD term. We feel that, at the current point of linguistic development, 'intersex' better recognises both the socially significant experiences of people with intersex characteristics and their representation in the LGBTIQ+ movement.

2 The significance of media technologies and broadcasting has been further emphasised following the resumption of sports without fans in stadiums after COVID-19 lockdown measures. As a result of the removal of spectators, sports events became entirely mediated spectacles.

3 The term 'non-cisgender' is imperfect as it reproduces a false dichotomy between trans and cis people. However, we use it here to encompass all identities that exist outside of the cisgenderist norm. The term 'trans' or 'transgender' can be used as an umbrella term to achieve the same thing, however, in this chapter 'trans' is distinct in our dataset from 'intersex' and 'non-binary'.

4 A search conducted between 21 March 2019 and 14 October 2020 for 'Transgender'+'-Sport', 'Intersex'+'Sport' and 'Non-binary'+'Sport', with search terms occurring at least three times in the article, brought back n=109, n=6 and n=4 articles respectively in the UK national press. The high number of transgender related sports articles is largely the result of coverage of World Rugby's decision to bar transgender women from competing in women's teams. There is a relative drop in intersex related articles in this time, most likely due to a shift towards the use of the term 'DSD' (a search for 'DSD'+'Sport' with the same parameters brought back 50 articles, the earliest in 2018). Non-binary athletes were discussed in four articles which remains low compared to transgender sports articles, however this is an increase compared to the seven articles that occurred prior to 20 March 2019.

5 Due to the limited number of articles referencing non-binary athletes there is only a small amount of empirical discussion of these identities.

References

Anderson, E. (2002). Openly gay athletes: Contesting hegemonic masculinity in a homophobic environment. *Gender & Society*, 16(6), 860–877. doi:10.1177/089124302237892.

Attenborough, F. (2016). A forgotten legacy? Towards a discursive psychology of the media. In C. Tileaga & E. Stokoe (Eds.) *Discursive Psychology: Classic and Contemporary Issues*. (pp.224–240). Oxon: Routledge.

Bennett, R. (2019, February 5). 'Women and non-binary' posters cause Cambridge student row. *The Times*.

Bermon, S., & Garnier, P-Y. (2017). Serum androgen levels and their relation to performance in track and field: Mass spectrometry results from 2127 observations in male and female elite athletes. *British Journal of Sports Medicine*, 51(17), 1531–1532. doi:10.1136/bjsports-2018-099700.

Billard, T. (2018). 'Passing' and the politics of deception: Transgender bodies, cisgender aesthetics, and the policing of inconspicuous marginal identities. In T. Duncan-Morgan (Ed.) *The Palgrave Handbook of Deceptive Communication* (pp.463–477). Palgrave Macmillan: Cham.

Blinde, E., & Taub, D. (1992). Homophobia and women's sport: The disempowerment of athletes. *Sociological Focus*, 25(2), 151–166. Retrieved April 10, 2020, from www.jstor.org/stable/20831616.

Bowcott, O. (2009, September 12). National: Intersex. *The Guardian*.

Braun, V., & Clarke, V. (2006). Using thematic analysis in psychology. *Qualitative Research in Psychology*, 3(2), 77–101. doi:10.1191/1478088706qp063oa.

Braun, V., & Clarke, V. (2019). Reflecting on reflexive thematic analysis. *Qualitative Research in Sport, Exercise and Health*, 11(4), 589–597. doi:10.1080/2159676X.2019.1628806.

Butler, J. (1993). *Bodies that Matter: On the Discursive Limits of Sex*. Oxon: Routledge.

Carey, J. (1989). *Communication as Culture: Essays on Media and Society*. London: Unwin Hyman.

CAS. (2019). Executive Summary. Retrieved from http://www.saflii.org/images/cassummary.pdf.

Chadwick, A. (2013). *The Hybrid Media System: Politics and Power*. Oxford: Oxford University Press.

Cleland, J., & Magrath R. (2020) Association football, masculinity, and sexuality: An evolving relationship. In R. Magrath, J. Cleland & E. Anderson (Eds.) *The Palgrave Handbook of Masculinity and Sport* (pp. 341–357). Cham: Palgrave Macmillan.

Connell, R.W., & Messerschmidt, J. (2005). Hegemonic masculinity: Rethinking the concept. *Gender & Society*, 19(6), 829–859. doi:10.1177/0891243205278639.

Cooky, C., & Dworkin, S. (2013). Policing the boundaries of sex: A critical examination of gender verification and the Caster Semenya controversy. *Journal of Sex Research*, 50(2), 103–111. doi:10.1080/00224499.2012.725488.

Cooky, C., Dycus, R., & Dworkin, S. (2013). 'What makes a woman a woman?' versus 'Our first lady of sport': A comparative analysis of the United States and the South African media coverage of Caster Semenya. *Journal of Sport & Social Issues*, 37(1), 31–56. doi:10.1177/0193723512447940.

Currah, P. (2006). Gender pluralisms under the transgender umbrella. In R.M. Juang, S. Minter, & P. Currah (Eds.) *Transgender Rights* (pp.3–31). Minneapolis: University of Minnesota Press.

Edwards, D. (2008). Intentionality and *mens rea* in police interrogations: The production of actions as crimes. *Intellectual Pragmatics*, 5(2), 177–199. doi: https://doi.org/10.1515/IP.2008.010.

Eklund, E., Berglund, B., Labrie, F., Carlstrom, K., Ekstrom, L., & Hirschberg, A. (2017). Serum androgen profile and physical performance in women Olympic athletes. *British Journal of Sports Medicine*, 2017(51), 1301–1308. doi:10.1136/bjsports-2017-097582.

Fausto-Sterling, A. (2000). *Sexing the Body*. New York: Basic Books.

Fausto-Sterling, A. (2018). Why sex is not binary: The complexity is more than cultural. It's biological too. *New York Times*. https://www.nytimes.com/2018/10/25/opinion/sex-biology-binary.html.

FIFA (2018, December 21). More than half the world watched record-breaking 2018 World Cup. Retrieved from https://www.fifa.com/worldcup/news/more-than-half-the-world-watched-record-breaking-2018-world-cup.

Fischer, M., & McClearen, J. (2020). Transgender athletes and the queer art of athletic failure. *Communication & Sport*, 8(2), 147–167. https://doi.org/10.1177/2167479518823207.

Gill, N. (2015, December 12). We are inter sex. *The Times*.

Graham, S. (2016, August 19). Mosquito pesticide linked to births of intersex children. *The Times*.

Hellen, N. (2018, April 22). Trans athletes face tougher entry rules in female events. *The Sunday Times*.

Halberstam, J. (2005) *In a Queer Time and Place: Transgender Bodies, Subcultural Lives*. New York: New York University Press.

Hogan, J. (2003). Staging the nation: Gendered and ethnicized discourses of national identity in Olympic opening ceremonies. *Journal of Sport & Social Issues*, 27(2), 100–123. https://doi.org/10.1177/0193732502250710.

IAAF. (2018). Eligibility regulations for the female classification (athletes with differences of sex development). Retrieved from https://www.worldathletics.org/news/press-release/eligibility-regulations-for-female-classifica.

Johnson, S. (2019, February 11). Highland Games in 'third gender' debate. *The Telegraph*.

Kelner, M., & Rudd, J. (2017, July 3). Caster Semenya could be forced to undertake hormone therapy for future Olympics. *The Guardian*.

Knott-Fayle, G., Peel, E., & Witcomb, G.L. (2021) (Anti-)feminism and cisgenderism in sports media. *Feminist Media Studies*. https://doi.org/10.1080/14680777.2021.1992644.

Lenskyj, H. (1994). Sexuality and femininity in sport contexts: Issues and alternatives. *Journal of Sport and Social Issues*, 18(4), 356–376.

Lenskyj, H. (2012). Reflections on communication and sport: On heteronormativity and gender identities. *Communication & Sport*, 1(1/2), 138–150. https://doi.org/10.1177/2167479512467327.

Lenskyj, H. (2013). *Gender Politics and the Olympic Industry*. Basingstoke: Palgrave Macmillan.

Lucas, C., & Newhall, K. (2018). Out of the frame: How sports media shapes trans narratives. In R. Magrath (Ed.) *LGBT Athletes in Sports Media* (pp. 99–124). Retrieved from https://ebookcentral.proquest.com.

Magrath, R. (Ed.) (2018). *LGBT Athletes in the Sports Media*. Retrieved from https://ebookcentral.proquest.com.

Messner, M. (1992). *Power at Play: Sports and the Problem of Masculinity*. Boston: Beacon Press.

Messner, M., Duncan, M., & Cooky, C. (2003). Silence, sports bras, and wrestling porn. *Journal of Sport & Social Issues*, 27(1), 38–51. doi:10.1177/0193-723502239583.

Messner, M., Michele, D., & Hunt, D. (2000). The televised sports manhood formula. *Journal of Sport & Social Issues*, 24(4), 380–394. https://doi.org/10.1177/0193723500244006.

Morgan, T. (2016, August 17). Denise Lewis: Semenya unfair on her rivals. *The Telegraph*.

Navratilova, M. (2019, February 17). The rules on trans athletes reward cheats an punish the innocent. *The Sunday Times*.

Ofcom. (2019). News consumption in the UK: 2019. Retrieved from https://www.ofcom.org.uk/__data/assets/pdf_file/0027/157914/uk-news-consumption-2019-report.pdf.

Pattinson, R. (2019, February 5). Students clash in gender gym row. *The Sun*.

Perraudin, F. (2017, March 14). Champion runner jailed for attempted murder of UK Athletics official. *The Guardian*.

Pidd, H. (2017, March 15). Jailed transgender fell runner thought UK Athletics was 'trying to kill her'. *The Guardian.*

Potter, J. (1996). *Representing Reality: Discourse, Rhetoric and Social Construction.* London: Sage.

Potter, J., & Wetherell, M. (1987). *Discourse and Social Psychology.* London: Sage.

Schultz, J. (2014). *Qualifying Times: Points of Change in U.S. Women's Sport.* Chicago: University of Illinois Press.

Sharpe, A. (2017). Queering judgement: The case of gender identity fraud. *The Journal of Criminal Law*, 81(5), 417–435. https://doi.org/10.1177/0022018317728828.

Sheridan, D. (2016, September 23). Transgender runner tried to murder athletics chief. *The Times.*

Shin, J. (2014). Clad with national identity: Parade uniforms of the Olympic Games. *International Journal of Fashion Design, Technology and Education*, 7(3), 208–244. doi:10.1080/17543266.2014.960900.

Shipman, T. (2017, July 23). Sex changes spark new dilemmas: Sport, prisons and schools are struggling to deal with the rise of transgender rights. *The Times.*

Silk, M. (2014). Neoliberalism and sports mega-events. In J. Grix (Ed.) *Leveraging Legacies from Sports Mega-events* (pp. 50–60). Basingstoke: Palgrave Macmillan.

Silk, M., & Andrews, D. (2001). Beyond a boundary? Sport, transnational advertising, and the reimagining of national culture. *Journal of Sport & Social Issues*, 25(2), 180–201. doi:10.1177/0193723501252005.

Singh, A. (2018, December 22). Navratilova accused of transphobia for saying gender matters in sport. *The Telegraph.*

Smith, L. (2017, March 15). Transgender athlete gets 18 years for murder bid. *The Mirror.*

Sonksen, P., Bavington, L., Boehning, T., Cowan, D., Guha, N., Holt, R., Karkazis, K., Ferguson-Smith, M., Mercetic, J., & Bohning, D. (2018). Hyperandrogenism controversy in elite women's sport: An examination and critique of recent evidence. *British Journal of Sports Medicine*, 52(23), 1481–1482. doi:10.1136/bjsports-2017-098464.

Spencer, N. (2003). 'America's sweetheart' and 'Czech-mate': A discursive analysis of the Evert-Navratilova Rivalry. *Journal of Sport & Social Issues*, 27(1), 18–37. doi:10.1177/0193–723502239582.

Statista. (2016, August 18). Olympic Games: TV viewership worldwide 2002–2016. Retrieved from https://www.statista.com/statistics/287966/olympic-games-tv-viewership-worldwide/.

Tredway, K. (2014). Judith Butler redux – The heterosexual matrix and the out lesbian athlete: Amélie Mauresmo, gender performance, and women's professional tennis. *Journal of the Philosophy of Sport*, 41(2), 163–176. doi:10.1080/00948705.2013.785420.

Valentine, D. (2007). *Imagining Transgender: An Ethnography of a Category.* Durham: Duke University Press.

Wetherell, M., & Potter, J. (1992). *Mapping the Language of Racism: Discourse and the Legitimation of Exploitation.* Hemel Hampstead: Harvester Wheatsheaf.

Wiggins, S. (2017). *Discursive Psychology.* London: Sage.

Williams, R. (2011, February 26) Oscar Pistorius and Caster Semenya's running battle to reach starting blocks. *The Guardian.*

Ziegler, M. (2019, January 11). Who should be allowed to compete as a woman? *The Times.*

Chapter 9

Ripping up the Rulebook

Challenges and Opportunities in Moving Beyond the Binary

H.J.H. Newman and G.L. Witcomb

Introduction

The number of people identifying as transgender or non-binary is increasing in the UK (Fielding & Bass, 2018) and worldwide (Arcelus et al., 2015). While these individuals continue to face stigma and discrimination, often perpetuated by misrepresentations in the media (Knott-Fayle et al., 2021), there is a gradual acceptance that sex assigned at birth (based on physical sexual characteristics) may not match the gender with which a person identifies. While this acceptance is positive and has influenced developments such as proposed reforms to the UK Gender Recognition Act (Government Equalities Office, 2018), it does raise a number of important issues that are more difficult to reconcile. One of these is participation in sport and the premise of fairness, on which the need for sex segregation is often based, and which serves to undermine transgender and non-binary people's right to participate.

In some competitive sports, attributes believed to be central to performance are used to group athletes into different categories. For example, weight categories in boxing and wrestling or handicaps in golf. In some sports, athletes are sometimes also segregated by age (e.g., junior, senior, and masters' categories). Such categorisations are often essential and sensible to ensure that athletes are set against each other in equitable ways. However, in most sports (e.g., boxing; WBA, 2019), these are secondary-level categorisations. The primary categorisation has happened prior to this; silently and without question. That is the categorisation based on sex.

Sex segregation occurs in many sports (see further Schultz, 2018; Chapter 2). It is argued that where there are physiological advantages of the male body that render mixed sex competition inequitable for women, and/or pose an unacceptable risk of injury (Pike, 2020), sex segregated categories are essential for ensuring fair and meaningful participation in the female category. However, it is also the case that in many instances within sport, for example where there is no clear physiological advantage or disadvantage, sex segregation is largely a result of historical sociocultural norms which have served to uphold traditional gender orders, often sexualising women's sports (Boykoff & Yasuoka, 2015)

DOI: 10.4324/9781003050568-9

and consequently sport has maintained its perceived sanctity as a male preserve (Hargreaves, 1994; Schultz, 2018). Consequently, sex segregation is deeply engrained in how we organise and practice sports (Anderson, 2008) to the extent that sport can be considered the last powerful institution upholding discriminatory, sexist ideologies (Milner & Braddock, 2016).

The sex segregation of sport causes particular problems for transgender people. For transgender women, and to a lesser extent transgender men, concerns that birth-sex physiology and puberty (Handelsman, 2017) may provide unfair advantages (depending on the sport) compared to their cisgender[1] competitors serves to exclude them from participating in their identified gender category. The situation is even more desperate for non-binary people who have no category to participate in at all, or are forced to choose between competing in a men's or women's category based on which causes them less discomfort, and whether policies and regulations allow them to. This is not only uncomfortable due to feelings of invalidation and being misgendered (Johnson et al., 2020), but can also raise issues related to fairness, particularly if prescribed testosterone is being used as part of medical transition due to it being a regulated substance (World Anti-Doping Agency, 2018).

Increasingly, suggestions of how sports can be more fully inclusive of transgender people have looked towards a total re-envisioning of competition that sees sex segregation eradicated (e.g., Kerr & Obel, 2017). Another example is Harper's (2017) suggestion that all athletes are subject to a scientifically determined performance-based metric that assigns them an 'athletic gender'. This may or may not align with their experienced gender, but this is argued to be less important if athletic gender is merely for participation purposes, and it is accepted that this does not affect self-identified and lived gender outside of the sporting arena. While this is a plausible possibility, for many individuals such incongruence between sporting-life and lived-life categories would be psychologically uncomfortable (Elling-Machartzki, 2017). Another sex- and gender-neutral classification idea suggested by Shin (2017) is to categorise athletes based on bioavailable testosterone, resulting in groups of high and low testosterone classes. However, this classification suggests that higher levels of testosterone result in greater athletic ability, which is widely debated and, as argued by Jordan-Young and Karkazis (2019), is wrongly misunderstood. A further possibility that may only be applicable to some individual sports is to classify athletes according to their capabilities, within a totally sex and gender-free arena.

The concept of performance-related categorisation is not new. Indeed, one only has to look to the Paralympics to see a functioning example of how such categorisation takes place. In para-sports, participants are categorised according to their functional movement capabilities, irrespective of sex. The Paralympics is a beacon of social inclusion and is the world's third biggest sporting event (after the Olympics and FIFA World Cup). Indeed, the 2016 Rio Paralympic Games saw 4,328 athletes from 159 countries, compete in 22 sports, with a TV audience of 4.1 billion people in more than 150 countries, and 2.15 million tickets sold (International Olympic Committee, 2020). Clearly, meaningful categorisations that allow for fair competition can take place irrespective of sex, and arguably able-bodied sport could be drawing upon some of these alternatives. This has been previously suggested by Kerr and Obel (2017) who used the example of the change in disability sport from a medical to a functional classification system to propose a model for able-bodied sport which involves classifying bodies based on functional ability across multiple traits as an alternative to sex segregation.

Thus, we argue that categorisations based on other attributes related to performance, rather than sex and/or gender as the primary and only categorisation, have three important advantages. Firstly, for applicable sports, it does not undermine the principles of fair and equitable participation for women, since participants are grouped according to ability. Secondly, removing sex segregation equalises the disparity (in importance, attention, funding etc.) observed between male and female sports, thereby elevating the status of female sports. Finally, and importantly, the removal of sex segregated categories opens the door for the participation of individuals of all gender identities, without the need for regulations to dictate under what circumstances (i.e., medical interventions) participation is permitted. The emergence of a small number of grassroots level sporting competitions that are not sex segregated, such as the one that forms the focus of this chapter, can provide valuable insight into the challenges and opportunities that arise when sex and/or gender is not the primary principle in the categorisation of athletes.

In this chapter we describe a sporting event, *Limitless*, that has embraced the idea of performance-related categorisation of athletes, and was developed to promote participation of all genders, with no sex segregation. Conceived and organised by the first author, in this chapter we provide a personal account of the coming of the event, followed by the findings of a qualitative investigation into the attitudes and opinions of those who took part or were spectators at the inaugural *Limitless* event in 2018.

Limitless

Limitless is a competition based on a sport usually referred to as Strongman or Strongwoman. Less commonly, the sport is referred to by the gender-neutral term 'strength athletics', which is the term we use in this chapter. Strength athletics is probably most well-known for its *World's Strongest Man* competition, which was established in 1977, and has been televised in a number of different countries, including the UK and USA. Strength athletics tests competitors' physical capacity in several different ways. A typical competition consists of 4–6 strength and power-based events which may vary between competitions, but typically are a combination of static tests of strength (such as the deadlift and overhead press), with more dynamic tests of strength (which combine strength, power, speed, and endurance; for example, the farmers walk and the vehicle pull).

Limitless arose through my own (first author) search for spaces to compete in strength-sports as a non-binary person. At the point of coming out as non-binary and beginning to take masculinising hormone treatment, I had been competing in strongwoman competitions for three to four years. Strength athletics is a relatively small sport with no official governing body, and so there were no formal rules or policies in place that would have necessarily stopped me from continuing to compete in strongwoman events. However, I began to feel increasingly uncomfortable with having to be prescribed a female label in order to compete in such events. Therefore, I decided to distance myself from strongwoman, and women's sport more broadly. However, this meant I struggled to find spaces to compete that felt right for me, having to choose between men's and women's categories, neither of which felt like a good fit. After discussions with my coach (who is also the owner of the strength and conditioning gym I was training out of), about my options and the lack of potential spaces for me to compete, we decided to host a competition at the gym that would be inclusive to anyone, regardless of their gender. *Limitless* was the result.

Limitless adopts the traditional format of a strength athletics competition (4–6 events, such as those described previously). However, instead of having 'men's' and 'women's' categories for competitors, there are three ability-based categories – Level 1, Level 2, and Level 3 – which increase in difficulty. In Level 1, competitors are required to lift the lightest weights, getting heavier for Level 2, and in Level 3 competitors are required to lift the heaviest weights. Anyone of any gender can enter any of the levels. Each competitor simply enters the category that best suits their ability-level, based on the prescribed weights to be lifted in each event. Entry level is self-selected, which is a standard entry procedure across most novice and intermediate level strength athletics competitions (Newman, 2020).

Limitless is held annually at a strength and conditioning gym in the Midlands, UK. The inaugural *Limitless* was held in 2018 and the venue is a strength-sport focused gym, open to anyone on a membership basis, that is primarily equipped for functional fitness, strength athletics, powerlifting, and Olympic weightlifting activities. *Limitless* is promoted via social media as a sporting event open to anyone, regardless of gender/sex, and hence, inclusive of all genders. In terms of competitor numbers, the inaugural *Limitless* was small. There were eight competitors; two non-binary people (one being the first author of this chapter), one genderfluid person, three cisgender women and two cisgender men competing across Levels 1 and 2. There were no entries for Level 3. The second competition, held in 2019, attracted a much larger 33 competitors across the three ability-based categories, the majority of whom were cisgender.

In the remainder of this chapter, we analyse competitor and spectator attitudes and opinions of *Limitless* using data from interviews that were conducted following the inaugural competition in 2018.

Opportunities and Challenges: Competitor and Spectator Attitudes and Opinions of *Limitless*

Despite the small number of competitors, the inaugural *Limitless* competition garnered much interest, both on social media[2] and from spectators on the day.

While all positive, we were interested in discovering more about both competitors' and spectators' attitudes and opinions of the event. While these data would be useful for understanding how the competition could be improved in future years, the main aim was to explore what individuals really thought about the concepts of non-sex segregated events, all-gender inclusive sports, and fairness in sport in relation to gender beliefs.

Thus, we conducted ten semi-structured interviews with competitors and spectators, including six of the other seven competitors on the day (excluding the first author), and four spectators. The six competitors interviewed consisted of three cisgender women, one cisgender man, one non-binary person, and one genderfluid person, with a mean age of 38.8 years. The four spectators interviewed were all cisgender women, with a mean age of 34.3 years. The interview asked participants questions related to 1) their participation and interest in the *Limitless* event, 2) the perceived success of the event, 3) their understanding or experiences of barriers to participation related to gender identity, and 4) their opinions on how sport can be more inclusive of gender diverse athletes.

The interviews were conducted by the first author in June and July 2018 (1–2 months post-competition) following ethical approval from Loughborough University ethics committee. Where possible, interviews were conducted in person at the gym where the competition was held. Where this was not possible, the interviews were conducted via telephone. The interviews lasted approximately 30 minutes each, were transcribed verbatim, and analysed using thematic analysis. Four themes were identified that highlight the complexity of sporting events that challenge the gender and/or sex binaries in sport. These themes are *Challenging the Binary versus Further Marginalisation* – which explores the potential trade-off between further inclusion and further segregation from mainstream sport that participants felt may occur through the development of events such as *Limitless; Support and Blind Acceptance* – which demonstrates the overwhelming support participants showed both for *Limitless* and broader inclusion of gender and/or sex diverse athletes, despite some admitting having never given the topic much previous thought; *Fear for Diminishing Women's Achievements* – which presents concerns some participants had around less sex segregation in sport and the impact it may have for female athletes; and finally *Overwhelming Challenge* – which conveys the weight of the challenge participants felt in attempting to reconcile potential conflicts between their two positions of support for the inclusion of gender and/or sex diverse athletes, and the fears of some for women's achievements. In this section of the chapter, we use these identified themes to further explore and discuss competitor and spectator attitudes and opinions of the inaugural *Limitless* competition.

Challenging the Binary versus Further Marginalisation

This theme explores the potential trade-off between further inclusion in mainstream sport and further segregation from mainstream sport that participants felt could occur for gender and/or sex diverse participants through the development of more events, such as *Limitless*, that are not sex segregated. When asked about their opinions of all-gender inclusion in sport, participants were overall supportive of less sex segregation, acknowledging the complexity and difficulty in providing opportunities for gender and/or sex diverse competitors in sex segregated categories. When discussing the potential benefits of less sex segregated sport, spectator Clara highlighted its importance for inclusion:

> 'It's just nice to be competing with anyone. And the best thing about it for me is you're not excluding people because the more rules and stipulations you put on, you know not just that male, female, weight category whatever else, each time you make a segregation you are excluding some people. And that's the thing do we actually want to be incorporating more and more rules? We should be encouraging people to compete.' *Clara, spectator, cisgender woman*

Clara's focus here appears to be on grassroots participation, and encouraging more people to take part, rather than elite sport. Many sporting organisations and governing bodies are now distinguishing between recreational and elite sport in their transgender inclusion policies (e.g., England and Wales Cricket Board, 2020). Clara's supportive view of less sex segregated sport was also echoed by Susan (*spectator, cisgender woman*), who said: 'It keeps everybody included, that to me is the most important thing not just in sport but in life in general… if those divides are taken down everybody can get involved.' Speaking specifically about *Limitless*, Susan also discussed the potential resistance to less sex segregated sport and the importance of awareness and visibility in breaking down barriers to the inclusion of gender and/or sex diverse people in sport:

> 'I think there were a few people there that weren't sure what to expect or how it was going to be and I think it definitely helped open other people's eyes and obviously it got quite a lot of social media attention which was fantastic. I didn't see any negative comments or feedback from it so I just think, hopefully you used a really good platform there to get your point across so to speak and you did. Everybody enjoyed it and I think for the people that were there and did look at it on social media it's broken down some barriers for them to know, you know, that it is okay to talk about it.' *Susan, spectator, cisgender woman*

Susan's suggestion here that some may need encouragement to talk about topics around the participation of gender and/or sex diverse people in sport is perhaps a sign of the highly contested and polarised views around transgender issues in the UK at the time (Peel & Newman, 2020); that the topic is seen as 'taboo' or that conversations about it are difficult to have. Other difficulties in implementing less sex segregated sport were expressed by participants, even though they were supportive of it. Tom, a competitor, expressed support for the categorisation of athletes in strength athletics by ability, but also drew attention to the potential difficulties in moderating who enters which category. However, he did also allude to this being a difficulty for strength athletics more broadly, including in other sex segregated competitions.

> 'It does work completely. You know, whether or not there should be some sort of, if the event was to become a very large event, you know some sort of qualifying. Just something like that where people – or they've got to show past competitions that are done or show how they competed there and then that way of like gauging it… it's the way that people in general may not stand by their abilities… that's, you know, the sport and industry in general, you know, not something that's a reflection on *Limitless* as I feel it did work really well with the weight categories.' *Tom, competitor, cisgender man*

Whilst supportive of less sex segregated sport, and of the categorisation of athletes by ability level, spectator Emma expressed concern as to how far the concept could go beyond smaller, less mainstream sporting events such as *Limitless*, due to the focus on money in elite sport and the financial implications of restructuring a sport in such a radical way.

> 'To be honest I think it's going to have some limits, but purely because of the money involved in certain sport. Particularly like football and things like that, the amount of money that goes into it and to make it a certain thing. It would be interesting to see how that develops over the next few years to be honest… It's so money driven sometimes like the essence of sport and the person who is doing the sport is lost really isn't it?' *Emma, spectator, cisgender woman*

Overall, the sense from both competitors and spectators was that they were supportive of a move towards less sex segregated sport, and were supportive of the ability-based model of categorisation used in *Limitless*. However, they also anticipated both logistical difficulties and resistance from others in the introduction of less sex segregated sport on a wider scale, particularly in elite and mainstream sport settings. It was recognised by some participants that sporting events with less sex/gender segregation are mostly smaller, non-mainstream sports as opposed to high profile mainstream sports. Hari (*competitor, gender-fluid*) listed some examples: 'There are some sports where the teams are mixed, like Quidditch… Ultimate Frisbee… Roller Derby… but none of them are mainstream.' This is arguably reflective of the potential challenges in the scope to develop less sex segregated sport identified by Emma earlier in this theme. In smaller, non-mainstream sports there are often fewer financial implications to restructuring competitions, and their often less organised and less governed nature means there is more freedom for organisers to structure their events in different ways. Karen (*competitor, cisgender woman*) also raised a point pertaining to the potential difficulties when sports and/or sporting events are high profile as opposed to when they are non-mainstream and lesser known, including the potential for competitors to take advantage of inclusive policies for reasons of competitive advantage: 'I guess in the elite level and national elite levels sort of, it's a bit different because people will unfortunately try and take advantage in every which way they can… you know at top levels of sport that's what they'll do.'

If the inclusion of gender diversity via less sex segregation is restricted to smaller, non-mainstream sports, one potential concern raised from this is the notion of further marginalisation; that gender and sex diverse people who wish to engage in sport are confined to small, non-mainstream sports and/or events and are further segregated from mainstream sport. One high profile example of a sporting event designed to have an inclusive environment specifically for LGBTQ+ people is the Gay Games (Federation of Gay Games, 2020). Events such as these often provide a safe space for gender and/or sex diverse people to engage in sport, something which has been found to be a facilitator to transgender sport and exercise engagement (Jones et al., 2017), but can also be viewed by some as a way of further segregating or marginalising gender and/or sex diverse people in sport and exercise.

Emma, a spectator, suggested that further marginalisation and/or segregation does not need to be the case in the emergence of events such as *Limitless*, describing how at the event the notion of 'difference' was not prominent, and instead the focus was on competing in the event, just as in any other sporting venture.

> 'We knew it was a competition organised in a different way, but it wasn't made a big deal of on the day, does that make sense? So this is a competition that is based on ability, we know the reasons why it's been organised in this way, but actually we're just going to enjoy it for what it is, and that's what I liked about it. The whole point of making it inclusive is not by saying "oh we're different because of these reasons", we're just here to do lifting and putting back down and that's what everyone did, and it was fun.' *Emma, spectator, cisgender woman*

For Tom, a competitor, the organisation of *Limitless* as a non-gendered competition that was designed to be inclusive of gender and sex diverse competitors caused some internal conflict and discomfort as to what his place could be in an event organised that way.

> 'I felt that with being just a white male of yeah, you know, the average Joe in the UK so to speak, going up against, like having to go up against female or transgender people I felt like I didn't know what my place was, do you know what I mean?' *Tom, competitor, cisgender man*

This alludes to the potential for events organised in this way to be perceived as 'events only for transgender people' as opposed to 'events for anyone', a perception that would increase the potential for further marginalisation, and a notion that we discuss further in the conclusion of this chapter. Overall then competitors and spectators interviewed perceived less sex segregated sport as having both potential positives for the inclusion of gender and/or sex diverse athletes through its challenging of the binary, but also potential negatives of further marginalisation and segregation if events are perceived only to be for those athletes.

Support and Blind Acceptance

This theme explores the overwhelming support that participants showed both for *Limitless* and the broader inclusion of gender and/or sex diverse athletes in sport, despite some admitting having never given the topic much previous thought prior to their involvement in the event. Overall, there was a positive response to the competition from both competitors and spectators, who described it as a successful event with an inclusive, supportive atmosphere. For both Alex and Hari, *Limitless* was their first experience of competing in a strength-based competition, and both had minimal involvement with strength-sport prior to the event. Alex (*competitor, non-binary*) described the spirit they felt amongst competitors and spectators as a key part of their experience of the day: 'it was pretty impressive and yeah just the whole way it was set up it was really interesting. The communal spirit, although it's a solo sport it doesn't feel like a solo sport. Yeah the whole thing was just really good fun.' This sentiment was echoed by Hari, who described the support they received from other competitors and spectators at the event.

> 'The atmosphere was amazing. Everybody was supportive, everybody was just happy to be there. They didn't care how much you lifted, it didn't matter how small you are, how big you are, everyone was going to cheer you on the same amount. Everyone was really nice and accommodating.'
> *Hari, competitor, genderfluid*

Clara (*spectator, cisgender woman*) expressed her support for the concept and structure of *Limitless* as being categorised by ability level as opposed to gender: 'it doesn't matter who you are, what you are, how heavy you are. Your own levels. If you want to have a go at that level it doesn't matter. Just have a go.' Laura, also a spectator at the event, further highlighted how she felt this structure helped to place emphasis on what she felt mattered more, the physical task at hand and the ability to complete it, rather than 'who you are' as a competitor.

> 'I'm all for it. I think it was great, it was brilliant, and it was nice to get loads of different people together… I think that it worked really well because

> it is about the weight and it's about your ability rather than who you are or what you are... If you know you can lift that weight it doesn't discriminate or doesn't target anyone in particular, just it's your level isn't it, your strength level.' *Laura, spectator, cisgender woman*

Laura's focus here on ability and the physical task at hand alludes to the perception that strength athletics lends itself particularly well to an ability-based model in that it is an individual, non-contact sport and is relatively objective – i.e., you can either lift a weight (for example 100 kilograms) or you cannot. Other sports may have different challenges – for example, ability-level may be more subjective. A sport like football could be one example of this, where it is common for there to be disagreements between people and their judgements as to who is the best player in a certain position. It could be argued that in these cases there is potential for the discrimination on the basis of sex and/or gender that Laura feels the ability-based model can help eradicate, as it could be disguised as ability-based selections. In other sports though, where ability-level can be measured using more objective performance-related markers, such as the weight lifted in strength athletics or qualifying times for a 100-metre race for example, this may be less of a concern.

Laura also indicated that the inclusive atmosphere of the event is in line with strength athletics as a sport more generally, which is known to have a strong sense of community (Newman, 2020). This suggests that the differing structure of categorisation of *Limitless* did not detract from what is widely deemed as one of the key characteristics of the sport more widely, its community spirit and support.

> 'My first competition I did, I did not know what to expect... Everybody had said about the inclusiveness and the support and everybody helps everybody. Until you go to a competition or get involved you don't really get that until you're part of it... By the end of the competition you've made new friends and you've got contacts, and everybody knows your name, and everybody is cheering for everyone and it's such a weird but really nice experience.' *Laura, spectator, cisgender woman*

This level of support and community spirit is something that is expressed as surprising to some who have not been involved in strength athletics before, which could be posited as being because of its 'intimidating' exterior, as it was labelled by Alex. This surprise was demonstrated by spectator Susan.

> 'The atmosphere surprised me. I know it was a competition, but it didn't feel like a competition because everybody was having so much fun and enjoying themselves and cheering each other on even if it was cheering the person that could've won or beat you but people still cheering them on. Cheering on people that I've never met before but just everybody was cheering on people they didn't know.' *Susan, spectator, cisgender woman*

The positive response to the event was, therefore, demonstrated by both the competitors and spectators that we interviewed after the inaugural *Limitless* event. The enthusiasm demonstrated for the event highlighted the community spirit and support amongst all in attendance on the day, but also indicated support for the non-gendered, performance-based categorisation of competitors in the event, as demonstrated in the previous theme.

In addition to their support of the *Limitless* event, all participants were also highly accepting of gender and/or sex diverse athletes, and inclusive sporting policies and events more broadly, demonstrating unequivocal support for gender and/or sex diverse athletes to be included in sport and physical activity. For example, Laura (*spectator, cisgender woman*) affirmed that 'there shouldn't be any exclusion' and Karen (*competitor, cisgender woman*) also expressed her views on inclusion: 'any kind of mixing- just makes the world a better place'. Similarly, Clara demonstrated her view that no one should be excluded from sport because of who they are.

> 'It's always been the definition of "you are this, you are that, you have to fit into that little box". There are more and more people who are becoming much more self-aware or actually you know I don't fit that f**king box, but why should they be excluded from doing something they love, whatever sport it may be. I don't think anybody should be forced to say well I can't do it because I can't go to that because it's not fair. We can have something where anyone can compete, it just makes it fairer for everyone and everyone competes in the same way.' *Clara, spectator, cisgender woman*

Susan, a spectator, acknowledged though that whilst she was also accepting and supportive of gender and/or sex diverse athletes, the issue of their inclusion in sport was not something that she had ever given much thought to before being involved in *Limitless*.

> 'Until you put the event together it wasn't actually something that really crossed my mind… it did make me think a bit more like how obviously it would make people feel if they're not comfortable in that specific box… it's not fair on other people that they've got to feel like they've got to fit into that box… without doubt I believe things should be based on ability… if that individual wants to take part against any other individual then they should be allowed, it's the individual taking part making the decision, not the rest of us. It keeps everybody included, that to me is the most important thing not just in sport but in life in general. People shouldn't feel they can't do something because of who they are.' *Susan, spectator, cisgender woman*

Tom (*competitor, cisgender man*) expressed a similar unfamiliarity with the topic prior to his involvement in *Limitless*: 'I'm just a white average male that was raised by mum and dad and I've not really had the exposure to any of these issues that people may have, you know.' The points raised here by Clara, Susan and Tom could be argued as indicating a blind acceptance of less sex segregated sport and the inclusion of gender and/or sex diverse athletes in sport – they feel strongly that they support inclusion but admit not having much prior knowledge about the complexities of doing so.

The support for the inclusion of gender and/or sex diverse athletes in sport was unanimous amongst all the competitors and spectators that we interviewed. The more difficult question for these participants was not the question of whether these athletes should be included, but rather the one of how this inclusion should take place, as we explore further in the *fear for diminishing women's achievements* and *overwhelming challenge* themes in the remainder of this section.

Fear for Diminishing Women's Achievements

Fear for women's achievements was highlighted by many of the participants we interviewed as an important consideration for performance-related categorisation in sport. As previously discussed, all the participants demonstrated unequivocal support for the inclusion of gender and/or sex diverse athletes, and support for less sex segregation in sport. This though did not mean that they did not foresee potential challenges in doing so. In particular, some participants highlighted potential difficulties for women's sport and the achievements of female athletes in the removal of sex segregation in sport.

For spectator Laura, her fears for women's sport were grounded on the basis of biological differences between men and women, and thus the potential disadvantage cisgender women might face if they are competing against a transgender woman.

> 'Obviously, a man is always going to be stronger than a lady that's just how they are… I don't know, it's difficult because they obviously want to live their life like a lady… and it's like their sport and they want to compete but by the same token it's slightly unfair… Because on like the one hand if that's how you know they feel that they want to live as a woman they should be able to do that and do everything else but then is it fair against other ladies?' *Laura, spectator, cisgender woman*

Laura's use of the terms 'lady' and 'ladies' here is interesting, given the drive in recent years to shift to the term 'women' rather than 'ladies' in sporting contexts due to the latter's connotations of physical fragility and reinforcement of sexist stereotypes (Tomas, 2021). Laura's assumption that 'a man is always going to be stronger' also reinforces these stereotypes. These fears for women in sport were also present for Laura when considering the notion of categorisation by ability as opposed to sex and/or gender in other sports such as athletics for example.

> 'My only thought would be that you know in some way it might make maybe ladies feel a bit less at the top of their sport, you know when you're in a group with a man who can run 100 metres 2 seconds faster than you and you're never going to beat him because of genetics and whatever, does it pose that problem, it might demean you know a lady's training or effort.' *Laura, spectator, cisgender woman*

In discussions around inclusion, testosterone – a regulated substance (World Anti-Doping Agency, 2018) – is often placed as the most important factor when considering the biological differences that Laura was referring to. Alex – a non-binary person assigned female at birth and taking prescribed testosterone – discussed this and their worries about therefore having an advantage against the cisgender women they were competing against in Level 1 of *Limitless*.

> 'I kind of, I do worry that I had an advantage because of my category obviously as I said I just wandered in and won, and I do worry that that was because I was the only one there who was demonstratively on testosterone. I don't like taking an illegal drug, so I felt a bit like a drug cheat… I don't know how true that is, there are some studies that sort of like testosterone isn't the most important thing etc. but then I know for myself that I have improved in strength through no real work on my own, through taking testosterone, so I am a bit conflicted with that one I think.' *Alex, competitor, non-binary*

For Jess, a competitor, the concerns around women's sport were more focused on how comfortable women may be in training and competing alongside men, and the preservation of single sex/single gender sporting spaces, than the biological differences and perceived advantages or disadvantages.

> 'I know like a lot of the women I work out with that are kind of like as strong as me but yeah they would never go and lift with the lads, or whatever, but I don't care I lift with anyone. But I think that's the only other thing so it might put, I don't know what guys think but for a female for sure it might put some females off certain sports. Because I think more yeah, I think more females like to just train and play with other females and I think that would possibly be one kind of drawback for sure.' *Jess, competitor, cisgender woman*

Tom, a competitor, though, described how he was prompted to think about his previous perception that men would always have an advantage over women after his closely fought battle for second place in Level 2 of *Limitless* with a cisgender female competitor.

> 'I thought to myself you know we are like neck and neck after the first event and wow you know I've really got to push myself and I felt like I

> really had to go for it to be able to just keep in front of her… just to be able to push me she's really trained hard, then it just makes me think you've really trained hard for this as well as I have and it's like we deserve to be able to compete on the same field definitely.' *Tom, competitor, cisgender man*

In this discussion, Tom suggested that this close competition with a cisgender woman had encouraged him to further consider his thoughts on how sport should or shouldn't be categorised. On one hand, the close battle described here between a cisgender man and a cisgender woman in the inaugural *Limitless*, and the placing of a cisgender woman above cisgender men in Level 2 of the second *Limitless* that was held in 2019, are both examples that challenge Laura's earlier assumption that all men will be stronger than all women and instead support the argument that biological differences between male and female bodies do not have to mean that the male body will always be stronger than the female body. However, on the other hand, considering the sex and/or gender make-up of the 33 competitors across the three performance categories in the second 2019 competition, cisgender women made up the majority of Level 1 and cisgender men made up the entirety of Level 3, with the most gender and/or sex diversity occurring in the middle category, Level 2. This is not to suggest though that there are not cisgender women in existence who are capable of entering Level 3, as can be evidenced by looking at the weights lifted by cisgender women in other sex segregated strongwoman competitions, particularly at national and international level (e.g., Lockridge, 2020).

In the introduction to this chapter, we proposed that, for applicable sports, this performance-based categorisation does not undermine the principles of fair and equitable participation for women, since participants are grouped according to ability. Secondly, we proposed that by removing sex segregation, it equalises the disparity (in importance, attention, funding etc.) observed between male and female sports. For those interview participants who placed focus on the biological differences between male and female bodies, there still appeared to be some concern for women's achievements in the sense that even if all competitors are grouped by ability, these matters of biology could mean that it is only 'male-bodied' athletes who are able to compete in the highest ability categories. Taking that perspective, this would be attributed to their biological make-up, meaning that they would be the ones who are the strongest and who can run fastest or be able to throw the furthest, for example.

Overall, participants' overwhelming support for the inclusion of gender and/or sex diverse athletes, combined with the fears of some for women's achievements, meant that many therefore felt it was an overwhelming challenge to consider how these two positions could be reconciled and appropriate methods of inclusion adopted in sport going forward, as we will discuss in the next, final theme of this section.

Overwhelming Challenge

Despite their unequivocal acceptance of gender and/or sex diverse athletes, many of the participants identified potential challenges to less sex segregation in sport, including but not limited to their fear for women's achievements. Their lack of awareness of how these challenges could be overcome presented the issue as an overwhelming challenge. For example, Laura (*spectator, cisgender woman*) voiced her lack of ideas as to how the challenge should be overcome: 'I don't know, it is difficult… it's a difficult one that… I think you could be debating it for many hours' and Karen (*competitor, cisgender woman*) also expressed the perceived difficulty of it for her: 'I don't think there is really any reason not to, I just think that it'll be quite challenging to do it, you know it's not going to be easy'. Susan, a spectator, also expressed the view that less sex segregation in sport would be more difficult at higher performance levels of sport than at grassroots and community level sporting opportunities such as *Limitless* due to the increased difficulties in regulating competitors by ability level.

> 'The trouble is the regulation at this level, at that level of that competition I think would have self-regulated because people would be going what were you doing in this competition or why are you in this group you should have been in that group… I think there'd be a certain amount of self-regulation and encouraging people to be in the right groups and so on, I think a little bit further up that's where the regulation would, will be more difficult definitely.' *Susan, spectator, cisgender woman*

When considering the biological differences that were raised by some participants in their fear for women's achievements, Susan displayed optimism at the possibility of this being able to be managed, but again admitted not knowing what that would look like or how it would occur.

> 'I don't really know that much about testosterone. Obviously, I know like males have it more than females, but as to the advantage it gives you over sport, surely there's going to be ways, there must be a way of managing that. I don't know how that would be but there must be a way of managing that.' *Susan, spectator, cisgender woman*

Similarly, Hari, a competitor, worked through their own thoughts aloud but also came to the conclusion that they didn't know what the best way would be to move forward in terms of inclusion and policies within sex segregated sport.

> 'That's quite difficult. There are probably quite a few options there so there's, if people are transitioning in a binary manner I feel they should be allowed to join whichever team they want to, but then I guess there'd be

problems if they were a trans woman maybe who hadn't yet changed over. Or you could have a third box to put them in but then again that wouldn't work either because I can't imagine there'd be many, no actually no that's bulls**t. I don't really know to be honest.' *Hari, competitor, genderfluid*

The uncertainty and lack of solutions that are presented here by Susan, Hari and other participants are reflective of the complexity of both including gender and/or sex diverse athletes in sex segregated sport, and introducing sporting events and opportunities that use performance-based categorisation or are otherwise not sex segregated. There are a number of other factors that might also need to be taken into consideration when looking to adopt a performance-related categorisation, for example in heavy contact and combat-based sports. One participant that we interviewed suggested that the safety risks often perceived in these types of sports could be negated in a performance-related categorisation in the same way that they currently are in a sex segregated categorisation – by continuing to also use a second categorisation based on athlete bodyweight (i.e., athletes would be categorised twice, on performance-related aspects and on bodyweight). It could also be argued that this is most feasible in larger sporting events where there are a high number of competitors. In smaller sporting events, the division of an already small number of athletes into even smaller sub-categories may pose different challenges. Some support for sex-integration in martial arts and combat sports (MACs) has been previously acknowledged by Channon (2014) who stated that the presence of men and women in the same training spaces in MACs in Western societies is already not uncommon, although the focus in this study was training spaces as opposed to competitive ventures.

For both the competitors and spectators we interviewed then, the prevailing thoughts were that gender and sex diverse people should be included in sport, it would be a positive shift to see less sex segregation in sport, and the ability-based model of categorisation worked well in the context of *Limitless*. However, those interviewed perceived there to be many potential barriers to a shift towards less sex segregated sport, and the question of how this shift is achieved is one steeped in overwhelming challenge.

Concluding Thoughts

In this chapter, we described *Limitless*, a sporting event that has embraced the idea of performance-related categorisation of athletes, and was developed to promote participation of all genders, with no sex segregation. We provided an account of the structure of the competition and how it came to be, before exploring the findings of a qualitative investigation into the attitudes and opinions of those who either competed in or were spectators at the inaugural event in 2018. We argue that the *Limitless* strength competition, which uses a performance-related categorisation system as opposed to one of sex and/or gender, provides an inclusive and supportive sporting opportunity for individuals of all gender identities. Both competitors and spectators from the inaugural *Limitless* competition demonstrated a high level of support for the event and its performance-related method of categorisation. Whether or not the ability-based model adopted in this case proves to be transferable beyond this setting, *Limitless* provides a space for marginalised athletes and individuals who may have limited opportunities to compete in other settings.

The aim of running the *Limitless* competition to this point has been to challenge the binary sex and/or gender-based model that most sport still uses to organise its competitions, and to experiment with other possible ways to categorise sport that could be adopted in more situations in the future. Another point of consideration for performance-related sport categorisation that we are able to reflect on using the example of *Limitless* is matters pertaining to the advertisement of events, how wording affects perception of such events and thus participant uptake to them. We noted previously that the second *Limitless* competition in 2019 attracted much larger numbers, but that to our knowledge the first author of this chapter was the only non-cisgender competitor in this event. The smaller representation of gender diversity in *Limitless 2.0* is likely to be a reflection of our changed approach to the advertising and marketing of the competition. Our message always aimed to be that *Limitless* was a competition open to anyone, but in our advertisement of the first *Limitless* we placed heavy emphasis on its inclusion of gender diverse competitors. For example, there were phrases in the description of the event such as 'this transgender and non-binary inclusive competition…'. Subsequent feedback from some members of the gym the competition was held at suggested that this put off several cisgender people from entering the competition as they did not want to take up spaces to compete that others may have needed more than them.

Taking on board the feedback from the first competition and aiming to increase the number of entrants, in the advertisement of *Limitless 2.0* we changed our approach in the hope of making it clearer that the competition was open to anyone, regardless of gender and/or sex. We did so by using less-specific messages about the suitability of the competition to gender diverse people and using more general phrases about it being open to anyone. However, we were also careful to maintain and make clear its description as 'all-gender inclusive'. It was noted earlier in this chapter that strength athletics has the potential to be an intimidating sport from the exterior, and so it is important that in our framing of the competition as open to anyone we do not lose the message that gender and sex diverse competitors will be welcome and that our aim is to provide an inclusive sporting space. Whether this broader advertising inadvertently served to exclude potential transgender competitors, who may have preferred an LGBT+ only event, is unknown. However, the large number of cisgender competitors suggests that the concept of non-sex segregated sport is appealing to all people, irrespective of gender identity, highlighting the fact that re-framing sports is not driven by a solely transgender-inclusive agenda, as some critics would suggest. The demographic of *Limitless* competitors in terms of gender representation, and the impact of the framing and advertisement of it on this, is something that we are continually reviewing, but we will always make it a priority for *Limitless* to provide a space for people who have limited other opportunities to compete. Therefore, no gender or sex diverse entrant would ever be declined the opportunity to compete, regardless of the numbers of competitors already registered.

The competitors and spectators interviewed after the inaugural *Limitless* did express support for less sex segregation in sport more broadly, however they identified several potential challenges in implementing this and a sense of overwhelming challenge when considering how this could be achieved. Reflecting on this, we argue that the removal of sex segregated categories in *Limitless* provides an opportunity for participation for individuals of all gender identities, without the need for regulations to dictate under what circumstances (i.e., medical interventions) participation is permitted. We also argue that for applicable sports, when necessary considerations have been made, performance-related categorisation does not undermine the principles of fair and equitable participation for women, as participants are grouped according to their ability. Lastly, we argue that by removing sex segregation, there is potential to equalise the playing field of male and female sports and increase participation.

Notes

1 In this chapter, we use the term cisgender to refer to those people whose gender identity matches the sex they were assigned at birth (i.e., those who are not transgender), and other than incidences where we distinguish between non-binary and binary transgender people, we use the term transgender as an umbrella term to refer to those people whose gender identity does not match the sex they were assigned at birth.

2 For novice and intermediate strength athletics events, Facebook is the primary platform for the promotion and advertisement of competitions (Newman, 2020). *Limitless* was advertised across the gym's social media channels, as well as within popular strongman and strongwoman Facebook groups.

References

Anderson, E. (2008). 'I used to think women were weak': Orthodox masculinity, gender segregation and sport. *Sociological Forum*, 23(2), 257–280.

Arcelus, J., Bouman, W.P., Van Den Noortgate, W., Claes, L., Witcomb, G., & Fernandez-Aranda, F. (2015). Systematic review and meta-analysis of prevalence studies in transsexualism. *European Psychiatry*, 30(6), 807–815.

Boykoff, J., & Yasuoka, M. (2015). Gender and politics at the 2012 Olympics: media coverage and its implications. *Sport in Society*, 18(2), 219–233.

Channon, A. (2014). Towards the 'undoing' of gender in mixed-sex martial arts and combat sports. *Societies*, 4, 587–605. doi:10.3390/soc4040587.

Elling-Machartzki, A. (2017). Extraordinary body-self narratives: Sport and physical activity in the lives of transgender people. *Leisure Studies*, 36(2), 256–268.

England and Wales Cricket Board. (2020). England and Wales Cricket Board policy on transgender people playing cricket. Retrieved from: https://resources.ecb.co.uk/ecb/document/2020/03/16/dbf9fbc2-d56d-429a-b48d-562064b1ecc8/2020-ECB-Policy-on-Trans-People-Playing-Cricket.pdf.

Federation of Gay Games. (2020). Promoting equality through sport and culture. Retrieved from: https://gaygames.org/Mission-&-Vision.

Fielding, J., & Bass, C. (2018). Individuals seeking gender reassignment: marked increase in demand for services. *British Journal of Psychiatry Bulletin*, 42(5), 206–210.

Government Equalities Office. Department for Education. (2018). Reform of the Gender Recognition Act. Retrieved from: https://consult.education.gov.uk/government-equalities-office/reform-of-the-gender-recognition-act/.

Handelsman, D.J. (2017). Sex differences in athletic performance emerge coinciding with the onset of male puberty. *Clinical Endocrinology*, 87(1), 68–72.

Hargreaves, J. (1994). *Sporting Females: Critical Issues in the History and Sociology of Women's Sport*. London: Routledge.

Harper, J. (2017). Athletic Gender, *Law and Contemporary Problems*, 80, 139–153.

International Olympic Committee. (2020). Paralympic Games. Retrieved from: https://olympics.com/ioc/ipc.

Johnson, K.C., LeBlanc, A.J., Deardorff, J., & Bockting, W.O. (2020). Invalidation experiences among non-binary adolescents. *The Journal of Sex Research*, 57(2), 222–233.

Jones, B.A., Arcelus, J., Bouman, W.P., & Haycraft, E. (2017). Barriers and facilitators of physical activity and sport participation among young transgender adults who are medically transitioning. *International Journal of Transgenderism*, 18(2), 227–238. doi:10.1080/15532739.2017.1293581.

Jordan-Young, R.M., & Karkazis, K. (2019). *Testosterone: An Unauthorized Biography*. Harvard University Press.

Kerr, R., & Obel, C. (2017). Reassembling sex: Reconsidering sex segregation policies in sport. *International Journal of Sport Policy and Politics*, 10(2). doi: https://doi.org/10.1080/19406940.2017.1406976.

Knott-Fayle, G., Peel, E. & Witcomb, G.L. (2021). (Anti-)feminism and cisgenderism in sports media. *Feminist Media Studies*. doi: https://doi.org/10.1080/14680777.2021.1992644.

Lockridge, R. (2020, November 13). 2020 America's Strongest Man and Woman results and highlights. *Barbend*. Retrieved from: https://barbend.com/2020-americas-strongest-man-and-woman-results/.

Milner, A.N., & Braddock, J.H. (2016). *Sex Segregation in Sports: Why Separate Is Not Equal*. Santa Barbara, CA: Praeger.

Newman, H.J.H. (2020). Becoming a Strongwoman: an auto/ethnographic study of the pursuit of strength and power, and the negotiation of gender aesthetics in the UK strongwoman community (PhD Thesis). Retrieved from: https://repository.lboro.ac.uk/articles/thesis/Becoming_a_strongwoman_an_auto_ethnographic_study_of_the_pursuit_of_strength_and_power_and_the_negotiation_of_gender_aesthetics_in_the_UK_strongwoman_community/12706238.

Peel, E., & Newman, H.J.H. (2020). Gender's wider stakes: Lay attitudes to legal gender reform. *Feminists@Law*, 10(2).

Pike, J. (2020). Safety, fairness, and inclusion: Transgender athletes and the essence of Rugby. *Journal of the Philosophy of Sport*, 1–14.

Schultz, J. (2018). *Women's Sports: What Everyone Needs to Know*. Oxford University Press.

Shin, P.S. (2017). Sex and gender segregation in competitive sport: Internal and external normative perspectives. *Law and Contemporary Problems*, 80, 47–61.

Tomas, F. (2021, February 2). Why I loathe the word 'ladies' in women's sport. *The Telegraph*. Retrieved from: https://www.telegraph.co.uk/sport/2021/02/02/loathe-word-ladies-womens-sport/.

World Anti-Doping Agency. Monitoring program 2018. Retrieved from: https://www.wada-ama.org/en/resources/science-medicine/monitoring-program.

WBA. (2019). Rules of World Boxing Association. Retrieved from: https://www.wbaboxing.com/wp-content/uploads/2020/10/World-Boxing-Association-Rules.pdf.

Index

Page numbers followed by 'n' refer to notes.

www.ingramcontent.com/pod-product-compliance
Ingram Content Group UK Ltd.
Pitfield, Milton Keynes, MK11 3LW, UK
UKHW020004200926
475702UK00015B/2469
* 9 7 8 0 3 6 7 5 0 6 2 8 5 *